REASON AND OBLIGATION

A Contemporary Approach to Law and Political Morality

R. George Wright

Lanham • New York • London

Copyright © 1994 by
University Press of America,® Inc.
4720 Boston Way
Lanham, Maryland 20706

3 Henrietta Street
London WC2E 8LU England

All rights reserved
Printed in the United States of America
British Cataloging in Publication Information Available

Library of Congress Cataloging-in-Publication Data
Wright, R. George.
Reason and obligation : a contemporary approach to law and
political morality / R. George Wright.
p. cm.
Includes bibliographical references and index.
1. Obedience (Law) 2. Law and ethics. 3. Law and politics.
I. Title.
K250.W75   1994   340'.115—dc20   93–37363 CIP

ISBN 0–8191–9339–9 (cloth : alk. paper)
ISBN 0–8191–9340–2 (pbk. : alk. paper)

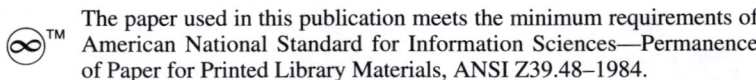
The paper used in this publication meets the minimum requirements of American National Standard for Information Sciences—Permanence of Paper for Printed Library Materials, ANSI Z39.48–1984.

Nothing seems to me less outdated than the classical emancipatory ideal.

—Jacques Derrida

Contents

Introduction		vii
Chapter 1	Gratitude and Political Obligation	1
2	The Logic of Contemporary Consent Theories	19
3	"Fair Play" Theories of Obligation	37
4	John Finnis on Obligation and the Natural Law	53
5	Does Moral Objectivism Matter?: Some Preliminary Responses	69
6	Polyphony, Dissonance, and Moral Objectivity	99
7	Can Debate Over Justice Be Progressive?	113
8	Conclusion: What Would a Sound Theory of Obligation Look Like?	139
Bibliography		149
Index		179

Introduction

Thoughtful persons have often wondered whether it might be morally permissible, or even morally required, to disobey a particular law. Some have confronted the broader question of a particular government's claim to legitimate authority. Of course, philosophers have discussed these questions more abstractly.

Philosophers have taken a number of approaches to the problem of legal and political obligation. The menu of basic alternatives has not changed much in two thousand years. Still, it is often difficult to classify philosophers by the differences in their approaches to legal and political obligation. This is for two reasons. First, the several popular theoretical approaches are not completely distinct. Each tends to merge with and overlap others at the margins. And second, each of the classic philosophers actually tends to recognize a variety of approaches. At least a hint of each of the major approaches appears in the work of most of the leading writers. The differences among philosophers is often really a matter of emphasis.

Listing some of the most common substantive approaches to legal and political obligation is not difficult. There are, to begin with, what might be called gratitude-based accounts. The theory in this case is roughly that obedience to a government may be the most appropriate response in light of the gratitude we feel, or ought to feel, toward the government or some group of persons for their efforts and sacrifices in conferring important benefits upon us. Next is a broad family of approaches generally known as consent or contract-based theories. On this view, obligation may be created by the right kind of consent or agreement to be bound. Then there are what might be termed "fairness-based" or "reciprocity-based" theories of obligation. Here, the idea is that we may owe an obligation of obedience in light of similar or reciprocal such sacrifices by other persons, presumably for the collective benefit. The emphasis here is on the general unfairness of being a free-rider. Finally, there is a wide range of what might broadly be called natural law theories. The basic idea here is roughly that there is some set of features of persons, the human good, societies, nature, and of the cosmos generally, or of the relations among these entities, that makes the exercise of governmental authority morally appropriate in at least some cases.

These are of course bare sketches, and the sketches sacrifice clarity for the sake of not unfairly excluding recognized versions of each of the above schools of thought. Each approach has been developed with subtlety unsuggested by these brief descriptions. But by no means do all leading theorists simply accept one or more of the above approaches. It may be that a plurality, or even a majority, of contemporary philosophers of obligation have actually denied that there is any broad moral obligation, even of a prima facie or defeasible character, to obey the law. While a few have argued that the exercise of state authority is morally illegitimate, more have argued that whatever moral duty we may have to do what a government requires of us reflects independent moral concerns, apart from the government's bare act of requiring us to obey. Thus we may be morally obligated not to assault others for reasons apart from the illegality of such acts. In other cases, we have a moral duty to do something the law commands not precisely because the law commands it, but because other persons are reasonably relying on our cooperation with some coordinating scheme, such as driving on the legally designated side of the road. In effect, many contemporary writers hold that the problems of legal and political obligation dissolve into general questions of justice and morality.[1]

It should be borne in mind that those who deny a general prima facie moral obligation to obey the law may counsel the same degree of disobedience, or even less disobedience, than those who do find such an obligation. It is certainly possible to argue for such an obligation to obey, but to find that obligation to be easily and often defeated by opposing moral considerations. On the other hand, one who denied such an obligation to obey might virtually always find convincing independent moral reasons for doing what the law requires. The practical importance of denying a general prima facie moral obligation to obey may thus be limited.

While each of the above general approaches has become more sophisticated over time, none has attracted a clear consensus. The deep explanation for this lack of consensus inescapably requires an examination of some basic issues in moral philosophy. This, in turn, reflects the absolutely crucial fact that each of the major approaches to legal and political obligation almost immediately raises and relies upon broad moral philosophical claims. None can be defended without explicit reference to some controversial basic moral philosophical claims. This is true of approaches that affirm, as well as those that deny, a moral obligation to obey the law. Thus the problems of legal and political obligation cannot be solved without solving deep problems in moral philosophy.

There is no need to tediously establish this claim seriatim with regard to each approach to obligation. The idea can be illustrated well enough by means of an example. As we will see below, the "fairness" or "reciprocity" approach developed by H.L.A. Hart and by John Rawls makes most normative sense if, as Rawls explicitly specifies, we assume that the society to which we are to contribute fairly in our turn is generally a morally just society.[2] Now, no one can be blamed for arguing that the existence of a moral duty of obedience may directly and crucially depend upon whether that society is morally just. But this obviously reduces the independent philosophical interest of the problems of legal and political obligation in isolation from the rest of political and moral philosophy. The interesting question turns out to be the logically prior question of a society's justness or injustice. Most of the interesting work must be done at that level, rather than on some independent question of legal or political obligation.

Of course, one might reasonably dispute whether Rawls' theory of justice is sound. As well, different interpretations of the "metaethical" status of justice also make Rawls' theory of obligation more and less attractive. That is, Rawls' reference to the idea of justice might be interpreted in several ways. For example, is justice something real, or is it conventional, or merely an arbitrarily affixed label? On some of these interpretations of what calling a society "just" involves, Rawls' theory may be attractive, and on other interpretations less so. It thus becomes essential to ask about the metaethical status of the idea of justice.

The other approaches to legal and political obligation each raise more basic moral philosophical issues at least as quickly, in ways crucial to their overall attractiveness as theories of obligation. Some of these questions will focus on the greater or lesser reasonableness of one normative claim as against some opposing claim. And again, it may be necessary as well to ask deeper metaethical questions. The interesting and central questions regarding legal and political obligation thus in fact turn out, in the main, to be basic questions of moral philosophy, including metaethical questions of the best understanding or most justifiable use of moral terms. To choose an example, it may in the long run do little good to say that a just society substantively requires equal shares, if we also believe metaethically that 'justice' is simply a label we may arbitrarily slap on any state of affairs.

This conclusion may be unwelcome, in that it holds real progress on issues of legal and political obligation hostage to resolving notoriously vexed issues of modern moral philosophy. But there is simply no other way. Sophisticated modern versions of each of the major approaches to legal and political obligation need not internally contradict themselves, or be demonstrably at odds with what we know of psychology, social life, or other factual matters. It may be only when we consider the moral attractiveness of competing approaches, or else when a particular approach to legal and political obligation takes a particular metaethical slant, that there arises a clear reason for accepting or rejecting that approach. Ultimately, disputes over the meaning, status, or the "reality" of terms such as 'just' and 'unjust' may bear crucially on "normative" disputes over whether one set of arrangements is more just than another.

Admittedly, this leads the inquiry into legal and political obligation straight into what is sometimes thought of as the morass of post-Humean moral philosophy. David Hume is, rightly or wrongly, often thought to have attempted to drive some sort of logical wedge between statements of fact and evaluative conclusions, or between "is" statements and "ought" statements.[3] What Hume was actually trying to show, and whether he succeeded, are controversial.[4] It is not much of an overstatement to claim that no two commentators have reached precisely the same conclusion on either of these questions.

From our standpoint, though, the real problem is not only the narrow one of whether from some set of factual premises about persons, needs, interests, values, motives, and wishes, or about society, nature, or the cosmos, one can rigorously infer some interesting evaluative conclusion about someone's moral obligation to obey. The real moral philosophical problem with which we must be concerned is unfortunately broader, and might be stated in this fashion: each of the general approaches to legal and political obligation, and each major variant thereof, apparently can be supported by some sort of plausible moral argument. Each such approach might impose lax or restrictive conditions on the existence of a moral obligation to obey, and might counsel obedience in most instances or else in only rare instances, depending upon how each approach is further developed.

If we are allowed to be arbitrary, we can simply endorse any approach we like, and any variant thereof. But if we wish to be reasonable, a broad lineal descendant of Hume's narrower problem stands in the way. This problem includes, but is broader than, any is-ought problem and also bears upon the practically important problem of metaethics referred to above. In brief, how do we reasonably know when we have the right approach to legal and political obligation? By what method can we reasonably and decisively adjudicate between conflicting but apparently plausible approaches? Each substantive or normative approach to legal and political obligation has apparent advantages and disadvantages. If we want to be rational, and to act morally, how can we commensurate or otherwise sort out the competing approaches in such a way as to reach a determinate reasonable result, at least where the approaches offer importantly conflicting advice? How can we conclude that, for example, one consideration counts for more in the logical or moral balance than some other consideration, or that some consideration must not be compromised?

Regardless of what one thinks about Hume's original problem, it is clear that moral philosophy offers no currently widely popular method for reasonably deciding among the conflicting approaches to legal and political obligation. Something can be said for each approach. But why one should opt for one resolution rather than another is, apparently, massively indeterminate from the standpoint of reason and morality.

Now, we must not expect too much from moral philosophy. There need be no reason to suppose that reason and morality must always in the end present us with some uniquely best answer or set of answers to every problem. It is hardly satisfactory, though, to face permanent logical and moral gridlock, in every respect, from the very start of the enterprise of trying to rationally choose among approaches to legal and moral obligation.

The chapters that follow do not arrive at a neat solution to the methaethical problems underlying issues of justice and obligation. For reasons to be argued for at various points below, a reasonable case can, however, be made for the overall superiority or special attractiveness of some versions of what metaethicists sometimes refer to as "objectivist" approaches to morality. Metaethical objectivist approaches to morality can be built into any of the best-known approaches to legal and political obligation. Metaethical objectivism is thus not itself some further alternative approach to the problem of obligation, but instead is merely one general family of ways of interpreting the moral language employed by all the competing theories of obligation. But if we wish to live under what we would now consider an attractive legal or political regime, it may be crucial to choose between metaethical objectivism and its rival approaches to the meaning or import of moral language.

The idea of an objectivist approach to morality, along with some of the most common metaethical alternatives thereto, is discussed in roughly the latter half of the book. The basic idea is roughly that some answers to moral questions are better than some others, independently of how any relevant person or group might want the answer to come out. Again, if this seems to range far afield, there is reason to believe that genuine and important progress on the narrower questions of legal and political obligation is impossible without such apparent detours. In particular, the acceptance or rejection of moral objectivism may make an important practical difference over time. This is so even though, as we shall see, there are huge differences among the substantive or normative approaches to obligation that might be adopted by metaethical objectivists.

Some objectivist approaches to morality can also be said to be theistic. Theistic moral objectivism would again involve a number of possible ways of interpreting the moral language used in any general approach to legal and political obligation. There are in fact an enormous number of possible theistically objectivist approaches to morality. Some are repressive, exclusionary, dogmatic, sectarian, divisive, or intolerant, for example, and others are not. Of course, in a democracy, no theistic argument should play a role in justifying or rejecting any constitutional or other legal result. But at the level of unofficial discussion among ordinary citizens, some theistic arguments make better claims to genuine public accessibility and to public rational justification through logic and investigation than others.

It may be, ironically, that it was Hume's dislike for theistic objectivist morality in general, or at least some versions thereof, that originally inspired the strictures on fact and value that have been referred to as Hume's Guillotine.[5] For many versions of theistically objectivist ethics, the employment of something like Hume's fact-value Guillotine is indeed immediately telling. Consider, for example, a theistic ethics that depends crucially on the mere issuance of moral commands, or on the issuance of moral commands backed by severe sanctions, or even, as a gratitude approach might argue, on an alleged moral obligation to obey anyone who has created us or brought us into being. Such theistic approaches simply cannot work. Without more, the fact that we have been commanded to do something by some extremely powerful person, or that we face enormous rewards or punishments depending upon our decision to obey or disobey, hardly constitute satisfactory accounts of a moral obligation to comply.

The theistic argument that we owe obedience to those who have created us is a more serious, but still plainly unsatisfactory, approach. We need, at least, to know something more about our creator. Dr. Frankenstein might have created a moral agent from spare parts. Perhaps some appropriate act of gratitude on the part of the created moral agent would be in order. But even if the created moral agent in question was created solely and exclusively by Dr. Frankenstein, and even if the created moral agent views life as an infinitely valuable gift, no real moral obligation of obedience follows. Dr. Frankenstein may, for example, be mad. His commands may, for reasons reflecting that madness, typically be morally objectionable in their substance. That he has created someone does not minimize this latter possibility.

These plainly defective theistic approaches to moral obligation do suggest, however, the possibility of a better version. Now, it is important to pause here. It is admittedly quite clear that for many, the very idea of a theistic ethics is simply a non-starter. Theistic ethics is commonly thought, quite understandably, to be simply implausible, anachronistic, divisive, undignified, anti-intellectual, immature, or to involve morally objectionable principles and outcomes, and to open the door to pointless, inherently interminable wrangling over its most basic presuppositions.

These concerns remain, even after we reiterate that theistic notions should not be relied upon to justify legal results or policies. Unfortunately, there is nothing that can be said quickly that can genuinely allay these concerns. The most obvious and important objections to the best sorts of theistic ethics are considered in separate chapters below. As it turns out, some theistic objectivist interpretations of the moral language of legal and political obligation offer certain attractions. It is certainly possible, though, that these apparent advantages can be matched by other, non-theistic forms of moral objectivism. The field certainly remains open for the development of a secular ethics that is superior overall.

The understandable general skepticism regarding all forms of theistic ethics lends an intriguingly "coherentist" flavor to the overall argument below. No single aspect of an argument for any theistic approach to obligation is plausible except in light of all of the other aspects of that argument. This means that this chapter's argument below that some theistic approaches to obligation are specially resistant to Hume's original fact-value guillotine, and to contemporary broader challenges, is unlikely to be persuasive until concerns over religious intolerance, exclusion, repression, and divisiveness, as well as the threat of perpetually non-progressive debate over basic theistic claims, can be allayed. But as a matter of the psychology of persuasion, those concerns cannot be allayed until the argument of this chapter below becomes plausible. The reader is therefore futilely urged to somehow read each chapter before reading any other chapter. In the alternative, the reader may simply set aside any theistic allusions below, and focus more broadly on the import of concerns such as the importance of moral objectivity in general.

In the meantime, we may for exploratory purposes simply assume for a moment that a particular kind of God exists, or has existed at any time necessary to the following argument. For purposes of clearly overcoming the challenges embodied in any version of Hume's Guillotine, we must ascribe two interesting minimum qualities to God.[6] God must first possess or have access to a certain degree of knowledge.[7] In particular, what each individual human being knows, or any group of human beings collectively knows, insofar as that knowledge is genuinely relevant to any moral decision, must amount to no more than a proper subset of God's knowledge. This might include knowledge of, among other things, the relevant parties' unexpressed desires, fears, motivations, and their concern for their own dignity and autonomy, as well as for human dignity generally.[8] And second, we must ascribe to God at least some sufficient degree of benevolence toward the relevant affected parties. Benevolence, as used here, encompasses some sufficient degree of judgment, or ability to decide well in the face of any relevant risks or uncertainties if any, in addition to wishing us well. Now, some may well argue that merely these qualities, without more, do not add up to a recognizable God. But that is not relevant to our purposes. These requirements of knowledge and benevolence could be clarified, elaborated, or strengthened in any number of ways. But the basic idea seems clear enough. If God is to be a moral authority for us, neither knowledge coupled with malevolence nor ignorance coupled with benevolence will suffice.

In combination, though, the above minimum ascribed levels of knowledge and benevolence would constitute God as a moral authority for us. This means in particular that no person or group of persons could reasonably override any known divine moral principle or judgment, if God is as minimally described above. What could we relevantly know or understand that such a God does not? If, by way of partial analogy, we were to compare the set of integers from one to four with the set of integers from one to six, a bit of matching will convince us that the first set is only a proper subset of the latter. How can the first set then reasonably be said to ever offer more in the way of problem-solving resources than the latter set?

Certainly it is possible that learning an additional fact may lead one to a worse decision than she would otherwise make. For example, learning that a favorite food is high in cholesterol may prompt us to avoid it, whereas if we knew the further fact that the cholesterol in question was actually "good" cholesterol, we would then continue eating the food, as we would if we were completely ignorant of its containing any cholesterol. But this general possibility does not provide any reasonable grounds for ever overruling one who wishes us well and who knows all we do, and more. If anyone prefers, we can add an additional assumption to the effect that God's additional knowledge does not tend to systematically lead to humanly predictable error patterns.

On the above assumptions, a law or moral principle that is consistent with divine nature or preferences[9] is itself not reasonably subject to human correction in favor of one that is not. No doubt it is still possible for us, inspired by the ancient example of Prometheus or the modern example of Nietzsche, to revolt against the postulated authority under one banner or another. Perhaps a benevolent God would ensure that we possess just this capacity. But on our assumptions, the grounds for such a revolt cannot be said to be reasonable.

There are, then, some theistic approaches to the morality of obligation that, on their own necessary assumptions, may escape at least the narrow, fact-value version of Hume's Guillotine. While positing the existence of the God described above looks like, and in a sense is, an alleged factual claim as to what "is," it is not difficult, on these assumptions, and with the assistance of other factual premises, to draw value-laden conclusions. The fact-value distinction obviously breaks down on the specified assumptions above. Whether any theistic objectivist approach to obligation can survive a broader challenge to its overall reasonableness of course remains to be seen.

Now, it is important to emphasize that other objectivist approaches to moral obligation that are explicitly non-theistic in character, or that are indifferent as between theism and non-theism, might equally avoid any version of Hume's Guillotine and therefore suffice in interpreting the moral language of some otherwise satisfactory approach to obligation. We again need not, and do not, argue that some theistic version of an approach to obligation is in any respect better than any or all objectivist, but non-theist, versions. Some such non-theistic version might work as well or better.

Whatever else might equally succeed, we can consider below whether some theistic versions of otherwise sound approaches to moral obligation may break the gridlock of plausible but normatively incompatible claims in which it is impossible to reasonably prefer one such approach to another.

Let us briefly reiterate what remains to be done. Roughly the first half of the book considers some of the most sophisticated contemporary "substantive" approaches to the problems of legal and political obligation. Each has been briefly introduced above. Each will be seen to depend almost immediately upon controversial basic substantive claims in moral philosophy. Each must be appraised ultimately on whether at least some version of each such approach to obligation can definitively establish its rational superiority over its rivals.

Because each of the contemporary approaches examined below raises such basic issues in moral philosophy, it becomes necessary to consider the general moral appeal of each approach, as well as the metaethical status of claims of fairness, justice, and obligation that might be made by each approach to obligation as well. We must, for example, consider not only what division of a social product would be just, but what it means to say, or in what ways it can properly be said, that a political society is just or unjust. The attractiveness of any and all theories of obligation may depend crucially on whether their basic moral vocabulary is to be understood, for example, in what might be called metaethically objectivist, relativist, noncognitivist, or pragmatist terms. Each of these metaethical views will be defined and appraised below. These so-called metaethical questions may well have predictable and important consequences in the real world. For example, a particular "fairness" approach to obligation may, if interpreted in a morally objectivist fashion, but not otherwise, be more attractive overall than a particular "contract" approach to obligation interpreted in some nonobjectivist fashion. Or vice versa. Or, it may do us little good in the long run to hold that the just society involves a roughly equal division of wealth, if we also hold that matters of justice are ultimately matters of arbitrary preference.

We then compare various forms of metaethical objectivism, relativism, noncognitivism, and pragmatism on the issue of their compatibility with or affinity for legal and political tolerance, pluralism, diversity, and inclusion. We will conclude at a minimum that some forms of objectivism, perhaps surprisingly including some forms of theistic objectivism, involve no disadvantage in this respect compared to other metaethical approaches. It will of course be important to bear in mind that within each family of metaethical interpretations, there will be much variety in attractiveness. Some metaethical objectivist approaches to obligation, such as Gandhi's, are more attractive than other equally objectivist approaches, such as those of Hitler or Stalin, or the theistic objectivism of Torquemada. It would be perfectly reasonable to think of life in a metaethically nonobjectivist society of some sort as less attractive than life with Gandhi, but better than life under Hitler. So for some purposes, we will want to know precisely what kind of objectivism or nonobjectivism we are in for. But there are, as we shall see, important lessons to be learned at the broad metaethical level.

Finally, we will directly confront an ultimate problem associated with theistic metaethics. Doesn't the use of any otherwise suitable morally objectivist theistic vocabulary at best invite an interminable, unpleasant, question-begging, ultimately pointless debate over the validity of basic theistic assumptions between dogmatists and their critics? The final substantive chapter suggests the surprising amenability of even some basic theistic assumptions to public, reasoned investigation. No doubt many varieties of objectivist and theistic morality are genuinely unattractive, for many reasons. Stalin's theory of obligation was objectivist, and Torquemada's theistically objectivist. But the door should be held open to the conclusion that whichever general substantive approaches to legal and moral obligation are otherwise most reasonable, there are advantages to interpreting such approaches in some sorts of metaethically objectivist, or even theistically objectivist, ways.

In a brief concluding chapter, we will tie together some of the themes discussed above and offer a few words on what legal or political regimes must do in order to qualify as objectively just in substance, or at least as sufficiently just to merit common obedience. The reader will be reassured to learn that no dramatically new understanding of the substance of justice and legitimacy is offered. It is implausible that what is objectively just should, in its broad outline, come as a surprise after thousands of years of philosophical exploration and debate. It is argued, though, that even with appropriate allowances for human ignorance and fallibility, we know at least dimly that questions of human dignity and the capacity for responsibility are central to the idea of the legitimate regime. And this conclusion would seem to morally require substantial redistribution of resources, freedom, and opportunities in favor of the least advantaged persons among us.

Obviously, it would be simpler to somehow arrive at and establish a fully satisfactory moral theory of legal and political obligation without recourse to more basic philosophical questions. But as one writer has expressed it, "the problem of explaining our political ties cannot be separated from the deeper problems of moral theory, difficult as those problems are."[10] If we wish to more adequately understand what is at stake in questions of legal and political obligation, we must following the arguments where they lead, even if that is into the realm of metaethics.

NOTES TO *INTRODUCTION*

1. See, e.g., A. John Simmons, Moral Principles and Political Obligations 193 (Princeton: Princeton Univ. Press 1979); Richard H. Fallon, Reflections on Dworkin and the Two Faces of Law, 67 Notre Dame L. Rev. 553, 576 (1992) ("it is natural but erroneous to believe that there is, at least in reasonably just regimes, a 'general' moral obligation to obey the law"); Larry Alexander, Law and Exclusionary Reasons, 18 Phil. Topics 5, 12, 19-20 (1990); J.L. Mackie, Obligations to Obey the Law, 67 Va. L. Rev. 143 (1981); Donald H. Regan, Law's Halo, 4 Social Phil. & Pol'y 15 (1986).

2. See John Rawls, A Theory of Justice 334 (Cambridge: Harvard Univ. Press 1971).

3. See David Hume, A Treatise of Human Nature book III, part 1, sec. 1 at 469 (L.A. Selby-Bigge ed.) (Oxford: Clarendon Press 1968). Robert Nozick has referred to the alleged gap between is and ought or between fact and value as a "famous chasm . . . in ethics that despite determined efforts no one has been able to leap across or bridge. . . ." Robert Nozick, Philosophical Explanations 535 (Cambridge: Harvard Univ. Press 1981). Of course, matters are hardly this simple, as Nozick himself recognizes.

4. Many contemporary writers on ethics have weighed in on these issues. The best narrowly focused collection is The Is-Ought Question (W.D. Hudson ed.) (London: MacMillan 1969). See also several of the papers in Hume (Vera C. Chappell ed.) (Garden City: Doubleday & Co. 1966). Professor Hudson's own original contribution can be found in W.D. Hudson, Hume on Is and Ought, 14 Phil. Q. 246 (1964). For a selection of more recent work in this area, see, e.g., David McNaughton, Moral Vision 54 (Oxford: Basil Blackwell 1988); Frank Snare, The Nature of Moral Thinking 83-89 (London: Routledge 1992); Steven W. Ball, Facts, Values, and Normative Supervenience, 55 Phil. Stud. 143 (1989); John Finnis, Natural Law and the "Is"—"Ought" Question, 26 Catholic Lawyer 266 (1981); Bruno Garofalo, A Note on the 'Is/Ought' Problem in Hume's Ethical Writings, 19 J. Value Inquiry 311 (1985); Toomas Karmo, Some Valid (but no Sound) Arguments Trivially Span the 'Is'-'Ought' Gap, 97 Mind 252 (1988); Charles R. Pigden, Logic and the Autonomy of Ethics, 67 Australasian J. Phil. 127 (1989); Janice L. Schultz, Is-Ought: Prescribing and a Present Controversy, 49 Thomist 1 (1985); Peter Simpson, St. Thomas on the Naturalistic Fallacy, 51 Thomist 51 (1987); Henry Veatch, Natural Law and the "Is"—"Ought" Question, 26 Catholic Lawyer 251 (1981).

5. See David Hume, A Treatise of Human Nature book III, part 1, sec. 1 at 469 (L.A. Selby-Bigge ed.) (Oxford: Clarendon Press 1968). The "guillotine" reference is from papers reaching opposing conclusions by Max Black and by D.Z. Phillips, reprinted in The Is-Ought Question (W.D. Hudson ed.) (London: MacMillan 1969).

6. It should be clear that this discussion is an exercise in moral philosophy, and not in the slightest an attempt to do responsible theology.

7. 'Knowledge' can be used in this context without entangling us in technical epistemological disputes over the nature of knowledge.

8. For those readers who suspect that this sort of God, or even the existence of any sort of objective ethical principles at all, is genuinely inconsistent with human dignity or with the moral value of autonomy, this matter is taken up briefly in chapter 5 below.

9. The logic of the argument above, on its assumptions, bypasses traditional concerns that morality cannot reasonably be based upon the subjective whim of some divine or less than divine actor. See, e.g., the argument of Richard Double, The Non-Reality of Free Will 168 (New York: Oxford Univ. Press 1991). There is of course a hugely important distinction between the mere existence of a principle that is consistent with the divine nature or preference, and the ability of some or all moral agents to somehow ascertain, appreciate, or establish the truth of that principle. This problem is discussed briefly in several contexts in succeeding chapters.

10. David R. Mapel, Democratic Voluntarism and the Problem of Justifying Political Bonds, 23 Polity 233, 235 (1990).

1
Gratitude and Political Obligation

Gratitude-based theories of political obligation are not currently fashionable among philosophers.[1] In some respects, this is surprising. Gratitude theory can draw as much support as rival theories from the sentiments of ordinary citizens. Gratitude theory can, no less than consent theory, trace its ancestry to Socrates' *Crito*.[2] Book-length discussions of the idea of gratitude, with some reference to gratitude in a political context, can be traced at least to Seneca.[3] The moral importance of avoiding ingratitude has been recognized by writers as otherwise divergent as Hume[4] and Kant.[5] As well, gratitude theory can be developed so as to show it to advantage, in some ways, with respect to rival theories of political obligation. Ultimately, though, the current unpopularity of gratitude theories transcends mere fashion. Gratitude-based theories are, as we shall see below, inherently problematic in certain crucial respects, and are incapable of providing a satisfactory account of political obligation.

Verbal formulations of the basic idea underlying gratitude-based theories are not difficult to produce. A.D.M. Walker has argued that "[p]olitical obligation . . . can be seen as an obligation of gratitude; our obligation to comply with the law is grounded in considerations of gratitude for benefits received from the state."[6] Such formulations, however, merely obscure, or at best raise without resolving, the crucial underlying issues. It is to those issues that we now turn.

Gratitude theories of obligation must address a number of basic problems. Questions as apparently simple as the circumstances under which gratitude is due quickly exhibit surprising complexity. For example, we must ask about what counts as a benefit sufficient to make gratitude appropriate. We must also ask whether it makes a difference whether the beneficiary's receipt of the benefit is compelled or otherwise unchosen. We must then ask whether it makes a difference whether the benefit conferred was antecedently owed to the beneficiary as a matter of right. A range of crucial issues arise with regard to the appropriate or necessary motives of the benefactor.

We must then go on to ask the even more crucial question of how much sense it makes to talk of compelled, or even merely demanded, expressions of gratitude. Problems concerning the proper manner and measure of expressing gratitude then arise. These problems implicate the fundamental question of in what, precisely, gratitude consists. Assuming that gratitude, whatever its nature, can be a matter of moral obligation in the first place, we must consider complicated issues of to whom a relevant obligation of gratitude might be owed, and to whom it might be repaid. How does a government fit in as benefactor or as a recipient of gratitude? How should we characterize the strength or weakness of obligations of gratitude with regard to governments? How, finally, should gratitude theory handle cases of unjust governments and of conflicting obligations of gratitude?

Each of these problems is susceptible, in turn, of multiple complications. What initially lends plausibility to gratitude theory, but contributes ultimately to its unacceptability, is the surprising lack of uniformity in descriptions of gratitude. Either gratitude is a protean phenomenon, or it somehow resists uncontroversial analysis to a surprising degree, given its familiarity. Scholars have noted the remarkable diversity in practice of gift relationships and of gratitude-like relationships.[7] This diversity actually ranges into sheer mutual inconsistency, either at the level of actual practice, or at the level of theoretical understanding. Thus while at least some version of gratitude theory may in turn offer a viable approach to one or more of the problems confronting gratitude theories of political obligation, no single version carries consistent conviction overall.

Each of the major issues noted above unavoidably implicates several of the others, so it is in a sense artificial to try to discuss them separately and consecutively. We may begin, in a way that inadvertently illustrates this interdependence, by focusing upon the apparently central idea of a benefit. Presumably, gratitude presupposes some sort of past, present, or future benefit. What counts as a benefit, however, may be unclear.[8]

Let us consider obvious candidates for the status of benefit in a political context, such as protection against assault by one's fellow citizens or defense against foreign invasion. Surely these are genuine benefits on all but the most idiosyncratic judgment. But gratitude theorists cannot simply assert that protection and defense in the abstract are benefits. No government provides protection or defense in the abstract. Gratitude theorists, along with "fair play" theorists, must confront a problem of level of generality. Governments provide particular levels of protection or defense through particular policies. A gratitude theorist must recognize that reasonable citizens may not find the actual level of protection or defense to be worth their actual personal costs in expressing what society deems proper gratitude for the benefits in question.

But there is another problem deeper than the fact that the benefit may not be deemed worth the expected gratitude. Particular levels of protection and defense flow from particular policies regarding surveillance, interrogation, crime prevention and detection, imprisonment, weapons choice, weapons production and testing, and strategy for use. Protection and defense therefore inevitably raise complex and controversial moral issues apart from any issue of paying for protection and defense through expressions of gratitude. Reasonable persons might, for example, find a nation's particular military policy to be morally objectionable, hence not a net benefit. Reasonable objection could be made to a non-defensive military capability, to a certain size military force, to insufficient civilian control, or to a policy of nuclear deterrence.[9]

Complicating this issue is that there seem to be cases in which gratitude is due even in the complete absence of any real benefit. Consider the case of a relative or friend who non-negligently, unsolicitedly, painstakingly knits us a sweater that turns out to be just barely too small to wear, or worse, which upon first wearing provokes an immediate allergic reaction, thereby imposing net disvalue upon the wearer.[10] Do we not potentially owe gratitude in such cases, even if we have received the opposite of a benefit? This kind of case hints at the slipperiness of the concept of gratitude. Ultimately, though, the problem of gratitude for non-beneficial acts is not crucial in our context. Once we shift the focus from gifts by doting relatives, it seems utterly implausible that unsuccessful attempts to benefit a group of persons could, by themselves, actually generate a sufficient moral obligation, based on gratitude, to obey a government.

What should the gratitude theorist say, though, of presumed benefits imposed upon or otherwise not chosen by the beneficiary? Some benefits are practically unavoidable. Professor A. John Simmons raises the possibility of someone who deliberately isolates herself geographically so as to receive no benefits, including protection, from a state.[11] But even assuming that no public goods or benefits of socialization or of defense "spill over" to the benefit of that exile, she may retain a valuable right to re-enter the state she left, should she change her mind. And even the very circumstance of her understanding this right, and its value, may reflect the continuing accrual of benefits, including education and protection, for which continuing gratitude may be owed.

The problem of unsought or inescapable benefits is thus surprisingly broad. And on mainstream understandings of the concept of gratitude, an unsought or unconsented-to benefit is either no benefit at all,[12] or not the sort of benefit[13] for which gratitude is owed, regardless of whether the "benefactor" has a benevolent intent or not. It would also be possible to hold that unsought benefits may create obligations of gratitude, but that those obligations are not strong enough to establish recognizable political obligations. It is worth noting that these analyses of gratitude involve the idea of consent. They thus involve adding at a crucial stage a central element of a rival theory of political obligation, consent theory. They may thereby ensure that gratitude theory is ultimately vulnerable to many of the same objections as consent theories of political obligation.

If it is difficult to sort out the implications for gratitude theories of unavoidable or unconsented-to benefits, the problem of preexisting moral rights and obligations is at least equally knotty. To put the matter simply, it is not clear why a "beneficiary" owes an obligation of gratitude to someone who, in conferring a "benefit," is merely recognizing an alleged antecedent moral right in the beneficiary to receive, from the benefactor, the good in question. If the benefactor is under an alleged independent, preexisting moral obligation to provide the good in question either to the beneficiary or even to someone in the general position of the beneficiary, it is far from clear why the beneficiary owes gratitude in return, or any gratitude beyond a merely nominal token.[14] Why should one be grateful for what one is owed? We may have a moral obligation to be reasonably courteous or civil to someone who has merely supplied us with our due, as in the case of the exchange of performances in the context of commercial contracts. But this minimal civility hardly suffices to generate a prototype of a satisfactory gratitude theory of obligation.

It is open to the gratitude theorist to deny that beneficiaries generally have moral rights to the benefits that are crucial to gratitude theories of obligation, or that benefactors have a moral obligation to supply them, but such theories would need to be worked out. It is possible to argue, for example, that everyone is owed respect, along with other basic rights and liberties, but not including defense and protection. Gratitude would therefore be appropriate for such benefits. If such a theory could be worked out, a gratitude theory of obligation would in this respect be possible and far from redundant.

The gratitude theorist might argue as well that even if everyone possesses the relevant antecedent moral rights, substantial gratitude may still be owed for supererogatory acts that deepen the value and meaningfulness of those recognized rights, as in the case of someone who generously contributes voluntarily to the education of a number of students, where education is already recognized as a moral right.

Finally, it may in certain cases actually be appropriate to express gratitude toward persons who have merely carried out their preexisting moral obligations.[15] Genuine gratitude, beyond mere admiration or respect, may be appropriate, for example, to a professional fire fighter who has entered a burning building to rescue a friend or relative, or to retrieve a valuable stamp collection. We may also, at least arguably, properly feel gratitude toward parents even for what they had a genuine moral obligation to do.

Gratitude in these cases may, however, reflect the social interest in encouraging socially useful behavior where it is difficult to clearly detect the difference between exerting extra effort and just going through the motions, or between supererogatory effort and morally required effort. In any event, it is difficult to imagine grounding a satisfactory theory of political obligation on gratitude toward anyone who merely recognizes and respects the moral rights of other persons.

The problem of gratitude toward benefactors who believe that they are merely doing what they are morally required to do provides a link to the broader problem of benefactor motive. It is ordinarily thought that one's gratitude should depend not only on the size of the benefit conferred, but on the benefactor's motive, or the spirit with which the benefit is conferred.[16] While this seems perfectly sensible in its own right, an emphasis on the motive of the benefactor fits poorly with our familiar intuitions concerning the grounds of an obligation to obey a governmental regime.

For one thing, it is simply difficult to believe that whether we are morally obligated to obey a government depends so crucially upon the motive or spirit underlying any relevant actions. If a governmental design is otherwise morally flawless, it hardly seems crucial that the designer's sole motive, for example, was hope of material reward, or the desire for an enhanced reputation. Of course, in most cases, the motives of the relevant actors will be a mixture of selfishness and unselfishness, but gratitude theorists are not entirely clear on whether, or to what extent, this reduces or eliminates any obligation of gratitude.[17]

Even if the benefactor's motive is crucial to political obligation, though, we must ask why typical benefactor motives do not actually undermine or minimize any obligation of gratitude. It has been argued from the time of Seneca, for example, that if one bestows benefits essentially in order to benefit in return, such a motive or purpose "supplies a just excuse to the ingrate."[18] A benefactor who looks to repayment reveals an apparent gift to have been, or converts an apparent gift into, a mere loan or advance.[19] In effect, the presence of such motives undermines the obligation of gratitude.

Such self-interested motives could be compatible with, say, a theory based upon obligations of "fair play" or reciprocity. We shall discuss such theories of obligation in chapter 3 below. But it is doubtful whether a gratitude theory of obligation can be built upon the foundation of self-interested or merely prudential acts incidentally benefitting others.

It is admittedly ironic, but hardly paradoxical, that acts of benefit to others undertaken solely with the intent to place those persons under an obligation of gratitude to return the favor, or to confer in return some other substantial benefit, are self-defeating. Any such intent to place others in the position of owing us gratitude tends to undermine just that obligation. Such motives may again be more compatible with "fair play" or reciprocity theories of obligation than with gratitude theories.

The crowning irony, of course, is that if the benefactor really is not looking to requital or repayment of the benefit, no enforceable moral obligation of gratitude seems logically to arise. As a recent writer suggests, "[i]f that for which gratitude is due was neither for sale nor a mere loan but was in some sense *gratis*, what sense does it make to feel indebted for it?"[21] But there is a further problem. Even if it does make sense to somehow feel morally bound to express gratitude toward or repay such a benefactor, what sense does it make for a government or anyone else to coercively intervene and compel an expression of gratitude in the form of substantial repayment, as a gratitude theory of political obligation would presumably require?

In most familiar governmental systems, many people comply with the law, pay taxes, or join the military not in a logically self-defeating attempt to place others under an obligation of gratitude to do likewise, but because these actions may be compelled or required by law. But if a person pays taxes or otherwise benefits others because of governmental coercion or fear of punishment if she does not, such motive again is not such as to rightly inspire gratitude in others, or to impose obligations of gratitude on others benefitted by her actions.[22]

In order to avoid this series of dead ends, the gratitude theorist is best off arguing that unselfishly motivated actions can create substantial obligations of gratitude, even though, or precisely because, the benefactor was not motivated by and does not insist upon repayment. The logic of such a claim may in a sense be mysterious, but it is at least supported by our familiar experiences with the social practice of gratitude. If most acts of benefit turn out to reflect a mixture of selfish and unselfish motives, the gratitude theorist must argue that the resulting obligation of gratitude, even if reduced or diluted in light of any selfish benefactor motives, is still strong enough to ground a sufficient political obligation in appropriate cases.

The gratitude theorist must still come to terms, though, with the problems and paradoxes of compelled expressions of gratitude. The gratitude theorist must certainly show why relevantly situated persons may be under a moral obligation of gratitude to obey a government in appropriate cases. But this is only the beginning. The gratitude theorist must then go on to provide a coherent moral justification for the government's enforcing or compelling the fulfillment of that moral obligation, if necessary, through imprisonment, threats of imprisonment, or other coercive techniques.

Now, if the government's rationale in compelling the discharge of moral obligations based on gratitude is not itself based somehow on the logic of gratitude, we do not have a genuine gratitude theory of political obligation. We might, for example, have a utilitarian theory that holds that it maximizes utility to compel people to do what their moral obligations of gratitude bid them do.

But if the government does try to point to the logic of gratitude in order to justify compelling people to do what gratitude suggests they do, major problems arise. Gratitude may be appropriate only insofar as our benefactor does not demand or compel requital of her benefit. And insofar as the government or anyone else seeks even as a third party to compel expressions of gratitude, the very logic of gratitude is jeopardized. Compelled gratitude may be no genuine gratitude at all.

Now, compelling gratitude need not involve the self-contradictory project of compelling someone to spontaneously feel a certain emotion. In the context of political obligation, the gratitude theorist is presumably less interested in gratitude as a state of mind or emotion than in gratitude as objectively embodied in some sort of act of repayment or requital.[23] But the problem of possible self-contradiction in coerced expressions of gratitude remains.

In some classic discussions of gratitude, compelled gratitude is actually not treated as strictly self-contradictory, at least in all cases, although compelling gratitude is thought at least to spoil the moral merit or virtue of the "gratitude" expressed thereby.[24] It has also been argued, though, that "[i]t is essential to gratitude that the grateful response be gratuitous: spontaneous and not required."[25] While benefactors may deserve gratitude, they generally hold no moral right to demand, let alone coerce, expressions of gratitude.[26] Thus we do not generally punish persons for failing to express gratitude.[27]

In contrast, though, generally "the state does not *request* compliance, it demands that citizens obey and . . . punishes them for not obeying."[28] But such attempts to enforce obligations of gratitude may be inherently self-defeating. One writer has observed that "the personified laws of the *Crito*, by being so demanding of gratitude, actually disqualify themselves as deservers of Socrates' gratitude."[29] Gratitude is not genuine gratitude if it is motivated by compulsion, or even by a desire for further benefits, as opposed to either an inclination toward gratitude or a sense of moral duty to express gratitude.[30]

This poses, it would seem, a serious problem for gratitude theories of obligation. Gratitude may at most give us a moral reason for obeying in appropriate cases, without also showing why a government has a moral right to coerce or compel obedience. To justify government compulsion, a gratitude theory would have to become a sort of "counterfactual" gratitude theory. Such a theory would seek to justify a government's compelling a person to do that which the person would have done had they properly expressed gratitude for the benefit in question. Instances of coerced "gratitude" could on such a theory be explained on any number of grounds. For example, enforcing a law against assaults could be thought to reflect basic natural law principles. But it is also possible that some acts of compelled obedience might be intended to promote the valuable social institution of genuine gratitude in other contexts. Gratitude may thus have at least some indirect, tangential role to play in a satisfactory theory of political obligation.

Even if gratitude theorists could overcome the problem of coerced gratitude, untidy loose ends would remain. Often, the manner or measure of repayment of an obligation of gratitude is unclear.[31] Gratitude may require an appropriate attitude, a token gesture, or a more substantial requital.[32] It has been argued that a proper response of gratitude, as opposed to the case of ordinary commercial debts, is to confer something more than, or something beyond, what we have received from our benefactor, if we can.[33] It has been said both that debts of gratitude are inextinguishable,[34] and that "benefactors are right to feel insulted if thanked too profusely just as if not thanked enough."[35]

Thus there seems to be no clear rule on how gratitude is properly expressed. No formula is universally applicable. Gratitude need not take the form, for example, of tendering to our benefactor value equivalent to that received, or of reimbursing our benefactor's costs in providing the benefit in question.[36] Arguably, proper gratitude sometimes need not reach even the lesser of the value of the benefit or the benefactor's cost in providing it, as when merely verbal thanks suffices to repay a small gift.[37]

This is a matter of some importance, because a gratitude theory of political obligation must again do more than identify some relevant debt of gratitude. Gratitude theory must also show that this debt of gratitude requires particular actions such as law obedience, tax payments, or military service on appropriate occasions.[38] Without such forms of obedience, no recognizable government is possible. But at this point, the skeptic may observe that "from the fact that a government requires obedience in order to subsist, it does not follow that any debt of gratitude to a government can be discharged only by obedience."[39]

Such an inference would indeed be a bit hasty. But it does seem clear that genuine gratitude does mean that we make special effort to weigh, and not to damage, the interests of our benefactor.[40] If we assume that a government has conferred great benefits upon us, at great sacrifice, it is difficult to realistically imagine appropriate acts of gratitude, genuinely safeguarding the interests of that benefactor, short of substantial obedience to just laws. Let us suppose we feel an obligation of gratitude toward someone who will shortly die unless we donate our own rare-type blood, as we conveniently could. Would it normally be considered an appropriate act of gratitude to insist instead upon providing the benefactor with an expensive new car? The scope or range of proper ways of displaying gratitude toward a government may analogously be limited.

This does not mean that the scope of one's obligation to even a just government is utterly unproblematic on a gratitude theory. Consider, for example, the case of someone who has been wounded in battle, voluntarily donates unusually high amounts of her income into the public treasury, and who refuses government assistance programs and regularly obeys most laws. If this citizen consistently violates, for one reason or another, say, the laws against jaywalking, can we say that in thus refusing to obey the law she is manifesting ingratitude? Would gratitude theory suggest that the more one has sacrificed for the state in various respects, the less one is morally obligated to the state in other respects? Perhaps not, if we focus on the strand of gratitude theory that emphasizes the sense in which obligations of gratitude may be "inexhaustible."[41] Perhaps in this respect gratitude theories hold an advantage over "fair play" theories that focus more narrowly on reciprocating equally or proportionately along with others.

We have, however, oversimplified grossly in taking for granted that it is some entity known as the government to whom the relevant obligation of gratitude is owed. Socratic personifications aside, governments as abstract entities do not appear to be capable of sacrifice, or at least of the sorts of sacrifice that might generate recognizable political obligations.[42] Nor is it entirely clear that governments can strictly be capable of benevolent motives in conferring benefits, or that we can be genuinely grateful toward abstract entities or institutions such as governments.[43]

Thus it is in some respects more accurate to say that the underlying object of our gratitude in this context is those natural persons who, perhaps with mixed and varied motives, have by their own actual efforts conferred on us the relevant benefits.[44] But while this approach avoids certain problems, it raises others. Can we simply presume that most of our fellow citizens who have relevantly sacrificed on our behalf would designate the current government, the regime, the Constitution, or some other entity as the proper object of our gratitude in the form of obedience, military service, tax payments and such? Have most of our fellow citizens explicitly or impliedly made such a designation? This seems implausible. It is at least as plausible that our benefactors were, in their turn, simply carrying out obligations of gratitude toward their own prior benefactors, in a continuous chain. Again, it is unclear why we owe obligations of gratitude toward those who only benefitted us in order to discharge their own prior obligations of gratitude. But if most people do not designate the present government as the third-party beneficiary of gratitude owed to them, by what logic can the present government claim a right to the gratitude actually owed directly to other citizens, individually and collectively? To put the matter colorfully, do not most of those who have benefitted us and who may deserve our gratitude die politically intestate? Admittedly, our own prior benefactors might well not have been able to benefit us had a government not organized their efforts. But other persons and other social institutions may also have been necessary conditions for the provision of such benefits. Would they have potentially conflicting claims on our gratitude as well?

What particularly complicates this matter is that our relevant obligations of gratitude appear to be owed not only within, but across, generations, including to cohorts now deceased who at some earlier time sacrificed on our behalf, or at least on "our" behalf as an anonymous member of a collectivity or nation. As a general rule, we might roughly assume that the further in the past the relevant sacrifice occurred, the less sympathetic to current regime policies and values the sacrificing party can be fairly assumed to have been. It is certainly possible that a person may sacrifice at time T_1 for the sake of a younger or future generation while expecting repayment in the form of obedience to some later government at T_2, whatever its policies and values might turn out to be. This might occur at least where there is, or is expected to be, substantial continuity of regime values. But it is again not clear why this should be presumed to be the case.[45] To the extent that our benefactors held or hold relevantly conflicting basic political wishes and interests, we will each have unavoidably conflicting obligations of gratitude.

Now, it is possible for a critic of gratitude theory to argue that even if we somehow owe obligations of gratitude to obey some relevant government, obligations of gratitude by their very nature are necessarily too weak to call for the kinds of substantial sacrifices governments typically require.[46] On such a view, gratitude may impose some obligations regarding government, but those obligations may not be stringent enough to underwrite burdensome compliance with the law.

It seems clear, though, that the contemporary view that gratitude can only involve weak moral obligations, or "quasi-obligations,"[47] is of only recent popularity. Even in the modern era, Kant wrote that ingratitude was among "[t]he three vices which are the essence of vileness and wickedness . . . ."[48] David Hume opined to similar effect that "[o]f all crimes that human creatures are capable of committing, the most horrid and unnatural is ingratitude."[49]

It is admittedly possible that ingratitude could be a grievous fault even if gratitude required only a modest performance at most. But it seems more plausible to suppose that the strength of an obligation of gratitude could vary from weak to strong, depending in part upon the degree of benefit conferred, whether the context is political or not.[50] If governments, or our fellows, confer a great benefit upon us at great sacrifice, a correspondingly great debt of gratitude may be owed.

This seems straightforward enough. But the feeling persists that obligations of gratitude toward governments are intrinsically too weak to validate the degrees of sacrifice upon which governments may insist. We may further account for this feeling, quite speculatively, in a number of ways. First, it is easy to forget that gratitude may require "repaying" far more than we have received.[51] We have, as well, rightly had little sympathy for Soviet-style arguments that emigration may be restricted on the grounds that would-be emigres have not fully repaid their obligations to the state. More generally, as the realm of rights has quite properly expanded historically, gratitude has correspondingly loomed less large, given the general view that gratitude is not appropriate where the government has merely recognized and respected our rights.[52] As the scope and importance of moral and legal rights expands, the importance of the institution of gratitude tends to diminish.

Relatedly, we may tend to assume that obligations of gratitude toward government must be weak, as they often come into conflict with and may be outweighed by obligations to other persons, or because such obligations are presumably defeasible, and can be overridden on proper moral grounds.[53] Gratitude theorists, though, need not make any claims to the contrary. That obligations of gratitude to obey governments can be overridden is a strength, not a weakness, of gratitude theory. At bottom, gratitude requires us to promote, if possible, the interests of our benefactor. Disputes may of course arise as to what is genuinely in our benefactor's interests. But it is certainly possible to deny that a government is invariably the best judge of the public interest, and gratitude theory need not require us to commit what we take to be immoral acts at the government's behest.[54]

This is not to suggest that conflicting obligations of gratitude pose no serious problems for gratitude theorists. They do. Consider the case of, say, a recent immigrant who owes much to the sacrifices of her parents. If the law requires her to act incompatibly with the interests of her parents, it is quite plausible that her obligations of gratitude to her parents outweigh her obligations of gratitude toward her new government. Yet the gratitude theorist of political obligation is unlikely to welcome this result. In contrast, some consent theorists of obligation might attempt to argue that in freely immigrating, one expressly or impliedly agrees to subordinate obligations of gratitude toward others to one's newly incurred obligations to the government. Whether such agreement is ever actually given, or is given in a morally justifiable way, is another matter.

As to the question of obligations to unjust governments, gratitude theory neither offers special insights nor faces unique problems. Presumably, obligations of gratitude can be overridden by a government's gross injustice, or by any special relationship between benefits accruing to oneself and acts of government injustice or oppression. Gratitude theory need not, on the other hand, deny all obligation to all unjust regimes, at least if the governmental injustice seems mild and remediable.[55]

While gratitude theories can, if we assume away all of the problems discussed above, thus be sensitive to questions of justified disobedience to law, such theories are not fully satisfactory even in this respect. The problem can be put in the following terms: that a person may owe a substantial obligation of gratitude to a government tells us very little about either the character of that government or about whether that person should generally obey the government in question. Some or all of the benefits derived from one's government may be crucially morally "tainted." Few imaginable governments confer no significant benefits on anyone, if perhaps only at the expense of oppressed minorities. Thus even if we ignore the cumulatively insurmountable problems discussed above facing gratitude theory, gratitude theory provides at best only modest contributions to resolving the question of whether a particular government is morally worthy of obedience.

NOTES TO *GRATITUDE AND POLITICAL OBLIGATION*

1. Defying this trend is A.D.M. Walker, Obligations of Gratitude and Political Obligation, 18 Phil. & Pub. Aff. 359 (1989); A.D.M. Walker, Political Obligation and the Argument From Gratitude, 17 Phil. & Pub. Aff. 191 (1988). For a somewhat "weaker" or less ambitious gratitude-based theory of political obligation, see Terrance C. McConnell, Gratitude ch. 6 (Philadelphia: Temple Univ. Press 1993).

2. See Plato, Crito 48b-52d.

3. See Lucius Annaeus Seneca, De Beneficiis, in 3 Moral Essays book VI at 400-03 (John W. Basore trans.) (London: William Heinemann Ltd. reprint 1958).

4. See David Hume, A Treatise of Human Nature book III, part I, sec. 1 at 466 (L.A. Selby-Bigge ed.) (Oxford: Clarendon Press 1968).

5. See Immanuel Kant, Lectures on Ethics 218 (Louis Infield trans.) (Indianapolis: Hackett Publishing 1963).

6. A.D.M. Walker, Political Obligation and the Argument From Gratitude, 17 Phil. & Pub. Aff. 191, 192 (1988).

7. See, e.g., Paul F. Camenisch, Gift and Gratitude in Ethics, 9 J. Religious Ethics 1, 1 (1981). For revealing, though quite disparate, discussions of gift relationships, see, e.g., Lucius Annaeus Seneca, supra note 3; Marcel Mauss, The Gift (Ian Cunnison trans.) (New York: W.W. Norton 1967); Richard M. Titmuss, The Gift Relationship (New York: Vintage Books 1972).

8. See, e.g., George Klosko, Four Arguments Against Political Obligation From Gratitude, 5 Pub. Aff. Q. 33, 34 (1991).

9. For one such extended argument, see John Finnis, Joseph Boyle & Germain Grisez, Nuclear Deterrence, Morality and Realism (Oxford: Clarendon Press 1987).

10. This example is suggested by Robert M. Adams, The Virtue of Faith 186 (New York: Oxford Univ. Press 1987).

11. See A. John Simmons, Moral Principles and Political Obligations 159 (Princeton: Princeton Univ. Press 1979).

12. See Lucius Annaeus Seneca, supra note 3, book II at 91 ("since that which I am forced to receive is not a benefit, that also which puts me under an obligation to someone against my will is not a benefit").

13. See A. John Simmons, supra note 11, at 175. See also id. at 177-78 (gratitude appropriate only for benefits we may be "taken to want"). On such a view, gratitude theories of obligation thus depend crucially on vital elements of rival, consent-based theories of obligation.

14. Kant is alleged to have had difficulties in reconciling general gratitude to our benefactors with what he took to be rights to receive or obligations to confer the benefits in question. See Victor J. Seidler, Kant, Respect and Justice 96 (London: Routledge & Kegan Paul 1986). See also Philip Abbott, The Shotgun Behind the Door: Liberalism and the Problem of Political Obligation 182 (Athens: Univ. of Georgia Press 1976); Fred R. Berger, Gratitude, 85 Ethics 298, 305 (1985) (gratitude itself as involving respect for the independent moral worth of other persons); Daniel Lyons, The Odd Debt of Gratitude, 29 Analysis 92, 96 (1969). Terrance McConnell has suggested that gratitude may be proper where someone has, at some personal risk, recognized one's right, where that right is not often respected. See Terrance McConnell, supra note 1, at 199. McConnell recognizes that in other contexts, gratitude may be proper where the benefactor has run no risk or has made no special exertion or sacrifice. See id. at 7. This seems right, in that we can owe at least modest gratitude to someone who has been especially considerate to us, where she could just as easily, if no more personally profitably, have done otherwise to our detriment.

15. See A. John Simmons, supra note 11, at 179. Simmons cites gratuitously assumed or supererogatory duties, as in the case of aid to a stranger, where the beneficiary presumably has no moral right to aid by any benefactor in particular.

16. See Thomas Aquinas, Summa Theologica II-II qu. 106, art. 5 at 54 (Fathers of the English Dominican Province trans.) (London: Burns Oates &

Washbourne Ltd. reprint 1935) ("repayment of a favour depends more on the disposition of the giver than on the effect"); Lucius Annaeus Seneca, supra note 3, book IV at 265 ("the motive of my action must be the interest of the one for whom the benefit is destined"); A. John Simmons, supra note 11, at 171 (discounting purely selfishly motivated actions as appropriate objects of gratitude); Victor J. Seidler, supra note 14, at 101 (on Kant's view, the obligation of gratitude depends in substantial measure on the degree of unselfishness exhibited by the underlying benefactor); A.D.M. Walker, supra note 6, at 219 ("the argument from gratitude forces us to consider the spirit in which the state provides benefits for its citizens. . . .").

17. See supra note 16. On this question, Thomas Hobbes takes a characteristically intriguing, if problematic approach. Hobbes argues simultaneously that gratitude rises to the level of a fourth law of nature, consisting in giving our voluntary benefactors no reasonable cause to repent of extending a benefit, and that all voluntary gifts can be presumed to aim at some good for the benefactor herself. See Thomas Hobbes, Leviathan ch. 15. at 209 (C.B. Macpherson ed.) (Harmondsworth: Penguin Books 1968). For a defense of the propriety of gratitude even in some cases in which the benefactor has been motivated in part by self-interest, see Terrance McConnell, supra note 1, at 201.

18. Lucius Annaeus Seneca, supra note 3, book I at 7-9.

19. But cf. Immanuel Kant, supra note 5, at 222 ("[t]he man who bestows favours can do so either in order to make the recipient indebted to him or as an expression of his duty."). One might reasonably ask Kant, though, why gratitude specifically is in order in either case.

20. See Lucius Annaeus Seneca, supra note 3, book I at 11. See also id. book II at 113.

21. Claudia Card, Gratitude and Obligation, 25 Am. Phil. Q. 115, 115 (1988) (emphasis in the original).

22. See Fred R. Berger, supra note 14, at 299.

23. For the distinction between these two dimensions of gratitude, see Thomas Aquinas, supra note 16, qu. 106, art. 4 at 53; Roslyn Weiss, The Moral and Social Dimensions of Gratitude, 23 S.J. Phil. 491, 491 (1985).

24. See Lucius Annaeus Seneca, supra note 3, book III at 137; Thomas Aquinas, supra note 16, qu. 106, reply to obj. 2 at 47; Francis Hutcheson, An Inquiry Concerning the Original of Our Ideas of Virtue or Moral Good, in 1 British Moralists 66, 161 (L.A. Selby-Bigge ed.) (New York: Dover Publications 1965).

25. George Klosko, supra note 8, at 41. See also Paul F. Camenisch, supra note 7, at 15.

26. See Fred R. Berger, supra note 14, at 300; Claudia Card, supra note 21, at 117, 120; Roslyn Weiss, supra note 23, at 492.

27. See Fred R. Berger, supra note 14, at 306.

28. George Klosko, Political Obligation and Gratitude, 18 Phil. & Pub. Aff. 352, 354 (1989) (emphasis in the original).

29. Roslyn Weiss, supra note 23, at 501 n.34.

30. See Immanuel Kant, supra note 5, at 221; Leslie A. Mulholland, Kant's System of Rights 161 (New York: Columbia Univ. Press 1990); Claudia Card, supra note 21, at 117.

31. See Claudia Card, supra note 21, at 116.

32. See A.D.M. Walker, supra note 6, at 200.

33. See Thomas Aquinas, supra note 16, qu. 106, art. 6 at 56.

34. See Immanuel Kant, supra note 5, at 222.

35. Roslyn Weiss, supra note 23, at 497.

36. See A. John Simmons, supra note 11, at 169.

37. For background, see id. at 170-71.

38. See id. at 185.

39. Id. at 187.

40. See id. at 168; A.D.M. Walker, supra note 6, at 203.

41. See supra note 34 & accompanying text. See also Thomas Aquinas, supra note 16, qu. 106, art. 6 at 56 (proper response of gratitude is to repay something beyond what we have received).

42. See George Klosko, supra note 8, at 41; A. John Simmons, supra note 11, at 188.

43. See A. John Simmons, supra note 11, at 188. But see A.D.M. Walker, supra note 6, at 197-99 (arguing for the possibility of benevolent institutional purposes and of gratitude toward institutions or collectivities).

44. See A.D.M. Walker, supra note 6, at 196.

45. Again, to the extent that anyone's efforts were motivated by selfish reasons, or even by a desire to place others under an obligation of gratitude, gratitude may not be a morally required response. We also set aside at this point the problems of gratitude toward foreign armies of liberation, as in the case of Allied armies in the later stages of World War II, or toward foreign governments or international organizations that have successfully intervened in one's country's affairs for genuinely humanitarian reasons.

46. See George Klosko, supra note 28, at 355; George Klosko, supra note 8, at 37; A. John Simmons, supra note 11, at 164.

47. See Paul F. Camenisch, supra note 7, at 2.

48. Immanuel Kant, supra note 5, at 218.

49. David Hume, supra note 4, book III, part I, sec. 1 at 466.

50. See Thomas Aquinas, supra note 16, qu. 106, art. 2 at 48; A.D.M. Walker, supra note 6, at 207; A.D.M. Walker, Obligations of Gratitude and Political Obligation, 18 Phil. & Pub. Aff. 359, 362 (1989).

51. See supra notes 34, 41 & accompanying text.

52. See supra notes 14-15 & accompanying text.

53. See A. John Simmons, supra note 11, at 184.

54. See Philip Abbott, supra note 14, at 133.

55. See Thomas Aquinas, supra note 16, qu. 106, art. 3, replies to objs. 5 & 6 at 52. An obligation of gratitude toward one's government might be tested by that government's injustice to oneself, or toward other people. Even worse, a government toward which one is grateful may call upon those grateful citizens to commit acts of injustice. For discussion, see Terrance McConnell, supra note 1, at 203.

2

The Logic of Contemporary Consent Theories

Few theories of obligation can match the intellectual pedigree of those that focus on consent. We may take consent theory to encompass the full scope of the social contract tradition. Given the breadth of this tradition, generalizing about consent theory becomes difficult. Setting aside all complications, though, the basic idea of consent theory seems clear enough. Whether one is morally bound to obey a particular government is thought to somehow depend upon whether one has in satisfactory fashion agreed or promised to do so. Consent may be a necessary or a sufficient condition for obligation. This rough idea has been developed in varied and sophisticated ways. However, even the most interesting contemporary consent theories are deeply problematic.

Some initial complications are familiar from legal practice. For example, if the idea of consent is to play an important role in justifying or in criticizing governments, the consent at issue must to some degree be given intentionally, knowingly, and voluntarily.[1] Beyond some vague and controversial point, coercion or lack of freedom either vitiates consent, or leaves us with no attractive explanation of why such coerced consenters are morally obligated to obey.[2]

At a minimum, then, consent theorists must give some guidance as to what sorts of circumstances undermine otherwise morally binding consent. This is not an easy task. Consider, for example, the labor-management context. One might imagine that techniques such as lockouts, plant closings, or prolonged strikes could be intended to break an opponent's will, or to coerce an opponent into accepting less favorable contract terms. Yet it is often supposed that labor contracts entered into on just such a basis may be not only legally but morally binding.

As the example of labor contracts suggests, it is unclear whether the presence or absence of consent-vitiating factors is mainly a matter of factual description or of moral evaluation. Are we to simply look for events such as the breaking of an opponent's will, or are moral judgments such as the proper scope of one's options, or of one's "background" rights, also crucial?

Simply put, is the kind of coercion, duress, or involuntariness that negates moral obligation mainly a matter of fact, or of value?

One way of approaching these problems is through a distinction carefully drawn by Professor Lea Brilmayer. Professor Brilmayer observes that "one consents to a transition from one state of affairs to another, rather than to a particular state of affairs as an absolute matter. Consent establishes only that an individual prefers the latter outcome to the earlier one, not that it is fair to hold the individual to either one."[3] Consent is thus comparative, rather than absolute. That one prefers some future state S_2 to one's present state S_1 hardly establishes the moral legitimacy of one's being originally placed in S_1, or the reduction of one's options to only those currently available.

These sorts of problems, though, do not seem insoluble in principle. As well, a consent theorist could suggest that a person who consents to S_2 in the way described by Brilmayer may be morally obligated at least not to arbitrarily retract that choice by simply reverting to S_1, even if S_1 and S_2 are both morally objectionable, as long as the choice between S_1 and S_2 itself was freely made. There may thus be some logical force to consent theory, even as a merely comparative concept, and even if we assume a background of unfairness and rights-violation.

Let us consider more generally what any plausible consent theory must involve. Professor Richard Flathman has offered a useful general schema in this regard. Flathman argues that if "circumstances are right for the question of consent to arise, for B to consent he must (a) know what he consents to, (b) intend to consent to it, (c) communicate his knowledge of what he is consenting to and his intention to consent . . . to the person or persons to whom the consent is given."[4]

This account requires some potentially controversial interpretation. It would seem, for example, that a consenter need not know the concrete substance of that to which she is consenting. A person might conceivably consent, for example, to obey a thick, but unread, criminal code or to obey all future laws duly enacted within a specified democratic constitutional framework. Flathman himself notes the familiar paradox "of achieving a better understanding of our intentions in doing X after we have done it."[5] The requirement that we know that to which we are consenting need not, therefore, be particularly demanding.

In other respects, complications arise quickly. In order to be morally bound under a consent theory, must one really intend to consent? Would it not suffice to intend to act in a way that one knows will be universally taken to mean that one is consenting? It is certainly conceivable that by convention, raising one's right arm under specified circumstances, or voting, could be universally so interpreted. In such a case, could one intend to vote without also intending to consent?[6] Or does voting in such a case simply amount to an act of consent, regardless of one's subjective state of mind? To the degree that a society is one of conflict and division, it becomes less plausible to infer that by voting, a person has intended to consent to the outcome, whatever that outcome may be, or to the resulting government, regardless of its basic policies and values. Of course, it may be precisely in circumstances of the greatest societal conflict that the public's interest in finding ways of moderating that conflict is greatest. But the greater the social conflict, the less reasonable it is to infer consent from any particular act. Consent theory may thus be of least help when it is most needed.

Claiming that voting necessarily involves consent—to a winning candidate, a regime, a constitution, a voting procedure, or anything else—may in some cases be implausible. One might vote solely to desperately fend off what one takes to be the slightly worse of two profoundly evil, threatening regimes.[8] To find consent in such a case stretches the idea of consent unduly. One might vote, as well, solely and precisely to express general dissent.[9]

Professor Peter Singer has attempted to reconcile some of the opposing considerations in the area of voting and consent. Singer argues that at least in a genuinely democratic system, based on equal power and fair consideration of interests,

> participating in a decision-procedure, alongside others participating in good faith, gives rise to an obligation to act as if one had consented to be bound by the result of the decision-procedure. So long as the participation is voluntary, actual consent is not required, but an express public refusal so to be bound would mean that participation, if still permitted, would not give rise to any obligation to obey the result.[10]

Thus Singer raises the possibility of a sort of quasi-consent or estoppel based in part on the raising of legitimate expectations, and in part on the independent moral force of democracy, equality, and fairness.

Now, Singer's approach may seem a step forward. But it is in any event a step away from consent theory. If Singer's analysis is sound, consent theory may require recourse to considerations of fairness, democracy, equality of power and their absence. Of course, the consent theorist need not claim that consent theory is self-contained and self-justifying. Consent theory is not defectively incomplete merely because it must recur to other, perhaps more general or more fundamental moral notions.

But if Singer is right, consent theory must depend upon ideas that constitute the core of prominent rival accounts of legal and political obligation. There are fairness theories of obligation, and natural law theories of obligation focusing on democracy and equality. Advocates of such theories can claim that if consent theory must in the end rely upon rival theories, consent theory is incomplete, and that we may simplify matters by eliminating the concern for consent and focusing instead on fairness or upon a democratic, egalitarian natural law theory. Now, fairness theories and natural law theories may themselves be defective or unacceptable for some reason. But there is no reason to believe that those defects can be neatly repaired solely by recourse, in turn, to consent theory.

As it turns out, there is much substance to the claim that consent theory is incomplete, in the sense of being dependent precisely on the crucial elements of prominent rival theories of obligation, in a way not paralleled by any dependence of those rival theories on consent. But for the moment, we must return to the task of illustrating the logic of contemporary consent theory.

We have seen that one's consent can arguably be given even where one does not know the concrete, substantive nature of that to which one is consenting. But this does not solve the problem of the indeterminacy of the scope of consent. Suppose one consents either by voting, by not voting even though one had the chance, by freely or unfreely accepting benefits from an ongoing government, or by continuing to reside within a territory when one could emigrate instead. In such cases, to what has one consented? To the taking of office by the victors? To a currently effective constitution? To a constitution as authoritatively interpreted? To all laws, current and future, promulgated thereunder? To only those laws necessary to generate the benefits of which one has availed oneself?[11] Or is the law a seamless, indivisible web for purposes of tracing benefits?[12]

The scope of one's consent, when given in these sorts of ways, seems inherently indeterminate.[13] Worse, the zone of indeterminacy of consent will tend to be the battleground between opposing political forces seeking to expand or contract the legitimate authority of the regime. Opposing political forces thus have a vested interest in differently characterizing the scope of one's consent.

Ironically, to the extent that opposing political forces can plausibly contest the scope of one's consent, one has consented only to that to which common, uncontested convention holds one to have consented. This follows from the requirement that one generally know what one is consenting to.

How can a consenter know to what she is consenting through an act such as voting if the implications of voting in this regard are hotly disputed? This may amount to a bias built into consent theory, but while this bias is convention-dependent, the bias is not in favor of the reigning political order. Instead, the bias in the case of disputed "conventions" is in favor of a narrow scope of consent, or of no effective consent at all. Of course, if one wishes to consent more clearly, more determinately, and more broadly, one may do so through express language, rather than relying upon less articulate acts such as voting, accepting benefits, or declining to emigrate.

This analysis, along with a bit of observation of public behavior, suggests that relatively few citizens of even liberal democratic societies have actually politically consented in any relevant respect.[15] This is often thought to be damaging to consent theory, in that it is often assumed that most citizens, at least of modern liberal democracies, are morally obligated to obey, despite their apparent lack of consent.[16] This is a problem for any theory based on actual consent, whether the consent is to be given expressly or tacitly. However, the obvious paucity of express consent has nevertheless often driven consent theorists to emphasize to the idea of tacit consent.

Professor John Simmons has offered the following account of tacit consent:

> Consent is called tacit when it is given by remaining silent and inactive; it is not express, explicit, directly and distinctively expressed by action, but rather is expressed by the failure to do certain things. . . . Silence after a call for objections can be just as much an expression of consent as shouting 'aye' after a call for ayes and nayes.[17]

Tacit consent is thus a genuine form of actual consent. But if the consent theorist looks to tacit consent because disappointingly few persons have expressly consented, tacit consent is of little help. Few persons seem as well to give tacit, but genuine, consent to a government or regime.[18]

We could, of course, impute tacit consent to most or all citizens by implausibly stretching the idea of tacit consent. It is often argued that in expanding the idea of tacit consent to encompass barely being within a particular territory, John Locke's theory of tacit consent loses its attractiveness.[19] This is partly a matter of a lack of clear understanding by the alleged consenters and other citizens of any such convention, or of any actual intent to signal one's consent via remaining within a given territory.[20] But it can also be argued that in many cases, the material and psychic costs of emigration are so great as to undermine our confidence that the choice to remain, and to thereby tacitly consent, is sufficiently voluntary for the consent to be valid.[21] Whether emigration is too high a price to ask may, again, be a normative, and not merely an empirical question.[22] But even if we decide that forced emigration is a legitimate governmental response to persons who refuse to consent, the high cost of emigration may lead persons to consent to what they know to be an unjust, oppressive regime, as long as emigration seems still worse.

Consent theory thus seems to have difficulty in showing that most citizens of modern liberal democracies have by any means genuinely consented, and are therefore bound to obey. Some contemporary consent theorists respond to this apparent problem not by stretching the idea of consent, but by conceding, if not insisting, that most citizens have not consented, and are not thereby bound to obey. One of the most interesting and sophisticated such responses has been offered by Professor Harry Beran.[23]

Professor Beran's theory, not surprisingly, emphasizes the moral importance of voluntarism and self-determination. Beran argues with respect to liberal democracies that "all relationships among sane adults in such a society should be voluntary."[24] He argues further that "normal adults are capable of and therefore have a human right to personal self-determination."[25] Beran is, within the scope of his book, unable to fully vindicate these claims. Surely liberal democrats should be suspicious of a principle of associational voluntariness. To the extent that persons decline to voluntarily associate with stigmatized, disfavored, or powerless groups, a voluntariness principle may tend to impair equality of opportunity for self-realization. And the mere existence of a human capacity for self-determination by itself hardly supplies a reason for establishing self-determination as a right. Humans have many conflicting capacities, the realization of many of which does not rise to the level of a right. Couldn't we choose to determine ourselves immorally? If so, we would need to morally supplement any theory relying on self-determination.

The possibility of immoral self-determination in general finds its analogue in the possibility of immoral consent, and of immoral refusal to consent. Clearly, persons may freely consent to an unjust regime that oppresses some distinct minority. Are the consenters thereby morally bound? Of course, consent theorists can reply that the obligation created by consent is defeasible, or subject to override in the case of unjust regimes. But the problem is that it is perfectly possible to consent precisely in order to achieve immoral ends, as in order to unjustly oppress some minority. It is not clear how this sort of consent creates even a defeasible obligation to help follow through on such a project through obedience.

Beran recognizes as well that one cannot generally point to one's refusal to consent in order to license one's immoral violations of law.[26] But unless

Beran's consent theory of obligation actually supposes that legal and political obligation is inconsequential, Beran must come to terms with the problem of unjust refusals to consent. Suppose some persons refuse to consent to a splendidly just government, which they nonetheless mistakenly take to be unjust. Their reasons for refusing to consent might point to the government's prohibition of murder, its concern for equality, or even its concern for self-determination. Are such persons not obligated to obey what we have stipulated to actually be a splendidly just regime?

Professor Beran seeks to address this and other problems through his distinction between the basis of political obligation and the justification of such obligation.[27] On Beran's view, the basis of obligation is said to be an essentially procedural matter, where the justification of obligation is essentially substantive. The basis of obligation is said to lie in the reasons for accepting the claim of some specific persons to legitimately rule over other persons. The basis of such obligation is said to be consent. In contrast, the justification of authority lies in why we ought, morally and rationally, to have government in the first place, or why we ought to consent to government in general. The justification of authority is said to lie in considerations such as the utility of the institution of government in general, its necessity if liberty is to be promoted, or perhaps in natural law reasoning.

Doubtless Beran is correct in noticing that the reasons for preferring government in general to a state of nature need not necessarily carry over into a preference for one particular government over its rivals. On the other hand, such a "carry-over" seems logical enough. Perhaps the clearest illustration would be through a utilitarian approach to obligation. Let us assume that there can be a satisfactory utilitarian account of why we should prefer government in general to a state of nature. Now, it is possible that the particular kinds of gains and losses that justify government in general may not also drive our choice of a particular government from among its competitors. But utilitarian considerations of one sort or another could clearly still lead us, even at this stage, in choosing a particular government or a particular constitution. From among the possible governments whose policies would promote utility, we could select the contender which if actually in power would be the likely utility-maximizer over some time frame, or the most prominent or salient contender, or the one with the greatest de facto power, or the most predictably stable. We could choose based on some utilitarian function of these and other considerations, or based upon only some simple utilitarian rule, with utility in turn governing this choice. There is certainly no reason to believe that a choice of a particular government based on utilitarian considerations need be self-defeating or impossible. The same may be said just as easily of, for example, a variety of natural law approaches to obligation as well.

Beran argues that "[t]he mere fact that a group would pursue the right political ends if in office cannot give that group the moral right to occupy it, since there may be two groups which wish to occupy the office, both of which would pursue the right ends equally effectively."[28] The utilitarian may respond, however, that utilitarian considerations can help break this tie. By analogy, two glasses of water identical in content may relevantly differ in their fragility, their proximity to one's hand, or their visibility. There is no reason why utilitarian approaches to obligation need run afoul of coordination problems, or problems of any other sorts, that can be solved only by introducing consent-based arguments.

Professor Beran's version of consent theory for liberal democracies points to voting, in appropriate cases, as an indicator of consent. In particular, Beran argues that "[v]oting in fair and effective elections puts voters under an obligation to comply with the government that is elected."[29] He specifies that this obligation is defeasible, or subject to override if the government enacts evil laws. Beran's theory deals most effectively with what might be called the revolutionary opportunist, who utilizes the suffrage mechanism but plans not to be bound by the electoral outcome. But it is less clear that Beran's theory is sensitive to what might be called the desperate revolutionary, who by voting seeks only to fend off the slightly worse of two options, both of which the revolutionary loathes. It is not clear that such a voter has consented to obey the electoral winner, even subject to override.

Beran argues finally that the high cost, or even the impossibility, of emigrating is irrelevant in the case of those persons who have otherwise freely consented, at least if they actually wish not to emigrate.[30] No doubt persons who do not wish to leave, for whatever reason, subjectively feel no lack of freedom in being barred from leaving. But the problem of the degree of freedom sufficient for a valid consent is not so simple. If citizens know that emigration is, let us say, legally prohibited, won't there be some cognitive dissonance-reducing tendency to adjust one's beliefs and desires, consciously or unconsciously, to avoid unnecessary conflict and frustration? One who knows that she is unable to exit may thus tend to decide that she really has no desire to exist. This sort of problem may call the validity of some persons' consent into question, whether or not the government propagandizes in favor of remaining.[31]

This, however, is a problem in the detail of consent theory. It does again point, though, to a deeper problem in any theory of actual consent.[32] Consent theory should be clear about its own presuppositions. In characteristically dramatic fashion, Friedrich Nietzsche raised the general question: "To breed an animal *with the right to make promises* . . . is this not the real problem regarding man?"[33] Nietzsche seems to be observing, at a minimum, that the institution of promise-making and promise-keeping is not free of controversial presuppositions. More prosaically, it has been observed that "[n]ot all claims, requests, or proposals create the conditions that make consent appropriate."[34]

It seems, for example, that there must be limits to the extent that pretenders can put us even to easily performed, low-cost acts of dissent from their would-be regime. Imagine, by loose analogy, a dissenting shareholder of a major corporation, who in addressing the annual meeting, announces that the insurgent slate will be considered adopted unless someone dissents by raising her hand within an hour. Surely the shareholders are not even morally bound by tacit consent if no hands are raised. The dissenting shareholder presumably lacks the moral and legal authority to require the other shareholders to tacitly consent or dissent in any fashion. Now, this may of course in part reflect preexisting authoritative rules of corporate governance. But there may be moral or "natural" limits to the extent that persons can be put to tacitly consent or cheaply dissent even in a state of nature. We should, for example, be spared the necessity of having to even cheaply dissent several times per week. This and other moral limitations, or presuppositions, of consent theory may in part reflect considerations central to rival theories of obligation, such as utility, fairness, or natural law. At the foundation of consent theories of obligation may thus again be: rival theories of obligation.

This can be illuminated more broadly by asking why it is typically believed that expressions of consent or promises to obey actually morally bind, at least defeasibly, when freely and knowingly given by competent adults. It is hardly surprising that the reasons point beyond consent theory itself. But more damagingly for the consent theorist, those reasons point in part to the central elements of competing accounts of legal and political obligation. It is again this sort of dependency in particular that raises the deepest objections to consent theory.

In this connection, Professor Lea Brilmayer has cautioned against casual moral explanations of obligation couched in terms of consent theory.[35] On Brilmayer's view, consent theory depends upon the notion of "territorial sovereignty."[36] Whether any viable consent theory of legal or political obligation actually depends upon the idea of territorial sovereignty may require a careful analysis of what territorial sovereignty entails, but Brilmayer does not fully explore this notion. There seems to be no reason to assume that putative states, or the recipients of political consent, must, for example, claim a monopoly on the authorization of the use of force, or even define the limits of their protective activity in territorial terms. Putative states need not claim any moral right or power to exclude outsiders, or even to punish law violations in any strict sense. A putative state might, instead, say only something like the following: "Obey us consistent with your moral rights or we will not provide the benefit of protection for you, except insofar as protection is an indivisible public good."

It is thus not clear that a putative state, as a recipient of consent, need claim territorial sovereignty in any obvious sense. But Brilmayer is clearly right in believing that consent theory is not presuppositionless. There is admittedly no consensus as to what, precisely, those presuppositions include. That depends upon one's view of the point or value of promising, generally and in a political context. The logic of promise-making and promise-keeping, and of consent, has been variously justified. For example, Kantian justifications that focus on not "using" people are possible.[37] Justifications in terms of the rendering of benefits to others or the incurring of detrimental reliance have been offered.[38] Enforcing promises may also promote or prevent harm to valuable specially developed voluntary relationships among persons, as well as the social institution of such relationships.[39] Or one might seek to justify the institutions of promising and of consent, no less than the institution of property rights,[40] in terms of facilitating human social interaction and human freedom in general.

Each of these theories of the logic or justification of consent is naturally understood in terms of one or more rival theories of obligation. Kantian concerns for treating a person as not merely a means are central to particular natural law or natural rights theories of obligation. Concerns for benefits and detrimental reliance suggest "fair play" or utilitarian theories. Concern for the value of special voluntary relationships might, in addition to the above theories, also bring perfectionist or developmental considerations into play. Human social interaction and freedom are again central to many utilitarian and natural law or natural right theories.

Of course, each of these explications of the logic of consent may be flawed. But even their refutation need not demonstrate the independent appeal of consent theory. We might, for example, take issue with the claim that there is some special linkage between consent theory and human freedom.[41] There could be genuine, voluntary consent to a regime that, at a minimum, does not generally and conspicuously value human freedom. As well, a generally morally sound and efficacious regime that exalts human freedom might not, for just that reason, attract free consent. As we saw above, nothing in consent theory requires that one's reasons for giving or withholding consent be logically or morally sound.[42] If there is really no foundation for consent theory in human freedom, so much the worse, we may reasonably conclude, for consent theory. And there is again no reason to suppose that what is distinctive about consent theory is necessary, and sufficient, to fix whatever is wrong about other sorts of theories of obligation.

NOTES TO *THE LOGIC OF CONTEMPORARY CONSENT THEORIES*

1. See A. John Simmons, Moral Principles and Political Obligations 77 (Princeton: Princeton Univ. Press 1979). Leslie Green argues concisely that "a binding promise must be both free and informed." Leslie Green, The Authority of the State 173 (Oxford: Clarendon Press 1990).

2. For references to much of the relevant literature on coercion, involuntariness, and binding consent, see Alan Wertheimer, Coercion (Princeton: Princeton Univ. Press 1987). See also Joseph Raz, The Morality of Freedom 148-49 (Oxford: Clarendon Press 1986); J.P. Day, Threats, Offers, Law, Opinion, and Liberty, 14 Am. Phil. Q. 265 (1977); Jeffrie G. Murphy, Consent, Coercion, and Hard Choices, 67 Va. L. Rev. 79 (1981); Robert Nozick, Coercion, in Philosophy, Politics and Society 104 (Peter Laslett, W.G. Runciman & Quentin Skinner eds. 4th series) (Oxford: Oxford Univ. Press 1972); David Zimmerman, Coercive Wage Offers, 10 Phil. & Pub. Aff. 121 (1981).

3. Lea Brilmayer, Consent, Contract and Territory, 74 Minn. L. Rev. 1, 3, 23 (1989).

4. Richard E. Flathman, Political Obligation 220 (New York: Atheneum 1972). Query whether one must communicate one's intention to consent, above and beyond simply communicating one's consent, or that one has consented. Only the latter seems necessary.

5. Id. at 228 n.12.

6. See John P. Plamenatz, Consent, Freedom and Political Obligation 144-56 (Oxford: Oxford Univ. Press 2d ed. 1968); John J. Jenkins, Political Consent, 20 Phil. Q. 60 (1970); Frederick Siegler, Plamenatz On Consent and Obligation, 18 Phil. Q. 256 (1968) (denying, as against Plamenatz and Jenkins, that voluntarily and understandingly voting in an election necessarily involves consenting, even if the voter knows that voting is widely taken as a sign of consent). See also Albert Weale, Consent, 26 Pol. Stud. 65, 71-72 (1978).

7. See Jules Steinberg, Locke, Rousseau, and the Idea of Consent 124 (Westport: Greenwood Press 1978).

8. See Leslie Green, supra note 1, at 171.

9. See Jules Steinberg, supra note 7, at 118.

10. Peter Singer, Democracy and Disobedience 133 (New York: Oxford Univ. Press 1974).

11. See Edward A. Harris, From Social Contract to Hypothetical Agreement: Consent and the Obligation to Obey the Law, 92 Colum. L. Rev. 651, 665 (1992).

12. See Kim Lane Scheppele & Jeremy Waldron, Contractarian Methods in Political and Legal Evaluation, 3 Yale J.L. & Humanities 195, 208 (1991).

13. See Edward A. Harris, supra note 11, at 675.

14. Again, assuming that we must know what we are consenting to, if half the population believes that by voting we consent to, say, a recently exiled regime, and the other half believes that by voting we are instead consenting to the new usurper regime, it seems reasonable to conclude that both sides are mistaken, and that in the absence of any clear convention, the simple act of voting cannot have either meaning.

15. See, e.g., Richard E. Flathman, supra note 4, at 209; Leslie Green, supra note 1, at 185; Carole Pateman, The Problem of Political Obligation 174 (Berkeley: Univ. of Calif. Press 1985); A. John Simmons, supra note 1, at 79, 93-94; Edward A. Harris, supra note 11, at 654-55.

16. See A. John Simmons, supra note 1, at 79; Edward A. Harris, supra note 11, at 683. But see Leslie Green, supra note 1, at 166 ("[i]t might be true that citizens are bound to obey only if they consent, and at the same time true that few of them are bound precisely because they have not consented"); George Klosko, Reformist Consent and Political Obligation, 39 Pol. Stud. 676, 676 (1991).

17. A. John Simmons, supra note 1, at 80.

18. See id. at 93-94.

19. See, e.g., id. at 79-83.

20. See Leslie Green, supra note 1, at 169 ("[o]ne who does not accept the authority of the state will not accept that peaceful residence in the country commits her to it").

21. See A. John Simmons, supra note 1, at 98-99; Lea Brilmayer, supra note 3, at 5. See also Don Herzog, Happy Slaves: A Critique of Consent Theory 226, 229 (Chicago: Univ. of Chicago Press 1989) (for consent to be valid, the alternative to consenting must be reasonable and not excessively costly).

22. Query whether the price for refusing to consent, without also posing any special threat to anyone, should be forced emigration, denial of police protection (to the extent reasonably possible), forced disarmament, or, perhaps, denial of civil privileges such as voting and jury service. This presumably matters, as many more persons may refuse to give consent if the price is relatively low. If, on the other hand, it is determined that the morally appropriate "baseline" for refusal to consent should be "returning" the non-consenter to a "state of nature," or denying police protection, another problem arises. We may say that if this denial of police protection is deserved or morally justified, it is non-coercive. See George Klosko, supra note 16, at 689. But it may still, even if non-coercive in this sense, be such as to vitiate consent. The threat of the denial, to the extent reasonably feasible, of police protection may be so intimidating as to inevitably motivate even the most oppressed, unjustly subordinated groups to consent, lest they certainly lose even their lives in the absence of police protection.

23. Harry Beran, The Consent Theory of Political Obligation 3 (London: Croon Helm 1987).

24. Id. at 37.

25. Id. at 23, 34.

26. See id. at 109.

27. See id. at 26-28, 33, 62-66.

28. Id. at 63. Michael Lessnoff deploys a similar argument against Hanna Pitkin's view that Locke is not so much a consent or social contract theorist as a natural law or natural rights theorist, for whom the crucial issue is whether a given government *deserves* consent. Lessnoff argues that social contract or consent theory is needed to handle cases of conflicting claims to sovereignty. See Michael Lessnoff, Social Contract 98 (Atlantic Highlands: Humanities Press 1986). But as our text illustrates, this need not be so. For Pitkin's argument, see Hanna Pitkin, Obligation and Consent—I, 59 Am. Pol. Sci. Rev. 990, 995-99 (1965). But cf. Charles Fried, Contract as Promise 14-15 (Cambridge: Harvard Univ. Press 1981) ("the usefulness of promising in

general does not show why I should not take advantage of it in a particular case and yet fail to keep my promise").

29. Harry Beran, supra note 23, at 76.

30. Id. at 98-99, 103.

31. Compare Onora O'Neill, Between Consenting Adults, 14 Phil. & Pub. Aff. 252, 259 (1985), in which Professor O'Neill implies that apparent consent may not be binding, however enthusiastically given, where the actions putatively consented to were, and were known by all relevant persons to be, inevitably to be undertaken whether anyone's consent was given or not.

32. Actual consent may be opposed to a Rawlsian-type hypothetical consent. Doubts have been expressed as to the sufficiency of hypothetical consent in grounding obligations. See, e.g., Vicente Medina, Social Contract Theories: Political Obligation or Anarchy? 142 (Savage, Md.: Rowman & Littlefield 1990); Edward A. Harris, supra note 11, at 679; Kim Lane Scheppele & Jeremy Waldron, supra note 12, at 201. For our purposes, hypothetical consent approaches can be represented by Rawls's general theory.

33. Friedrich Nietzsche, On the Genealogy of Morals 57 (Walter Kauffmann & R.J. Hollingdale trans.) (New York: Random House 1967) (emphasis in the original).

34. Richard E. Flathman, supra note 4, at 213. Professor Simmons has listed five prerequisites to the validity of tacit consent. These include the known appropriateness of consent, the availability of an appropriate time and means for expressing dissent, a known time limit on the expression of dissent, the availability of reasonable and reasonably easily performed means of dissenting, and finally that "the consequences of dissent cannot be extremely detrimental to the potential consentor." A. John Simmons, supra note 1, at 80-81.

35. See Lea Brilmayer, supra note 3, at 35.

36. See id.

37. See, e.g., Charles Fried, supra note 28, at 16. Fried argues that "a liar and a promise-breaker each *use* another person. In both speech and promising there is an invitation to the other to trust, to make himself vulnerable; the liar and the promise-breaker then abuse that trust." Id. (emphasis in the original).

38. See Patrick S. Atiyah, Promises, Morals, and Law 143 (Oxford: Clarendon Press 1981). Atiyah argues, therefore, that "perhaps it is not the promise itself which creates the obligation, so much as the accompanying incidents." Id.

39. See Joseph Raz, Promises in Morality and Law, 95 Harv. L. Rev. 916, 925-28, 937 (1982). Raz criticizes Atiyah's claim that promises do not generally create new independent moral obligations, but merely evidence or admit the existence of logically prior moral obligations. See id. at 925-27. Raz's own argument, though, tends to establish the dependence of consent theory on rival theories of obligation. For further development of Raz's approach, see Joseph Raz, supra note 2, at 85-87, 175.

40. See Randy Barnett, A Consent Theory of Contract, 86 Colum. L. Rev. 269, 297 (1986).

41. Such a claim of a special linkage between consent and freedom is raised, for example, in Don Herzog, supra note 21, at 222; Kim Lane Scheppele & Jeremy Waldron, supra note 12, at 205.

42. See Richard E. Flathman, supra note 4, at 231-32.

Before moving on, a word or two should be said about the "consent" theory developed, with remarkable sophistication, by David Gauthier. Gauthier's primary concern is not with the legitimacy of government, but with the deeper question of a viable social morality for "adults," where adults are apparently defined partly in terms of a willingness to abandon all objective morality. See David Gauthier, Moral Artifice, 18 Can. J. Phil. 385, 385 (1988). Gauthier also abandons any reliance on non-self-interested sympathy or sociality. See id. The most extended exposition of his "rational choice" approach to constructing morality is David Gauthier, Morals By Agreement (Oxford: Clarendon Press 1986). Through techniques such as a version of Robert Nozick's "Lockean Proviso" and what Gauthier refers to as "constrained maximization," along with the "principle of relative minimax concession" in bargaining based on our initial endowments, we are to arrive at some determinate, stable way of distributing the net utility gains accruing from social cooperation.

It is fair to say that at a number of crucial stages of the argument, Gauthier builds in extremely controversial assumptions as to appropriate "baselines," rights, fairness, rationality, motivation, and psychology. These assumptions are questionable on grounds of empirical plausibility as well as normative moral appeal. See, e.g., Allan Gibbard, Constructing Justice, 20 Phil. & Pub. Aff. 264, 267, 270 (1991); Robert Goodin, Review of Morals By Agreement, 54 Economica 272, 273 (1987); Gregory S. Kavka, Review of Morals By Agreement, 96 Mind 117, 199-20 (1987).

Let us offer only a single brief illustration. For Gauthier, the constraints that morality imposes on the rational pursuit of self-interest must be consistent with mutual contractual benefit. See Morals By Agreement, supra, at 16, 232; David Copp, Review of Morals By Agreement, 98 Phil. Rev. 411, 412 (1989). But Professor Jean Hampton speaks for many in arguing that

> *regardless* of whether or not one can engage in beneficial cooperative interactions with another, one owes that person respectful treatment simply in virtue of the fact that he is a person. Not all value is subjective; in particular, the value which human beings have is objective, and demands one's respect, whether that human being is an infant with whom one will never have reason to cooperate, an elderly man past his prime, or an adult whose talents one finds of no particular use.

Jean Hampton, Can We Agree On Morals?, 18 Can. J. Phil. 331, 352 (1988) (emphasis in the original). While many reject the idea of moral objectivity, it does strike most of us as implausible that we can fairly despoil future generations, whether through current consumption financed by massive long-term debt or through irresponsible environmental policies, as long as the resources or welfare available to those not in a position to bargain with us does not fall below some specified modest baseline.

The deeper, more speculative problem, though, is whether a purely constructed, subjectivist morality really serves the long run interests of even those whose initial endowments, protected against force and fraud, have left them relatively well-off after bargaining has been successfully concluded. Those who see no morally objective reason to exert themselves unduly for the sake of future generations, or anyone else, may come to find that rational prudence permits behavior unexpected by or undesired by Gauthier. See Allan Gibbard, supra, at 267, 270-71. Over the long haul, as writers from Joseph Schumpeter to Daniel Bell have argued, the ideology of sheer self-interest, bereft of sympathy, sociality, or any objective grounding, may not sustain an attractive, diverse, productive society. See Wayne J. Norman, Review of Moral Dealing: Contracts, Ethics, and Reason, 101 Ethics 370, 372 (1992). For further discussion of the long-term unattractiveness of metaethically subjectivist societies, see infra chapter 5. For further discussion of Gauthier's work, see Contractarianism and Rational Choice: Essays on David Gauthier's Morals By Agreement (Peter Vallentyne ed.) (Cambridge: Cambridge Univ. Press 1991); The New Social Contract: Essays On Gauthier (Ellen Frankel Paul ed.) (Oxford: Basil Blackwell 1988); Symposium on David Gauthier's Morals By Agreement, 97 Ethics 715 (1987).

3

"Fair Play" Theories of Obligation

Of late, so-called "fair play" or "reciprocity-based" approaches to obligation have been increasingly popular. A number of sophisticated contemporary versions of fair play or reciprocity theory have been developed.[1] The particular version currently most prominent on the intellectual landscape is that of John Rawls.[2]

Rawls's theory of obligation does not begin with considerations of fair play or reciprocity. For Rawls, the morality of obedience is largely dependent upon prior questions of societal justice. Rawls argues that "[f]rom the standpoint of the theory of justice, the most important natural duty is that to support and to further just institutions. . . . [W]e are to comply with and do our share in just institutions when they exist and apply to us. . . ."[3] This does not mean that no unjust law can ever be morally binding. Rawls specifies that "[w]hen the basic structure of society is reasonably just, as estimated by what the current state of things allows, we are to recognize unjust laws as binding provided that they do not exceed certain limits of injustice."[4]

Rawls seeks to expand his theory beyond the asserted natural moral duty to comply with applicable just institutions. Rawls then introduces the element of fair play or reciprocity into the analysis. Under what Rawls refers to as the Principle of Fairness:

> a person is under an obligation to do his part as specified by the rules of an institution whenever he has voluntarily accepted the benefits of the scheme or has taken advantage of the opportunities it offers to advance his interests, provided that this institution is just or fair, that is, satisfies the two principles of justice.[5]

By "the two principles of justice," Rawls refers to his conclusions that "[e]ach person is to have an equal right to the most extensive total system of equal basic liberties compatible with a similar system of liberty for all"[6] and, secondly, that "[s]ocial and economic inequalities are to be arranged so that they are both . . . to the greatest benefit of the least advantaged, consistent with the just savings principle, and . . . attached to offices and positions open to all under conditions of fair equality of opportunity."[7]

Whether Rawls's Principle of Fairness, emphasizing the voluntary acceptance of benefits, really strengthens or extends his "natural duty" approach to obedience is open to doubt.[8] Regardless, Rawls's view of political obligation remains vitally dependent upon a logically prior assessment of the degree of justice of the basic structure of the society in question. However Rawls's theory of obligation is interpreted, most of the interesting questions of the morality of obligation are "pushed back" to the level of questions about societal justice.

Rawls's recent work has often been interpreted as taking a pragmatist, as opposed to metaphysically objectivist, turn. Rawls recognizes that his explicitly political, broadly liberal democratic conception of justice cannot hope to avoid all controversial metaphysical, religious, or other deep philosophical questions.[9] Nevertheless, Rawls has of late deemphasized the truth or falsity of moral claims in the quest for a consensus on crucial liberal democratic moral principles. Rawls is motivated in this partly by his belief that "as a practical political matter no general moral conception can provide a publicly recognized basis for a conception of justice in a modern democratic state."[10]

This change, however, does not mean that Rawls now wants the theory of obligation to be independent of conceptions of justice and injustice. Rawls's recent work continues to assume that reasonable persons capable of engaging in fair social cooperation will be willing and able to do their part, where they have reasonable assurance of others' doing their part, as long as the relevant institutional arrangements or practices are perceived to be just and fair.[11]

Justice as fairness within a democratic society aims at "a fair system of cooperation between citizens regarded as free and equal."[12] That fair system of cooperation is to be arrived at through bargaining under fair conditions, where fairness disallows the exercise by some persons of special bargaining advantages, such as great wealth, over other persons.[13] The imposition of a "veil of ignorance," for the sake of neutralizing such bargaining advantages, is thought to result in the selection of Rawls's two principles of justice referred to above.[14] In particular, as we have seen, justice requires among other things that "[s]ocial and economic inequalities . . . be to the greatest benefit of the least advantaged members of society."[15]

Whether we focus on the more metaphysical or less metaphysical version of Rawls's theory, it is difficult to conclude that a satisfactory account of political or legal obligation is at hand. There would of course be a vicious circularity if the idea of justice were thought to include the justice or injustice of revolution, civil disobedience, conscientious refusal, emigration, or other matters of obligation. If this were so, justice and obligation would each require that we first understand the other. But Rawls need not be interpreted in this way. Rawls does, however, rely generally on a coherentist methodology of "reflective equilibrium."[16] On this sort of coherentism, the plausibility of the theory of justice might depend as much on the plausibility of the theory of obligation as the converse, and neither would in this sense be privileged or foundational relative to the other.

Resolving the senses in which justice is and is not foundational with respect to obligation, though, does little to reduce the serious difficulties Rawls must confront. Rawls' theory of obligation is crucially dependent upon his theory of justice.[17] Most of the standard criticisms of the derivation or the substance of his theory of justice seem translatable into the context of Rawls's theory of obligation.[18] After all, Rawls's crucial point is not simply the generic claim that the obligation to obey depends upon whatever justice may turn out to require. Rather, it is that the obligation to obey depends upon the substance of the particular two principles of justice actually endorsed by Rawls.[19] And Rawls cannot avoid the controversiality of his two principles of justice by noting, doubtless correctly, that there may be many ways of arriving at or defending those two principles.

People are, it seems fair to say, equal in some arguably morally relevant respects, and unequal in others. We are, for example, unequal in our reluctance to impose suffering on other people. Rawls is doubtless correct in arguing that people are equal in the sense of equally possessing the capacities, to at least the minimal degree necessary, to be fully cooperating members of a society.[20] But as Professor Jean Hampton has pointed out, "not only is there no consensus on Rawls's conception of justice in our society, but, more disturbingly, there is no consensus on the idea that all human beings deserve equal respect."[21] Even if there were, happily, such a consensus, Rawls's two principles of justice would amount to only one among many approaches claiming compatibility with the idea of equal respect for persons.

Rawls's focus on mitigating the inequalities attributable to social or economic factors, as opposed to basic physiological, medical, or "natural" factors, has been cogently criticized, for example, by Professor Will Kymlicka.[22] If the latter factors are no more morally deserved than, say, social standing at birth or inherited wealth, then perhaps redress is morally called for. Perhaps compensation for "natural" disadvantage is the morally appropriate societal response, as opposed to mere nondiscrimination. More broadly, there are a host of important reasons to conclude that Rawls's two principles of justice are actually insufficiently egalitarian in their implications, and certainly not excessively egalitarian.[23] In general, the massive critical literature on Rawls leaves us with no reason to find his chosen principles of justice particularly attractive.

It should be noted as well that some have found Rawls's two principles of justice to be excessively egalitarian. Probably the best-known exposition of this view is that of Robert Nozick in *Anarchy, State and Utopia*.[24] Nozick does not, on his own understanding, repudiate the idea of the moral equality of persons, or for that matter, Kantian respect for the dignity of each person.[25] Nozick nevertheless rejects the redistributive potential of Rawls's two principles of justice.[26]

On Nozick's view, Rawls's full account of the obligation to obey, based on fair play as well as on a natural duty to cooperate with just institutions, would still be defective even if Rawls were right about his two principles of justice. Nozick denies in particular that there is any general moral obligation based on reciprocity or fair play to obey a government, or more broadly, to reciprocate for genuine benefits from the operation of otherwise just public institutions.[27] There do seem to be cases in which the voluntary receipt of modest benefits provided at little cost do not clearly give rise to a moral obligation to reciprocate. In some such cases, a word of thanks or a sincere intention to be specially benevolent might suffice as a moral response. Obedience, or general support, might not seem morally mandated.

Nozick's rejection of the fair play-based elements of Rawls's theory of obligation has been amplified by others. Professor Anthony D'Amato, for example, considers the case of someone who has received an undoubted benefit as a result of the workings of some social scheme. Couldn't such a person view what she has received as a genuine good, but less so than something attainable only in the absence of the social scheme in question? Couldn't such a person respond to such a benefit, or to others' sacrifices in providing such a benefit, by means other than direct cooperation with the social scheme? Couldn't a sincere and adequate gesture of thanks take many different forms? The response might equal the value of the benefit to the recipient, the market value of the benefit, the opportunity cost to the providers, or the providers' subjective assessment of the value of the benefit. Finally, couldn't a conscientious person determine that the power to set limits to her obligations via the giving or withholding of her consent is, in the case at hand, the highest moral good or right?[28]

None of this is to deny the enormous influence of Rawls's discussions of justice, of a natural duty to cooperate with applicable just institutions, or even of his discussion of fair play and obligation.[29] Equally undeniable, though, is the breadth and cogency of the objections raised against Rawls's approach at all stages of his argument. That not all objections to Rawls's theory are mutually compatible hardly rehabilitates that theory. As we have seen, Rawls has sought to cope with the difficulty of establishing the truth of his theory by deemphasizing the role of truth, at least as a criterion of theory selection. Instead, Rawls recommends his two principles of justice not because of their alleged moral truth, but because those principles are allegedly useful in developing, with a minimum of coercion, a stable morally-based societal consensus.

At this point, though, Rawls must confront a large question: why should we expect a greater consensus on Rawls's particular substantive moral principles than on somewhat more egalitarian, somewhat less egalitarian, or on otherwise divergent moral principles?[30] If there are no clear pragmatic grounds for choosing Rawls's principles over many incompatible alternative sets of principles, we may have little choice but to return to the questions of truth and metaphysics that Rawls seeks to bypass.[31]

Rawls realistically concedes the possibility that his project might fail, in that in our society no reasonable and workable conception of justice may attract an uncoerced overlapping consensus. This concession has been defended as merely indicating a healthy sense of fallibility.[32] But this amounts to fallibilism in an unusually strong and problematic sense. In its more familiar sense, fallibilism involves the modest recognition of our susceptibility to error in discerning what is truly just. Surely it goes beyond fallibilism in this sense to set aside truth or falsity as theory selection criteria, or to hold open the possibility that for our pluralistic society, no general solutions to the problems of justice or obligation may be available. It instead seems more reasonable to continue to suppose, along with traditional liberal fallibilism, that one or more sets of arrangements may be just, but that we might be mistaken as to what justice requires, or unable to implement what we take to be just institutional arrangements.

Rawls's approach to justice and obligation has attracted a great deal of attention, but his is not the only sophisticated contemporary theory incorporating considerations of fair play or reciprocity. Professor George Klosko, for example, has done thoughtful work along these lines. As we have seen, Rawls begins with a distinction between just and unjust regimes, and posits a natural duty of obedience with respect to the former. In contrast, Klosko posits a prima facie obligation to obey in the case of any rule of law providing important benefits, but then specifies that such an obligation may be overridden where obedience would involve committing injustice or supporting unjust institutions, or where a particular law is unjust or conflicts with the public good.³³

Thus Klosko differs at least technically from Rawls in requiring a moral theory of obligation that is to some extent prior to and independent of the theory of justice. But Klosko's approach too displaces much of the interest in the problem of obligation. Where Rawls shifts the interest "backward" into a prior general theory of justice, Klosko shifts much of the interest "forward" by making it relatively easy to create, but then defeat, prima facie moral obligations to obey. For both Rawls and Klosko, the general theory of justice and public morality is where much of the crucial action concerning obligation takes place.

This is not to deny that Klosko's analysis of fair play or reciprocity in the creation of obligations is of interest. Klosko's theory, for example, controversially deemphasizes the role of voluntariness in the creation of obligations. Consider, for example, Klosko's reference to the good of national defense: "If A benefits from the protection his fellow citizens provide, he has an obligation to cooperate in their efforts. He can be obligated to serve in the armed forces or to help finance them with tax payments or both."³⁴ Klosko argues specifically that "as long as the benefits in question are sufficiently large, someone 'who by simply going about his business in a normal fashion' benefits unavoidably from a cooperative scheme does indeed incur an obligation to contribute to the scheme."³⁵

A fair play theorist such as Klosko presumably wants at a minimum to deny that obligations are normally the result of voluntary consent. It is possible for a fair play theorist to concede that persons voluntarily receive certain benefits from their government. Such a fair play theorist could simply deny that the voluntary receipt of benefits typically involves broad consent to a government. But fair play theorists often find obligations to obey not only where there has been no consent to obey, but where there has been no consent even to receive the benefits in question.

Along such lines, John Stuart Mill argues that quite apart from any fictional social contract, "everyone who receives the protection of society owes a return for the benefit. . . ."³⁶ Mill gives no indication that for such an obligation to attach, the benefit must have been received voluntarily. Kent Greenawalt has made a similar point more explicitly: "If someone is delighted to receive a benefit, understands the cooperative scheme by which it is supplied, and believes that his required contribution is a fair share, then he may be in the same position as someone who has genuinely chosen to receive a benefit he could freely refuse."³⁷

In considering such cases of alleged nonconsensual obligation, does the sheer size of the benefit conferred matter? If so, how? Some have argued that it does matter, quite apart from whether everyone receives or values the alleged benefit. Edward A. Harris, who endorses a fair play approach to obligation,[38] asserts that "when the benefits produced by the scheme are sufficiently substantial, the involuntary participant can incur obligations of fairness to contribute to the scheme."[39]

Harris uses the distinction between large and small benefits to limit the applicability of Robert Nozick's claim that the benefits flowing from a rotating public address system do not impose a moral obligation to cooperate with the scheme. Even if each of us enjoys the programs, voluntarily or involuntarily, Nozick's claim that no obligation to cooperate is created may be right. But this may be only because the benefits from such a scheme are too insignificant. Listening to such programming is normally far from indispensable, and far from what Rawls would call a primary social good.

But does the substantiality of the benefit really make the difference by affecting what reciprocity requires? Factors such as the substantiality of the benefit, or the voluntariness of its receipt, may merely help determine whether we have a "natural" moral duty under the circumstances to cooperate, apart from any considerations of fair play or reciprocity.

Might we not have a "natural" moral duty, for example, to risklessly save a stranger's life, but not to risklessly trim a stranger's hangnail, or to play announcer on a public address system? The importance or triviality of the benefit helps determine whether a moral duty exists, but not via considerations of fair play, reciprocity, or benefitting in one's turn. If, as some "fair play" theorists concede, we may have a moral obligation to cooperate with a scheme even where we have no chance of personally receiving any benefit from that scheme,[40] the best explanation may be through a "natural duty" approach, as opposed to a fair play or reciprocity theory.

By way of further example, let us consider George Klosko's discussion of auto emission controls. Klosko argues that one may have an obligation, under appropriate circumstances, to comply, along with one's fellows, with specified auto emission regulations.[41] As Klosko of course recognizes, the emission regulations are at bottom an attempt to address health and other effects of unregulated emissions. But do we really need a fair play or reciprocal benefit analysis to generate a prima facie moral obligation in such cases, or even to morally criticize free riders?

Instead, it may be simpler and more plausible to recur to some sort of natural prima facie moral duty not to knowingly participate, unjustifiedly, in the imposition of a significant health risk on other persons. No doubt the contribution of any individual polluter to a health risk, in general or with respect to any particular victim, may be minimal. But there is no reason to suppose that there can be no natural moral duty in such cases. There might even be some moral duty at work even if everyone else is polluting, and we are not benefitting from anyone's restraint. Reciprocity or fair play thus may not be crucial. Natural moral duty may, for example, bid us not be even formally or technically associated with any racist organization, even where the incremental harm done by our membership in particular is minimal. Thus natural moral duties need not be confined to cases in which an identifiable person individually imposes a substantial risk on some other identifiable person. Such duties can also exist when others are not doing their fair share.

The idea of benefit must be explored as well. Klosko offers a sophisticated account of what constitutes a benefit in the first place. Some goods, such as national defense or environmental protection, may be worth at least the average recipient's effort, if not everyone's effort, in providing them. In the case of such goods, it may also be impossible or unduly costly to provide the benefits only to particular people, while excluding others. Klosko recognizes that in an intellectually or culturally diverse society, there may not be unanimous agreement on what sorts of things are good even in the abstract. Klosko focuses, therefore, on what he calls "presumptively beneficial" goods in an assumed society of shared values and priorities, in much the same way Rawls does.

Klosko then defines "presumptively beneficial" goods as "necessary for a minimally acceptable life. In other words, they must be desired by rational individuals regardless of whatever else they desire, even though this account presupposes a background of generally accepted values and beliefs."[42] Again, some rational persons may be pacifists, or may consider environmental protection, as opposed to one's spiritual fate, to be inconsequential. Such persons are, on Klosko's account, assumed not to affect the analysis.

The major remaining problem for Klosko, then, involves the "level of generality" at which goods are described. In the abstract, national defense and environmental protection may qualify as ordinarily worthwhile, nonexcludable, presumptively beneficial goods. But virtually no citizen is called upon to decide whether national defense and environmental protection deserve support. Citizens typically face practical questions of obligation with regard to particular defense or environmental policies, reflecting a particular level of defense or environmental protection, at some particular moral and economic cost.

Thus citizens typically must decide, for example, whether they are morally obligated to support an army of a particular size or capability, with a particular history and current strategy, or to help fight a particular war in a particular way, or to pay taxes to support such a war, or to cooperate with a compulsory military draft or registration system, again of a certain sort, under particular circumstances. Some minimal level of defense, observing appropriate moral limitations, may be a presumptively beneficial good. But that is rarely the question. Even if we assume that some minimal defense is good, that does not help much in developing a fair play account of the real questions of moral obligation citizens must confront.[43] Assuming that because of shared values, citizens will tend to think homogeneously about such issues, or about environmental regulations, would simply be unrealistic.

The "level of generality" problem would thus seem to further limit the utility of Professor Klosko's fair play approach. Klosko does argue for placement of the burden of proof in a way that might advance his cause. He suggests that in cases in which the value of a putative good is disputed, "the burden of proof is on the recipient to show why he believes that the goods are undesirable."[44] This placement seems controversial, though. Perhaps it is based on the assumption that the majority is more likely to be right about not only the popularity of an alleged good, but about its real value or indispensability as well. But it is, after all, the majority that proposes to forcibly coerce the minority into cooperating with the social scheme in question. Wouldn't the cause of individual liberty or autonomy therefore be served by requiring would-be coercers to justify their coercion?

Even if each of the problems noted above could be solved, fair play theories would still have to confront what can be called the "relevant baseline" problem. Let us suppose that a government supplies a person with a good that she does indeed want. Before we conclude that a fair play-based obligation to cooperate exists, though, we would presumably want to know, for example, whether that same good would be freely available in a "state of nature," or in the absence of the cooperative scheme in question. If so, why should any moral obligation to cooperate attach? We need a reason why some chosen set of circumstances should provide the relevant baseline.

To illustrate the baseline problem, Ronald Dworkin has argued that it asks too much to find an obligation to cooperate only if the putative obligor is better off, given her receipt of the good in question, than she would be under any practical alternative scheme.[45] But Dworkin argues as well that it asks too little if an obligation is to be imposed whenever the "beneficiary" is, in that respect, better off than she would be in some bleak, atomistic state of nature.[46] Such baseline problems are not insoluble in principle, but they often lead to substantively controversial, if not apparently arbitrary, results.[47]

In sum, the most interesting "fair play" theories of obligation tend to be underdeveloped, unconvincing, or unnecessary insofar as they focus on fair play. The fair play elements of such theories tend not to directly address the most interesting questions. Such questions tend to be shunted aside into controversial broad theories of justice. Insofar as fair play theories recognize that problems of legal and political obligation can be adequately addressed only along with basic moral issues, they are on the right track.

NOTES TO *"FAIR PLAY"* THEORIES OF OBLIGATION

1. See, e.g., George Klosko, The Principle of Fairness and Political Obligation (Lanham, Md.: Rowman & Littlefield 1992); Richard J. Arneson, The Principle of Fairness and Free Rider Problems, 92 Ethics 616 (1982); Kent Greenawalt, Promise, Benefit, and Need: Ties That Bind Us to the Law, 18 Ga. L. Rev. 727 (1984); Edward A. Harris, Fighting Philosophical Anarchism with Fairness: The Moral Claims of Law in the Liberal State, 91 Colum. L. Rev. 919 (1991); H.L.A. Hart, Are There Any Natural Rights?, 64 Phil. Rev. 175 (1955); George Nakhnikian, The Principle of Reciprocal Obligations, 55 Phil. Stud. 195 (1989).

2. See John Rawls, A Theory of Justice (Cambridge: Harvard Univ. Press 1971). Rawls's theory has been revised in ways relevant to problems of obligation in a series of articles. See, e.g., John Rawls, Justice as Fairness: Political not Metaphysical, 14 Phil. & Pub. Aff. 223 (1985); John Rawls, The Idea of an Overlapping Consensus, 7 Ox. J. Legal Stud. 1 (1987); John Rawls, The Domain of the Political and Overlapping Consensus, 64 N.Y.U. L. Rev. 233 (1989). Much of Rawls' work over the past two decades has been compiled, in revised and expanded form, in John Rawls, Political Liberalism (New York: Columbia Univ. Press 1993).

3. John Rawls, A Theory of Justice 334 (Cambridge: Harvard Univ. Pres 1971).

4. Id. at 351.

5. Id. at 342-43.

6. Id. at 302.

7. Id.

8. See Nancy Hirschmann, Rethinking Obligation: A Feminist Method for Political Theory 93-94 (Ithaca: Cornell Univ. Press 1992).

9. See John Rawls, Justice as Fairness: Political not Metaphysical, 14 Phil. & Pub. Aff. 223, 223 (1985).

10. Id. at 225. For discussions of Rawls's pragmatic turn, see, e.g., Kai Nielsen, John Rawls' New Methodology: An Interpretive Account, 35 McGill L.J. 572,

597-98, 601 (1990); Joseph Raz, Facing Diversity: The Case of Epistemic Abstinence, 19 Phil. & Pub. Aff. 3, 9, 15 n.34 (1990).

11. See John Rawls, The Idea of an Overlapping Consensus, 7 Ox. J. Legal Stud. 1, 22 (1987).

12. John Rawls, The Domain of the Political and Overlapping Consensus, 64 N.Y.U. L. Rev. 233, 241 (1989). See also id. at 240.

13. See John Rawls, supra note 9, at 235.

14. See supra notes 6-7 & accompanying text.

15. John Rawls, supra note 12, at 251 n.43 (citing John Rawls, supra note 9, at 227).

16. See, e.g., John Rawls, supra note 9, at 228.

17. See, e.g., Jonathan Wolff, What Is the Problem of Political Obligation?, 91 Proc. Aristotelian Society 153, 167 (1991).

18. See Gerald Doppelt, Is Rawls's Kantian Liberalism Coherent and Defensible?, 99 Ethics 815, 847 (1989).

19. See supra notes 6-7 & accompanying text.

20. See Jean Hampton, Should Political Philosophy Be Done Without Metaphysics?, 99 Ethics 791, 796 (1989).

21. Id. at 813.

22. See Will Kymlicka, Contemporary Political Philosophy 72-73 (Oxford: Clarendon Press 1990).

23. See, e.g., R. George Wright, The High Cost of Rawls' Inegalitarianism, 30 Western Pol. Q. 73 (1977).

24. See Robert Nozick, Anarchy, State and Utopia (New York: Basic Books 1974). In his more recent work, Nozick briefly and generally repudiates, to an indeterminate extent, his earlier atomistic, property rights-based libertarianism. See Robert Nozick, The Examined Life: Philosophical Meditations 286-96 (New York: Simon & Schuster 1989).

25. See Robert Nozick, Anarchy, State and Utopia 31 (New York: Basic Books 1974).

26. See id. at 161 (Nozick's "Wilt Chamberlain" example of the alleged justice of unequal rewards flowing from natural talent, effort, and market choices).

27. See id. at 93-95 (Nozick's hypothetical rotating public address system case).

28. See Anthony D'Amato, The Obligation to Obey the Law: A Study of the Death of Socrates, 49 S. Cal. L. Rev. 1079, 1104-05 (1976).

29. A mere sampling of recent book-length works appreciative of Rawls's efforts might include, for example, Rex Martin, Rawls and Rights (Lawrence: Univ. Press of Kansas 1985); Thomas Nagel, Equality and Partiality (New York: Oxford Univ. Press 1991); Thomas W. Pogge, Realizing Rawls (Ithaca: Cornell Univ. Press 1989).

30. See Jean Hampton, supra note 20, at 797; Patrick Neal, Justice as Fairness: Political or Metaphysical?, 18 Pol. Theory 24, 44 (1990). See also George Klosko, Rawls's "Political" Philosophy and American Democracy, 87 Am. Pol. Sci. Rev. 348 (1993).

31. See Patrick Neal, supra note 30, at 44; Joseph Raz, supra note 10, at 31.

32. See Kai Nielsen, supra note 10, at 600.

33. See George Klosko, The Moral Force of Political Obligations, 84 Am. Pol. Sci. Rev. 1235, 1246-47 (1990).

34. Id. at 1243.

35. George Klosko, Presumptive Benefit, Fairness, and Political Obligation, 16 Phil. & Pub. Aff. 241, 249 (1987).

36. John Stuart Mill, On Liberty ch. iv, at 141 (Gertrude Himmelfarb ed.) (New York: Penguin ed. 1974).

37. Kent Greenawalt, Promise, Benefit, and Need: Ties That Bind Us to the Law, 18 Ga. L. Rev. 727, 757 (1984). Presumably the "fair share" requirement means only something like the belief that one's own assessment is not disproportionate to the assessment imposed on other people; if it meant that one considered it fair that one pay one's share, the theory so formulated would be of reduced interest as an alternative to consent theory. A person

who admits to the overall fairness of a practice, including the moral demand that she appropriately support that practice, is essentially estopped from generally denying the moral legitimacy of such a practice. Most dissenters from a practice would presumably not be willing to make such an admission.

38. See Edward A. Harris, supra note 1, at 944.

39. Id. at 953-54.

40. See id. at 950-51 (discussing the work of Kent Greenawalt); George Klosko, The Principle of Fairness and Political Obligation, 97 Ethics 353, 355 n.7 (1987) ("it is not necessary that each individual participant benefit").

41. See George Klosko, supra note 35, at 250. Klosko's argument in this regard is effectively critiqued in A. John Simmons, The Anarchist Position: A Reply to Klosko and Senor, 16 Phil. & Pub. Aff. 269, 271-72 (1987).

42. George Klosko, supra note 40, at 355.

43. Compare A. John Simmons, The Principle of Fair Play, 8 Phil. & Pub. Aff. 307, 335 (1979) (many persons, "faced with high taxes, with military service which may involve fighting in foreign 'police actions,' or with unreasonably restrictive laws governing private pleasures, believe that the benefits received from governments are not worth the price they are forced to pay.")

44. George Klosko, supra note 40, at 355 n.9.

45. See Ronald Dworkin, Law's Empire 194 (Cambridge: Harvard Univ. Press 1986).

46. See id.

47. See, e.g., Richard J. Arneson, The Principle of Fairness and Free-Rider Problems, 92 Ethics 616, 623 (1982). Arneson's fair play theory requires, among other things, that the scheme of cooperation in question provide benefits that are worth their costs to each recipient. It would seem to follow that on Arneson's fair play theory, no moral obligation attaches where an individual sincerely, if eccentrically, considers her accruing benefit to be insufficient. Arneson's argument, more fully, holds that

> where a scheme of cooperation is established that supplies a collective benefit that is worth its cost to each recipient, where the burdens of cooperation are fairly divided, where it is unfeasible to attract voluntary compliance to the scheme via supplementary private

benefits, and where the collective benefit is either voluntarily accepted or such that voluntary acceptance of it is impossible, those who contribute their assigned fair share of the costs of the scheme have a right, against the remaining beneficiaries, that they should also pay their fair share.

Id.

4

John Finnis on Obligation and the Natural Law

In *Natural Law and Natural Rights*[1] and elsewhere,[2] John Finnis develops a theory of legal and political obligation that blends ancient, medieval, and modern elements. Finnis does not pretend to offer precise, exhaustive guidance as to when obedience or disobedience to authority is morally appropriate. The moral status of disobedience will often depend upon culture and context. Finnis does offer a general framework for thinking about legal and political obligation. He elaborately traces the moral and practical logic of obligation from what he takes to be its roots in human goods.

Human goods, Finnis argues, cannot be deduced or inferred from descriptions of human nature. More broadly, human goods cannot be deduced from any set of theoretically knowable facts, even though human goods would be different if human nature were different. Finnis also denies that human goods are intuited, since we do not perform some intuitive act of apprehending human goods in the absence of data and experience. Rather, human goods are known to us as obvious or as self-evident, through what Finnis calls non-inferential acts of understanding.

Finnis' talk of the obviousness or self-evidence of human goods has led to a certain amount of confusion.[3] Finnis' basic idea is that our inability to point to a more basic reason for wanting to do something need not mean that our wanting to do that thing is arbitrary, unjustified, or unintelligible. Some reasons for acting can be said to be self-justifying or to require no (further) justification. Those reasons refer to what Finnis considers basic aspects of human flourishing, beyond which no further informative explanation is possible or logically called for.

Consider the case of someone shining a flashlight at her front lawn after midnight. Let us suppose she has been asked why she is acting in this way. Her possible responses fall into several categories. Some responses would be intelligible and satisfying, but only because special background assumptions are at work. Thus if she says "I'm looking for my house key," no further probing will ordinarily seem appropriate, but only because we automatically fill in some assumed facts, values, and purposes.

Some responses to our question, however, would be unintelligible or unsatisfying. Thus if she says "I'm just directing flashlight rays at the grass. There's no further purpose or ulterior motive at stake, it's just something I'm doing for its own sake," we will likely be mystified. If she insists that she is acting freely and not as part of some compulsive ritual, we might suppose that some aspect of play, relaxation, aesthetic experience, or learning must, despite her denials, really be involved.

Midway between these cases would be responses that become intelligible and satisfying only upon further explicit clarification. Thus if she tells us "I'm looking for an acorn," we may be initially mystified, but eventually satisfied by her explanation if she further reports that she needs an acorn to finish off her list of scavenger hunt items.

Finally, some responses are thought by Finnis to be intelligible and satisfying on their own, without further elaboration, inquiry, or special assumptions. Thus if she says "I'm exploring the relationship between temperature, humidity, and dew formation, just because I'm curious," no further substantive explanation will, according to Finnis, normally be called for or possible. Finnis regards the satisfaction of such curiosity, or the pursuit of knowledge for its own sake, as a basic, intrinsic human good.[4] Thus if pressed, she would ordinarily be able to offer no genuinely deeper explanation for her actions beyond a mere generic, abstract reference to the good of knowledge. Doubtless she might be able to discuss why she has chosen to focus on meteorological dimensions of knowledge in particular, or why she has chosen to pursue knowledge at this point rather than some other basic human good. But these further responses would not imply that her reference to curiosity or the good of knowledge was somehow inherently problematic, incomplete, or mysterious. Knowledge is thus a basic human good. Of course, that an action is understandable, as undertaken in the pursuit of knowledge, does not mean that it was morally or prudentially defensible under the circumstances. Knowledge is, in itself, a premoral basic human good. The pursuit of knowledge may not always be morally appropriate.

Finnis argues that the good of knowledge is thus not inferred or deduced from any set of propositions. The obviousness, self-evidence, or underived quality of the good of knowledge, including the example above, reflects the fact that explanations of our actions in terms of the pursuit of knowledge are normally taken to be unproblematic and explanatorily self-sufficient.

On Finnis' view, it is thus possible to gain insight into at least premoral forms of good while conceding what we have elsewhere taken to be Hume's point about the non-derivability of any interesting "ought" (or good) from any set of purely factual premises. Finnis does not try to leap across the chasm between factual claims and valuational, purposive, action-guiding principles. Of course, if human nature were radically different, so would human goods. But Finnis does not argue inferentially from nature to goods. More broadly, he does not argue from theoretical or speculative reason to practical reason. He starts and stays on the practical, action-guiding side of the chasm, relying upon underived, noninferential insight into forms of the human good.

Finnis thus departs from those natural lawyers who claim to derive values from facts, or perhaps more accurately, who concede Hume's argument, but insist that statements regarding human nature can simultaneously be action-guiding statements as well. On their view, apparently factual statements describing human nature may be inescapably value-laden. Such natural lawyers might claim that we really desire things only insofar as the satisfaction of our desire is truly perfective of us. Thus the fact of human desire may be said to itself be importantly valuational.[5]

But Finnis, again, does not take that route. Finnis argues that the value of knowledge cannot be inferred from such alleged facts as, for example, any human consensus on its value, any universality of the desire to know, the evolutionary survival advantage conferred by knowledge, or any fit between knowledge and any unique factual attribute of human beings as a species.

Finnis focuses on knowledge for its own sake, as opposed to knowledge as a means to some extrinsic end. This focus is certainly understandable. Knowledge as a means to some further end would hardly qualify as a "basic" good. The focus on knowledge as an end in itself also deflects certain criticisms of the claim that knowledge is a basic good. For example, while knowledge of the fissionability of plutonium may be put to purposes destructive of any attractive human values, this possibility need not impeach the pursuit of knowledge of nuclear physics for its own sake. Finnis assumes that a clear distinction can be drawn between knowledge and the good or bad uses to which it is presumably contingently put.

On the other hand, focusing on knowledge for its own sake implies that we must think of knowledge as a good apart from its role as a means to such presumably good things as self-control, mastery of nature, enhanced self-esteem, technical progress, happiness, useful inventions, or pleasure. Presumably there is a difference between simply wanting to know something, and wanting to know something only for the sensation of pleasure that may accrue from knowing.

In the latter case, pleasure rather than knowledge would seem basic. But Finnis does not recognize pleasure as a basic human good. This may seem controversial. If we are asked, in a wide variety of contexts, why we are doing what we are doing, the answer "because it gives me pleasure to do so" will seem as logically complete, intelligible, self-sufficient, and satisfying as any answer referring to any basic good recognized by Finnis. In fact, it seems often possible to dig beneath explanations in terms of knowledge and uncover deeper explanations in terms of pleasure. If it were not pleasurable, the activity of learning for its own sake might hold limited appeal. Pleasure does not seem to be inherently scarce, divisive, a "zero-sum" good, or dependent upon any other human good. The problem of pleasure for Finnis, though, is that the attainment of a sensation of pleasure may indeed be an intelligible reason for action, but not fulfilling or perfective of human beings in the way Finnis expects will be true of basic goods generally.

Perhaps pleasure is too generic or cross-categorical for certain explanatory purposes, though. Almost any sort of act, selfish or altruistic, might produce some kind of pleasure, of some moral quality, in the actor. Some pleasurable sensations might be objected to on moral or prudential grounds. But we might similarly object to the pursuit or experience of knowledge in some circumstances.

Let us consider, though, a different sort of problem for Finnis. The idea of basic human goods is the foundation of Finnis' theory of obligation. But are there really any culturally or historically invariant basic human goods as Finnis uses the term? No doubt the forms in which we pursue goods will be culturally dependent. But, for example, is knowledge a basic good for humans regardless of cultural context? If not, Finnis' natural law theory might turn into a powerful defense of some form of moral relativism.

There is certainly something logically odd about an excessively broad denial that knowledge is a good. Claims, for example, that no proposition about knowledge is worth uttering, or that no knowledge is worth communicating, for itself or as a means to some further end, seem self-refuting when made for their alleged truth value. But denying that knowledge is usually good, let alone a basic good, does not commit one to any such self-refuting claim. Thus even if Finnis could somehow construct parallel self-refutational arguments concerning other basic goods besides knowledge, this would contribute little to the defense of his theory of basic goods.

When we reflect on the possible kinds and circumstances of knowing, the value of knowing in and for itself seems at least to require substantial qualification. Normally, using a flashlight to help count and thus know the total number of blades of grass in one's front lawn will seem a trivial or pointless act. If someone explains that they are not interested in such knowledge for the sake of, say, thickening their lawn, or for relaxation, but merely for the sake of the knowledge itself, the act of grass blade counting may then have some nominal point, but will also seem devoid of any real moral or premoral value. This would be so even if there were no other demands on the blade-counter's time.

Common sense tells us, therefore, that knowledge for its own sake can be trivial. As well, knowledge for its own sake often involves distraction from other activities; the upset of persons whose knowledge we have cruelly, prematurely, or tactlessly increased; an informational overload that impairs decisionmaking; or the pathological intellectualization of problems requiring more direct confrontation. Knowledge is sometimes attainable only at a high cost in privacy. Often, it is only our ignorance of the obstacles we will inevitably face in some worthy undertaking that allows us to be motivated to undertake the effort at all. Examples of each of these phenomena are obvious. Instances of even the self-defeating character of knowledge are not difficult to spot: many golfers know more about their golf swing than is good for them as golfers.

Now, Finnis insists that the good of knowledge is limited by a ceteris paribus or "other things equal" clause. Depending upon the circumstances, knowledge may not be a good, or at least not practically or morally advisable under the circumstances. But Finnis' "other things equal" clause must not be too broad, lest it trivialize the claim that knowledge in itself is a good. If we use the ceteris paribus clause to rule out a wide range of frequently encountered cases, we may begin to wonder why we shouldn't just consider knowledge itself as inherently neither good nor bad, and as either good or bad depending, sensitively, on the relevant circumstances.

But has anyone ever really denied that knowledge for its own sake of, for example, the basic principles of nature is a good? No one in the Platonic-Aristotelian tradition could do so. Plato admittedly recurs to mythology not just for the masses, but for his ideal political elite as well, if possible. But we can assume that Plato's reliance on indoctrination of literal falsehoods is for the sake of conveying deeper truths. However, one could easily envision Rousseau in some moods, or a nineteenth century Romantic, exalting the noble savage or the rule of passion over knowledge and reason. An individual or group might prefer a life in which passion overrules reason or knowledge, without being logically committed to the belief that even this preference itself is knowably sound, or that it is good to know even that passion should prevail over knowledge, let alone any other truth. We can imagine cultures that generally distrust reason and view attempts to gain knowledge as generally hubristic, doomed, or destructive of higher values. Such cultures could be Romantic, hyper-fallibilist, postmodern, Nietzschean, traditionalist, Spartan, or theologically motivated.

In order for Finnis to make a convincing case that knowledge for its own sake is a good, basic or otherwise, Finnis must, it would seem, appeal more directly to facts or assumptions about the world. Only such an appeal could give us clear reason to believe that, for example, the pursuit of knowledge is not chimerical, arbitrary, prideful self-delusion, or destructive of our better selves. If knowledge is a good, it is only because the world is a particular kind of place, and because we have a particular kind of relation to that world. Now, Finnis might again grant that if the world or our relation to the world were otherwise, knowledge might not be a good. But to work in our context, this would have to amount to a vital concession. It would appear that to really justify knowledge as a human good, we must unavoidably and crucially recur to matters of theoretical reason, to matters of fact, and to metaphysics.

The idea of human flourishing through pursuit of the basic goods, including knowledge, provides the crucial first step in Finnis' account of legitimate political and legal authority. Some of Finnis' basic goods apart from knowledge, such as friendship or sociability, themselves point toward a civil order. More importantly, though, all basic human goods can, in practice, ordinarily be effectively realized only in some sort of coordinate community. The efficient pursuit of knowledge outside of coordinate community is, as Hobbes recognized, unlikely at best. In principle, this coordinate community might take the form of a continuous unanimous democracy in which legal and political authority could be said to be absent. But the obvious inefficiencies in any such system drive the community toward some form of authority.[6]

Legal and political authority for Finnis are therefore not necessarily a mere reflection upon human selfishness or, for that matter, a mode of resolving vital conflicts of basic interests.[7] The need to coordinate with others for the sake of human flourishing reflects, more basically, the unnecessary costs of each of us using, for example, our best good faith independent judgment as to which side of the road to drive upon. Authority can arise legitimately because it is practically necessary in order to promote the fulfillment of basic human goods. It is not hard to see the safe promotion of basic human goods as a moral obligation. While Finnis believes that we cannot commensurate or quantitatively maximize the satisfaction of basic human goods, he believes at least that we can recognize when we are vitally promoting basic human goods or preventing their promotion. The common good, in the form of the rich fulfillment of human goods generally, may as a practical matter require that authority be exercised. All persons relevantly situated may thus acquire a moral obligation to comply with authority.

Coordinative authority for the sake of the efficient realization of human goods thus might arise without explicit contract or consent. Let us suppose that we find ourselves in a situation in which social coordination would seem generally advantageous, but there is as yet no recognized legal or political authority to provide that coordination. Consider a case in which everyone agrees upon the need to quickly empty a multiple-doored building of its occupants, while providing for the simultaneous entry of new occupants. If the various individuals and groups involved simply use their best good faith judgments as to ingress and egress, or try to actually negotiate, the result will be massive inefficiency.

One person, though, may happen somehow to be in a particularly salient position. She may be visible to all. She may have the only bullhorn. She may have set the rule on the last occasion for coordination. Or she may have come closest to authoritatively setting the rule among several arguably salient actors in the last failed attempt at coordination. Salience of an actor is thus really a matter of a relatively great likelihood that persons who are open to some efficient solution to a coordination problem will acquiesce in a solution signaled or proposed by the actor in question.

A person who is in a position of salience has a distinctive practical opportunity, and indeed a moral obligation, to establish some fair, just, and rights-respecting convention that promotes the common good. Fulfilling that obligation requires selecting, and making salient, one of the possible solutions to the coordination problem at hand. To complete the example above, designating the North and South doors for exit, and the East and West doors for entrance, may be a just solution, even if no more so in the abstract than some other arrangement.

Now, Finnis' theory has so far said nothing about coercive sanctions for refusing to follow any coordination solution. Some may therefore deny that a genuine political or legal system obtains in the circumstances Finnis has thus far described. But there has been progress toward developing a theory of a moral obligation to comply with designated coordination solutions that are otherwise just.

Finnis notes in particular that ongoing mass coordination problems are typically more complex than, say, problems of whether one individual promisor should breach a promise made to an individual promisee. The most reasonable thing for most of us to do, in many mass coordination situations, is to follow any apparently fair saliently designated solution, rather than using our best autonomous judgment to derive and follow some allegedly technically superior solution. A certain degree of deference on the part of most persons is thus appropriate beyond the deference we normally show in deciding whether to keep ordinary promises to individuals.

Of course, the mere salience of a proposed solution does not guarantee the justice of that solution. For Finnis, the ideas of justice, the common good, and natural or human rights are closely related. Some rights are, on Finnis' account, exceptionless and absolute. Finnis does not call for universal deference to rulemakers in this respect. Thus reason may allow or require disobedience to authority in certain cases.[8] Whether disobedience to a particular rule or to a regime in general is morally justified will, according to Finnis, normally be determined in part by considerations of circumstance.

Finnis notes, interestingly, that the moral logic of obedience to authority extends beyond consideration of the moral character of the rules themselves. There is also in Finnis' argument a "fairness" or "reciprocity" strain. Presumably, many of us derive a very broad range of important benefits from the exercise of authority and from the general legal compliance of others. We could not flourish as well in the absence of such compliance by others. According to Finnis, fairness requires acceptance by us of certain reciprocal burdens and restraints, in the form of broad adherence to law. Persons who defy authority may thus be acting, unfairly, as "free riders." We have generally discussed fairness or reciprocity-based theories of obligation above.

Of course, governments as well as individuals are capable of acting unjustly. In general, a government commits commutative injustice, according to Finnis, when it violates any absolute moral right, such as what Finnis takes to be the absolute, exceptionless moral right never to be lied to when a factual communication is reasonably expected. Finnis does not claim that such a right is self-evident or obvious. We shall take up the question of the defense of basic moral principles briefly below. In the meantime, it should be noted that for Finnis, commutative justice also requires that the government not deny any non-absolute moral right which could in practice be exercised or fulfilled consistent with the public welfare and with the appropriate exercise by other persons of the same as well as other rights.

Interestingly, Finnis recognizes no general human right to social freedom. Freedom is not a basic human good. Of course, some minimal degree of freedom is presupposed by the idea of moral or immoral action itself. Beyond this, Finnis emphasizes that the virtues of the rule of law itself, in limiting arbitrary governmental action and in promoting predictability, are conducive to individual dignity, self-direction, and freedom of action. And there are of course many ways of pursuing various human goods. But this hardly amounts to a distinctive emphasis on freedom.

Finnis values freedom, but sees freedom solely as an instrumental good. Finnis argues that whatever denial of freedom paternalism may involve does not necessarily violate what he considers the self-evident principle that each person is entitled to equal concern and respect, or at least that merely arbitrary departures from equal concern and respect are unjustified. This may open the door to Finnis' refusal to consider freedom of action and choice to be among the basic human goods.

In a way, this seems understandable. If knowledge itself, for example, is a good, it will usually seem good whether it is freely acquired or forced upon us. That persons are compelled to attend school raises many interesting moral issues, but does not of itself necessarily impeach the goodness of the knowledge gained. Most good things remain good even if our receipt of those good things is constrained.

But having a choice among all (other) possible goods may itself be a good. Often, we want things only, or more strongly, if our having them is not coerced. And sometimes, we want freedom itself, apart from the particular things freedom allows us to do. Finnis thus seems mistaken in viewing freedom as simply an instrumental good. We might want freedom of action and choice even if our being free somehow meant that our menu of choices was confined to less desirable objects of choice than those items now available to us under constraint. Consider that it is possible reasonably to want political freedom, or self-determination for a colony, even if it turned out that such freedom would result in somewhat less of all the things that Finnis recognizes as basic human goods.

It is certainly possible to deny that freedom is a basic human good. Admittedly, not all persons and not all societies seem to want any sort of political freedom. But explanations of our actions in terms of pursuing the good of freedom may be as deep, intelligible, satisfying, and as logically complete as an explanation in terms of any (other) basic good. As Finnis recognizes, not everyone values knowledge for its own sake or some other of Finnis' basic goods.

It may admittedly be possible to offer some further explanation of our desire for freedom, perhaps in terms of human dignity. But if the good of freedom is in this sense non-basic, the good of knowledge can hardly be basic either, as we might just as well explain our quest for knowledge in terms of human dignity. Finnis, it might be noted, believes that one must not act directly against, or with no other intent than to impair, any basic good. Recognizing freedom as a basic good thus might, to some degree, enhance the status and protection accorded to freedom by a just political order. In turn, an increased emphasis on political freedom might more securely entrench democracy within Finnis' system.

The possibility of a marriage of basic elements of Finnis' theory with crucial elements of the broad liberal tradition should thus not be overlooked. Finnis has gone so far as to recognize harmony between one's choices and one's behavior as a basic human good. He seems to have in mind the difference between "living a lie" and living with authenticity. But this basic good could also be interpreted more broadly, providing more substance for a Finnisian liberalism.

There is more to the just political order than commutative justice, though. Finnis recognizes as well the claims of distributive justice. Distributive justice, according to Finnis, does not require reductions in wealth disparities for the sake of equalization as such. But such reductions might be proper, on Finnis' theory, for other reasons. In particular, it might be proper to coercively transfer some portion of A's wealth to B, if B's using that increment would promote the basic goods of B and of others more than A's using the same increment would promote the basic goods of A and of other persons.

On Finnis' logic, it would be necessary, as noted above, to justify such transfers on grounds that do not require the commensurability of basic goods. It is meaningless, according to Finnis, to talk of maximizing the realization of basic goods in any situation. Finnis argues, however, that we should, over some limited range of distributions of goods, give a defeasible preference to certain persons in view of their greater need. Recognizing greater and lesser need is not thought by Finnis to require any impossible commensuration of goods. Thus we can legitimately cut into A's plentiful basic good of play, or of excellence in work and play, in order to fund B's primary education and the basic good of knowledge, at least in certain cases.

One complication is that despite Finnis' claim to the contrary, we should not hierarchically prefer the basic human goods to human goods that are not basic. It may seem sensible to prefer the basic good of life, for example, to the non-basic, merely instrumental good of property. But one need not be a utilitarian to accept some risk to life in exchange for greater wealth. Even the Golden Rule could counsel such an exchange.

One important problem is that some instances of some basic goods may seem frivolous, while some instances of some non-basic goods, such as property, may seem morally important. A diary, yearbook, photograph, wedding ring, or one's modest home or farm may be items of property. Perhaps they were not even produced by their owner. But in some cases such items can, as Hegel recognized, legitimately be important to their owner's personal identity, without warping their owner's consciousness or injuring the interests of others. Depriving their owner of such items without just reason may be more immoral than, say, arbitrarily depriving someone of some increment of the basic good of excellence in work or play.

Or so someone might reasonably argue. Whether Finnis wishes to accommodate such complications or not, he must offer some morally objective grounds for his choice. And it would again seem, as on Finnis' more basic claims discussed above, that the best justification for whatever course Finnis might take may require more direct recourse to facts or assumptions about nature, human and otherwise. The best resolution of such issues will not generally be obvious or self-evident, or rigorously inferable from what Finnis takes to be self-evident. And if several alternative approaches to broad, vital questions of ethics and political philosophy can seem no less justified than Finnis', then Finnis' theory may seem incomplete and inadequately defended as it stands.[9]

The problem Finnis must confront is thus twofold. Finnis first must establish the objectivity of any principle on which he relies, such as that of the basic goods or the Golden Rule, without any crucial appeal to "theoretical" reason, or to what we can know about the world or human nature. Should Finnis be forced into such appeal, he would then have to confront what he assumes to be the gulf between fact and value. But even if Finnis could somehow vindicate the objectivity of a principle like the Golden Rule, he would still have to show, again without any crucial appeal to theoretical reason or to nature, how the Golden Rule selects for one set of plausible solutions over another in at least some interesting set of cases. There may seem little value in an objective Golden Rule if we cannot show why one approach to a legal or political problem is genuinely more compatible with that rule than some other plausible approach. We would at least need to know objectively why it is really unimportant that the Golden Rule, for example, is of limited value in picking out determinate sets of solutions to moral problems. Whether Finnis can do this without crucial reference beyond the bounds of his own system seems doubtful. This is not, certainly, a matter of demanding specific marching orders from a political philosophy, or of pretending that there are necessarily determinate answers to all apparently moral dilemmas.

Consider, for example, the law of inheritance and the taxation of testamentary transfers. On Finnis' approach, the law should, all else equal, exclude arbitrary preferences of family members for their own relatives. Should the law then consider an attempt to pass along the bulk of a large estate to one's own offspring an arbitrary preference? Does the Golden Rule counsel against such a bequest, or against the law's enforcing such a bequest? Finnis argues that, among other things, the statuses we have assumed with regard to other people may prevent a preference from being genuinely arbitrary. But then, as we have seen, the criterion of need is morally relevant in some class of distributive justice cases.

It would be unreasonable to expect Finnis to vindicate some unique solution to questions of wealth distribution, or of the obligations of citizens with regard to governments that maintain narrow concentrations of wealth. Particular circumstances may modify general rules. But it may not seem unreasonable to ask for some sort of determinate general guidance, for example, for landless peasants who wonder whether they are morally obligated to respect legal rules that prevent large landed estates from being divided into numerous potentially profitable small farms. And we will again need to know why Finnis' guidance is better than some alternative approach. As above, if this sort of general guidance is really for some reason unnecessary, we will need to know why.

Let us summarize briefly our main conclusions regarding Finnis' theory. Even minimal determinate guidance on questions of obligation and the adequate defense of the most basic elements of Finnis' general theory require that we venture beyond what Finnis considers either self-evident or derivable from the self-evident. Recourse to what we can discover, via theoretical reason, in the realm of fact seems indispensable. Such recourse may be indispensable in arriving at moral conclusions of useful specificity. More importantly, though, more direct reliance on theoretical reason may be necessary to defend any elements of Finnis' theory at all with the maximum attainable logical assuredness.

NOTES TO *JOHN FINNIS ON OBLIGATION AND THE NATURAL LAW*

1. See John Finnis, Natural Law and Natural Rights (Oxford: Clarendon Press 1980). This chapter focuses on the work of John Finnis in light of the detailed elaboration of Finnis' approach. The importance of Finnis' work is seen in its clear kinship to more recent work outside the natural law tradition. A number of Finnis' crucial assumptions and arguments are, for example, developed in Jeremy Waldron, Special Ties and Natural Duties, 22 Phil. & Pub. Aff. 3 (1993).

2. Finnis' other relevant writings are numerous. A useful selection might include John Finnis, Fundamentals of Ethics (Washington, D.C.: Georgetown Univ. Press 1983); John Finnis, Moral Absolutes: Tradition, Revision, and Truth (Washington, D.C.: Catholic Univ. of America Press 1991); John Finnis, Joseph Boyle & Germain Grisez, Nuclear Deterrence, Morality and Realism (Oxford: Clarendon Press 1987); John Finnis, Natural Law and Legal Reasoning, in Natural Law Theory: Contemporary Essays 134 (Robert P. George ed.) (Oxford: Clarendon Press 1992) (see also 38 Clev. St. L. Rev. 1 (1990)); Germain Grisez, Joseph Boyle & John Finnis, Practical Principles, Moral Truth, and Ultimate Ends, 32 Am. J. Juris. 99 (1987); John Finnis, The Authority of Law in the Predicament of Contemporary Social Theory, 1 N.D. J.L. & Pub. Pol'y 115 (1984); John Finnis & Germain Grisez, The Basic Principles of Natural Law: A Reply to Ralph McInerney, 26 Am. J. Juris. 21 (1981); John Finnis, Natural Law and the "Is"—"Ought" Question: An Invitation to Professor Veatch, 26 Catholic Lawyer 266 (1981).

3. The fullest, clearest, and most generally useful explication of Finnis' theory of self-evident basic human goods is contained in Robert P. George, Recent Criticism of Natural Law Theory, 55 U. Chi. L. Rev. 1371 (1988).

4. For a sampling of critical responses to Finnis on knowledge as a self-evident basic human good, see, e.g., Russell Hittinger, A Critique of the New Natural Law Theory 46 (Notre Dame: Univ. of Notre Dame Press 1987); David A.J. Richards, Review of John Finnis' Natural Law and Natural Rights, 93 Ethics 169, 170-71 (1982); Robert M. Scavone, Natural Law, Obligation and the Common Good: What Finnis Can't Tell Us, 43 U. Toronto Faculty L.J. 90, 99 (1985).

5. For examples of such critiques of Finnis' approach, see, e.g., Ralph McInerney, Ethica Thomistica 37-38, 51-52 (Washington, D.C.: Catholic Univ. of America Press 1982); Henry Veatch, Natural Law and the

"Is"—"Ought" Question, 26 Catholic Lawyer 251, 258-59 (1981). See also Vernon Bourke, Review of John Finnis' Natural Law and Natural Rights, 26 Am. J. Juris. 243 (1981). For comparisons of Finnis' approach with that of Aquinas, in addition to those sources cited above, see, e.g., Jean Porter, The Recovery of Virtue 43-45 (Louisville: Westminster/John Knox Press 1990); Jean Porter, Basic Goods and the Human Good in Recent Catholic Moral Theology, 57 Thomist 27 (1993); Janice L. Schultz, 'Ought'-Judgments: A Descriptivist Analysis from a Thomistic Perspective, 61 New Scholasticism 400 (1987); Janice L. Schultz, Is-Ought: Prescribing and a Present Controversy, 49 Thomist 1 (1985); Peter Simpson, Practical Knowing: Finnis and Aquinas, 67 Modern Schoolman 111 (1990); Peter Simpson, St. Thomas on the Naturalistic Fallacy, 51 Thomist 51 (1987).

6. For discussion of Finnis' emphasis on social coordination in justifying legal authority, see Leslie Green, Law, Co-Ordination and the Common Good, 3 Ox. J. Legal Stud. 299 (1983). See also Leslie Green, The Authority of the State 102-05 (Oxford: Clarendon Press 1990).

7. For an expression of concern over whether Finnis' theory overemphasizes commonality of interest at the expense of conflicts of interest, see Valerie Kerruish, Philosophical Retreat: A Criticism of John Finnis' Theory of Natural Law, 15 U. W. Aust. L. Rev. 224, 234-35 (1983).

8. For discussion, see Ruth Gavison, Natural Law, Positivism, and the Limits of Jurisprudence: A Modern Round, 91 Yale L.J. 1250, 1276 (1982). See also John Finnis, Moral Absolutes: Tradition, Revision, and Truth (Washington, D.C.: Catholic Univ. of America Press 1991).

9. Several writers have raised the question of whether Finnis' theory is metaphysically unduly sparing. See, e.g., Russell Hittinger, A Critique of the New Natural Law Theory 195 (Notre Dame: Univ. of Notre Dame Press 1987); Lloyd Weinreb, Natural Law and Justice 109 n.* (Cambridge: Harvard Univ. Press 1987); Vincent M. Cooke, Moral Obligation and Metaphysics, 66 Thought 65, 69 (1991); Robert M. Scavone, Natural Law, Obligation and the Common Good: What Finnis Can't Tell Us, 43 U. Toronto Faculty L.J. 90, 102 (1985) ("It may be . . . that to be truly coherent Finnis's theory demands some source of value that transcends man. . . ."); Jeremy Shearmur, Natural Law Without Metaphysics: The Case of John Finnis, 38 Clev. St. L. Rev. 123, 129 (1990) (asking whether Finnis' theory can "stand without those links to metaphysics and an understanding of the world that were so much a feature of those approaches to natural law of which Finnis is critical"). Cf. Russell Hittinger, Review of Jean Porter's The Recovery of Virtue, 8 Faith & Phil. 549, 553 (1991) ("I am not sure that Aquinas' method of unifying the central

concepts of morality can be adequately understood without bringing theology to the center of attention"); James M. Rhodes, Right by Nature, 53 J. Politics 318, 327-28 (1991) (arguing that even Aristotle's theory of moral and political obligation may ultimately have depended on theistic notions); Robert J. Roth, Moral Obligation—With or Without God?, 59 New Scholasticism 471 (1985); Robert J. Roth, Moral Obligation and God, 54 New Scholasticism 265 (1980).

5

Does Moral Objectivism Matter?: Some Preliminary Responses

In their recent survey of contemporary ethics, Stephen Darwall, Allan Gibbard, and Peter Railton note the increasing diversity and sophistication of contemporary metaethical positions.[1] This chapter surveys a few of the most currently popular metaethical alternatives to moral objectivism. The object is not to attempt to refute any such position. The remarkable and increasing sophistication of the various approaches to metaethics ensures that none can be convincingly refuted. It is instead to suggest that no prominent alternative to moral objectivism is likely to prove particularly attractive in practice over the long term. If an attractive and viable objectivist morality can be found, the choice between moral objectivism and its alternatives therefore matters in practice.

The relevant metaethical terminology is not used consistently by philosophers. But a few basic distinctions can be drawn. The idea of moral objectivity is sometimes linked to the existence of natural or non-natural moral properties,[2] or to the mind-independence of moral principles.[3] But talk about moral properties is too far removed from anyone's ordinary language to provide reliable guidance. This is not an attempt to evade arguments damaging to moral objectivism. In fact, if we set aside the issue of the plausibility of theism, it is possible to argue that the best explanation for the ability of natural persons to apprehend non-natural moral properties would be theistic.[4] And talk of the mind-independence of moral objectivity merely invites a series of subtle and for our purposes inessential distinctions as to ways in which this is, and is not, the case.[5]

Let us say instead that moral objectivism claims at a minimum that some answers to some moral questions are better than others, where the superiority of an answer is thought not to be ultimately arbitrary from a rational perspective. Analogous claims could be made regarding moral theories, principles, characters, virtues, and so forth. Or, if it becomes more suitable for some purpose, we can think of moral objectivity as implying the possibility that a person might hold a moral belief that is mistaken even though that belief is consistent with all of the relevant beliefs currently held by that person or by some relevant group of persons.

The idea here is in part to allow moral objectivism to be compatible with either coherentism or foundationalism in epistemology,[6] while still classifying the so-called "quasi-realist" approaches to metaethics discussed below as non-objectivist. We may say that moral objectivity aims at apprehending moral principles that are attuned to the broadest logically relevant circumstances in which the moral decisionmaker finds herself. This formulation brings out the compatibility of moral objectivism and coherentism. Now, none of these formulae will suffice for all purposes. But it is precisely the point of this chapter that practical consequences of metaethical views count more than labeling and classification.

Moral objectivism is, understandably, often thought to oppose approaches such as moral relativism. While this contrast is often sound, there may well be versions of moral relativism that fall within some reasonable understanding of moral objectivism.[7] In general, moral relativism would emphasize something like the dependence of moral right and wrong on the norms or beliefs subscribed to by particular groups of persons. For moral guidance, one turns to what some particular group thinks, or should on their own terms think, about the matter in question. The term "moral subjectivism" is probably equivocal as between the limiting case of moral relativism, where the size of the group shrinks to one,[8] and being either a synonym for or a particular form of moral noncognitivism. Moral noncognitivism holds roughly that moral claims cannot be true or false in the robust sense to which moral objectivism aspires.[9]

Moral relativism is currently held with rigorous consistency only rarely, but it is frequently held on an inconsistent basis, and is of enormous current influence.[10] Many leading moral relativist philosophers make dramatic concessions to moral objectivity, and hold only limited versions of moral relativism.[11] Even limited versions of moral relativism may, however, prevent us from making moral claims which might otherwise be widely considered appropriate. Consider, for example, a person who might, at minimal cost, save a number of innocent lives, but who has no stake in the consequences of or reactions to her decision whether or not to save those lives. Under even the limited relativism of Professor Gilbert Harman, for example, we are still prevented from saying precisely that the potential rescuer would do moral wrong in choosing to not carry out the rescue.[12]

Some sort of moral relativism might help avoid the cruelty, insensitivity, and oppression of across-the-board moral uniformity. It might be, as well, that relativism can help promote the interests of oppressed social groups.

Whether relativism can do these things better than some forms of moral objectivism, however, of course remains to be seen. This issue is discussed in chapter 6 below.

A basic problem for relativism is that it is widely felt that morality should occasionally regulate or restrain, and not merely promote, the prudent assertion of the interests of at least some groups, as we shall discuss a bit further below. It seems implausible that many purely group-based moralities would tend over the long term to require that the group itself exercise self-restraint beyond that which seems merely prudent. Knowing that a bit more self-restraint may be objectively required of course does not guarantee that we will act in accord with that knowledge. But mere empathy unsupported by any moral principles transcending those of one's group is not likely to be sufficient to run a large and diverse society for any length of time, even if we all belong to more than one morally relevant group.

Consider a division-of-the-housework example.[13] On an objectivist analysis, it may well be the case that both parties ought to assume responsibility for the housework. Those objectivist moral principles which have purported to deny this may be false, and showable as false.

In the relativist society, on the other hand, a fellow group member might chastise a shirking husband on the grounds that their shared group-based morality, whatever its metaphysical status, required, say, equal division of housework. But this merely brings to the fore the problem of group definition, group jurisdiction, and defection. There is, as a matter of moral logic, very little to stop the self-interested husband from announcing that at least for housework purposes, he is to be considered not as a member of group A, which believes in equal sharing of household duties, but as a member of another relevant group B, which bars or exempts husbands from discharging such burdens.

Each person belongs, revocably or irrevocably, to many arguably relevant, partially overlapping groups.[14] Why may not the relativist husband claim that relevant gender, class, regional, or age group-norms render his contributions improper or morally optional? This is not to abandon morality, or relativism, or to demand to know why one should be moral. It is simply to opt for one set of group-based moral principles over another.

Now, it is possible for someone to complain that in defecting, the husband may have breached some moral rule of the group from which he has defected concerning defection itself. This might be so. But the husband may be in circumstances under which he inescapably must violate some rule of some group in which he holds membership. We must ask the relativist a bit more about group rules concerning group membership, exit, and cases of conflict with rules of other groups. Are such rules binding only within the group, as opposed to being objectively binding? If so, they are of little use. One can just as easily defect from those rules as well. If, surprisingly, the relativist wants to say that the boundary-maintenance, exit, and conflict rules of some group are objectively binding, we will want to know why, and we will want to know how that squares with moral relativism. By way of contrast, some moral objectivists may say on at least some occasions that if one falls into a particular classification, one has certain moral obligations, even if one also falls into different, competing classifications as well.

Nor does relativism capture our sense of the relation between oppressing and oppressed groups. It simply does not strike most progressive-minded persons as adequate to reduce the morality of oppressing and oppressed groups to one of the pursuit of group interest. Nor do oppressed groups tend to make only group-based or relativist arguments when appealing to third parties.

Someone might want to concede these problems, but still argue that moral relativism has other virtues. Consider the obvious and persisting diversity of moral belief. Such diversity exists broadly among persons of experience, intelligence, sensitivity, and good faith, whether those persons are of similar or different backgrounds. Isn't some form of moral relativism involved in the best explanation[15] of this undeniable phenomenon?[16]

On this, there is much that might be said. The issue is obliquely discussed in the following chapter in the context of tolerance, pluralism, and diversity. For now, it should first be remembered that moral objectivism does not imply an answer for every moral, or every apparently moral, question, let alone some uniquely best answer universally applicable across history and cultures. While some utilitarians, for example, might imagine that there is in principle some morally best, utility-maximizing response to every problem of choice, even a theistic objective morality need not be so ambitious.[17]

Some theistic approaches, for example, might assume that not all choice problems significantly implicate what a particular theology deems essential, such as someone's salvation, and that only those that do can be considered genuinely moral problems. It might be that in many sets of circumstances, the moral value of some or all of the obvious competing choices can be said to be indeterminate. Or a range of equally acceptable answers may emerge. What appears to be a moral dilemma may for a number of reasons actually pose no genuine moral issue. Moral objectivity need not imply any determinate set of answers, let alone any single best answer, to all problems of social and personal choice, however painful or serious such a problem may be.

It is also certainly possible, on a wide variety of objectivist ethical approaches, to conclude that for fallible creatures such as ourselves, in many instances the high cost of obtaining relevant information swamps the difference in moral value between two options under consideration. Consider, for example, the real or apparent moral problem of to which of two apparently worthy charities one should donate one's money—if one is not to divide one's gift. In such a case, there may be no readily ascertainable morally best answer, even though different sets of people may suffer or even die depending upon the choice made.

It is possible as well for a theistic objective morality to endow individuals and groups with the maximum degree of freedom, autonomy, and moral law-making capacity compatible with God's assumed nature and the assumed relationship of God to human persons. Theistic as well as nontheistic objectivism might also emphasize the general undesirability of moral indoctrination or the hegemonic imposition of uniform belief, perhaps for the sake of autonomy or human dignity. There is, after all, great diversity in people's natures, basic preferences, inclinations, aptitudes, interests, opportunities, and circumstances. Various sorts of theistic and nontheistic moral objectivism might view rich diversity of moral belief and practice as a vital moral goal, instrumentally or for its own sake. It may be objectively true that different groups should, perhaps even regardless of their preferences in the matter, act in significantly different ways. Moral objectivism can thus foster moral diversity. Each of these considerations goes some distance toward reducing the sense that there is a greater degree of moral diversity in actual practice than moral objectivism can plausibly account for.

Does the absence of moral progress, or the slow pace thereof, count decisively against any objectivity of morals?[18] Certainly there has been progress in and an effective resolution of, for example, the erstwhile debate on chattel slavery. This is more than a matter of the mere political defeat of or economic irrelevance of slavery. There has, as well, been as much of an advance toward consensus on the value of free elections over the past fifty years as has occurred in some areas of the physical sciences, such as in the interpretation or meaning of quantum mechanics. Even on persistently contentious issues such as the propriety of the death penalty, the scope of the debate has narrowed considerably, as the class of crimes for which death may be inflicted has generally been reduced. Of course, none of this is to claim that apparently increasing consensus is not at all attributable to, say, changes in economic interests or the overall balance of political power. But in some important respects, our moral views have seemed not merely to change, or even to merely reach consensus, but to progress.

The nagging problem remains, though, of just how much moral progress an objectivist should predict. The enforced uniformity or apparent consensus engendered globally by crude territorial colonialism has been reduced, and there may be increasing absolute disparities in income and wealth among rich and poor nations.[19] These developments might tend to enhance global moral disagreement. But then, factors such as the homogenizing effect of Western mass media might tend to increase moral consensus. As well, there can be clear moral progress, as in the gradual emancipation of women from various forms of oppression, even though there may be less consensus on the rights of women than obtained several hundred years ago. An at least apparent consensus may be engineered around false principles. Progress in moral thinking can therefore take the form of increasing moral disagreement, as oppressed groups begin to articulate their grievances.

It is therefore difficult to argue that moral objectivism suffers by comparison with its rivals in accounting for an observed degree of moral diversity or lack of progress. If moral debate seems nonetheless to compare unfavorably to scientific debate, that perception may in part be illusory,[20] and be otherwise explainable in ways consistent with moral objectivism. Crucially, surrendering one's longstanding political privileges for the sake of justice is typically more painful, and more inspiring of ingenious moral evasion, than giving up a mere hypothesis about the physics of the world in which we have no vested interest. And the holders of unjust privilege are not generally susceptible of conversion once and for all, as a group. For every holder of unjust privilege who can be persuaded by reference to objective moral principles to surrender those privileges, there may be someone morally blinded by the desire to newly acquire such privileges.

It should be noted, finally, that much of the objectivist response to challenges to objectivism based on moral diversity or lack of moral progress long antedates the modern era,[21] in which the rise of relativism and noncognitivism has drawn attention to this issue. Thus it is implausible to characterize the objectivist response to critics of objectivism as contrived, or as an *ad hoc* response to an unanticipated lack of moral progress.

Do the more distinctively noncognitivist approaches fare better as against moral objectivism than does relativism? Consider first the "quasi-realism" of Simon Blackburn.[22] Blackburn urges, probably correctly, that the sophisticated noncognitivist can, with utmost sincerity, say anything that ordinary people say in the realm of morality. This is one reason why a generally satisfactory definition of moral objectivism is difficult to come by.

The noncognitivist can say, for example, that there are real obligations and values, and among these is that racism or sexism is wrong, regardless of who approves of it or desires to engage in it. But by saying that there are real obligations, the noncognitivist means merely to ascribe to such obligations as much reality as they can correctly be said to have according to the noncognitivist, which is not much. By saying that racism is wrong, independent of anyone's preference for racism, the noncognitivist means only to express or report an attitude, say, that the effects of racism on its victims are bad, and that such effects should control over other considerations, such as the desire for personal gain, that might counsel in favor of racism. Crucially, the noncognitivist ultimately leaves morality hanging at the level of mere attitudes. And as long as the attitude taken toward any particular consideration is consistent with one's other relevant attitudes toward other considerations, we can rationally take whatever attitude we care to. In the long run, most people may tend, as long as the matter is morally arbitrary, to take the attitudes that leave them in the good graces of the powerful, or those with most control over their lives.

Thus while the noncognitivist can probably say anything that ordinary language allows objective moralists to say, we should not be misled. What is possible in principle need not be historically stable in practice. At an early stage, a noncognitivist society would doubtless look and sound much like a morally objectivist society of some sort. But given certain limits on the plasticity of human motivation, the noncognitivist society will likely tend to lose its appeal for us as the attractiveness of ultimately arbitrary pro-attitudes toward self-sacrifice begins to pall for members of the noncognitivist society.

This argument will be expanded below in the context of discussing the recent work of Jeremy Waldron. But at this point, we should consider two interesting responses by Blackburn to the claim that the noncognitivist society would tend in what most of us would view as unattractive directions. Blackburn first points out correctly that the altruistic noncognitivist is not necessarily being irrational, and that noncognitivist selfishness, even when constrained by prudence, is no more inherently rational than noncognitivist altruism, over any length of time.

But this is irrelevant. No one supposes that the noncognitivist society tends to decay because persons stop acting irrationally and start acting rationally. Certainly, on the noncognitivist account, persons are in a sense more rational to the extent that they begin to act more consistently with their gradually deepening awareness that there is no objective morality, all the implications of which may not immediately sink in. But when a person throws off the shackles of her prior socialization and simply decides to act more selfishly, on the basis of more selfish attitudes, she is not necessarily being more rational. It is not necessarily more rational to keep what one has than to give it away to a stranger even in the absence of any objective moral reason to do so. The problem is not one of differential rationality, but of the predictable frequency with which less altruistic behavior will be chosen.

This is not to deny that real happiness, or even the most desirable sorts of pleasure, are to be found in group affiliations, in broad identification with others, in loving relationships, or in service. Individual identity is inherently social identity. People exist only connectedly. Atomism is false.

But the regrettable fact is that given a morally objectively undetermined choice between self-sacrifice, particularly in favor of persons or groups to which we do not have strong affective bonds, and the omission of such self-sacrifice, all else equal, the more likely choice is obvious. If there are no real moral reasons for one to either keep one's paycheck or to send a portion of it to an unseen needy stranger, the likely result is as clear as it is regrettable. Even governments that have appealed to a mixture of threat, coercion, and various sorts of allegedly objective moral principle have occasionally not prevented excessive selfishness. It is difficult to believe that a noncoercive appeal based on a repudiation of the objectivity of morals is likely to be successful in the long term. One needs no special reason, as an individual or group, to be selfish.

Blackburn's second response is that persons "who cannot put up with" the ultimate arbitrariness of the values we happen to confer on the world "have a defect" in their sensibilities,[23] and that we ought not allow such persons to hold moral philosophy hostage to their defects. But this misses most of the problem. The primary concern of our response to Blackburn is not for the relatively few sensitive souls who in one way or another break down in the transition to the morally noncognitivist society. Rather, our primary concern must be, as we have briefly seen above and will see in further detail below, for the majority who do adapt in predictable ways.

Of course, Blackburn's arguments do not exhaust the store of arguments available to moral noncognitivists. Recently, Allan Gibbard has offered an explanation of why most societies talk in apparently moral objectivist terms even though, Gibbard believes, the idea of moral objectivity is ultimately not rationally defensible. Under Gibbard's noncognitivism, to call an action morally right, for example, is simply to express a state of mind. In particular, one is expressing one's acceptance of a system of norms requiring or permitting that action, on whatever grounds, arbitrary or not.[24]

Thus Gibbard reduces claims of moral objectivity to demands that one's listeners come to share one's own acceptance of certain norms.

Gibbard expects substantial limitations on the extent to which people will argue for, or act on the basis of, the idea of letting moral norms vary according to anyone's mere immediate preference. This is because such thinking and behavior would tend to dissipate the collective advantages of the social coordination directly or indirectly selected for in a Darwinian evolutionary competition. Moral talk that is apparently objective in character tends to promote the kinds of coordination that confer survival advantage. Thus it tends to persist.

One obvious problem, though, is suggested by loose analogy to the fact that con games tend to work less well if all relevant persons recognize the con. Up until recently, we have coordinated socially not necessarily for the sake of survival advantage, but because we have tended to believe that it was objectively morally right to do so. If it is not objectively right to do so, we would appear to have several options. We are, as even ardent sociobiologists recognize, perfectly capable of acting in selfish or altruistic ways that plainly tend to reduce our genetic fitness.[25] We might wish to think of morality less in terms of coordination for the sake of greater joint payoffs, and more in terms of redistribution of rights, resources, and welfare. It has often been thought, certainly, that there is more to morality than coordination and conflict avoidance in a narrow sense. Giving money individually to an aged, suffering stranger with no immediate family is hardly a matter of coordination and may well have no favorable impact on anyone's genetic fitness. Yet this might be the right thing to do. Gibbard's emphasis on coordination and survival value is hardly wired into our brains or otherwise inevitable. Nor should we expect sheer instinctive, non-moral empathy to increase sufficiently to take up all of the eventual slack.

After a lapse of time, there would predictably be an increasing tendency for persons disabused of the illusion of moral objectivity by Gibbard's evolutionary explanation to be guided, unless coerced otherwise, by the prudent pursuit, over the short or long term, of metaphysically unproblematic gratifications. Sacrifice on behalf of strangers is not common enough even under most regimes of objective morality. To expect it to persist uncoerced at even those levels once the recognition sinks in universally that there is no objective moral reason to endure such sacrifice is, unfortunately, unduly optimistic.

Admittedly, the consequences to the starving stranger of not receiving assistance may seem somehow severe. And the noncognitivist moral language of the would-be recipient is no less valid than the expressed selfish desires of potential donors. But the selfish person, in declining to make the donation, commits no logical error under noncognitivism, because the arguments of the starving stranger have no objective weight or moral incumbency.[26]

Let us turn to contemporary pragmatism, in which the desire to do without the distinction between moral cognitivism and moral noncognitivism is of the essence. In our context, do pragmatic approaches work? Our argument above against noncognitivism on "pragmatic" grounds can be refitted to challenge pragmatism's claim to be pragmatic.

Probably the best-known contemporary pragmatist political theorist is Richard Rorty. Without embracing any competing skeptical metaethics, Rorty proposes to abandon the search for any objective moral principles. Moral rights, goods, and oughts cannot transcend the nonphilosophical practices of living communities. Rorty has written that "I do not think there are any plain moral facts out there in the world, nor any truths independent of language, nor any neutral ground on which to stand and argue that either torture or kindness are preferable."[27] Rorty suggests in particular that we "avoid the self-deception of thinking that we possess a deep, hidden, metaphysically significant nature which makes us 'irreducibly' different from inkwells or atoms."[28] More generally, it is self-deceptive to claim that we can attain to knowledge; we know only under optional descriptions.[29] And one thing we know—presumably under an optional description—is that anything can "be made to look good or bad, important or unimportant, useful or useless, by being redescribed."[40]

Rorty's pragmatism is thus not a form of relativism, at least in the ambitious sense of relativism under which one competing idea is said to be "really" as good as another.[31] Since Rorty's own logic forbids traditional argumentation,[32] Rorty merely offers or invites us to consider alternative conversations of greater or lesser resonance or appeal. Some of these conversations may sound superficially familiar, in light of their talk of moral rightness and goodness, but these and related usages will have been "sociologized"[33] into mere intraconversational references or mere discursive strategies. Their familiar metaphysical content will have been drained off. The category of the morally wrong reduces to that which the relevant conversational group simply does not do.[34]

What is particularly ironic is that Rorty offers this revolutionary overthrow of metaphysics in order to promote essentially the same moral and political values emphasized in familiar, metaphysically laden liberal political theory. Rorty's utopia features, in accord with liberal tradition, an attractive flowering of equality, freedom, delight in diversity, expanded empathy, and an aversion to cruelty and humiliation.[35] Whatever limitations, conflicts, or ambiguities may arise among these values is presumably to be somehow resolved, again without purported objectivity. And precisely in its literal "de-moralization," it is inhospitable to the rise of any moral fanatic. One might argue, though, that Rorty's denial that we are irreducibly different by nature from inkwells may inadvertently tend to serve some tyrant's cause. If we are like inkwells, only more complicated, we presumably have no more inherent dignity or value than complicated inkwells.

Rorty informs us that if we wish to trade in a metaphysical liberal culture for a pragmatic, metaphysically evacuated liberal culture, there can be no guarantees as to the stability or persistence of liberalism or any appealing successor thereto.[36] It is plainly impractical for the pragmatist to ironically mimic Plato's noble lie through a scheme in which an elite appreciates the appeal of pragmatism, but the masses are socialized into something like traditional metaphysics. Nor is it likely that we can consistently compartmentalize our intellects, commitments, and motivations in such a way as to take pragmatism seriously only in circumstances in which it is beneficial or harmless, but not otherwise.[37]

Rorty does offer what looks like an argument for the belief that his utopia would not be unstable in some way we would now take to be disastrous. This is that just as the historical weakening of religious faith has strengthened the bonds of liberal society, so the further, complete demise of moral objectivity would have no disastrous effect.[38] Setting aside the perhaps in some respects controversial premiss, we are left with an argument of the general form that since doing X has not led to disaster thus far, doing Y & Z beyond X probably will not either. Life, however, offers counterexamples.

Perhaps the basic response should be this: at least some theistic and nontheistic objectivist accounts can, if their premises are fully accepted and internalized, provide a logically complete and potentially motivating account of why one morally ought to engage in self-sacrifice for the sake of a stranger. But human nature is not infinitely plastic, and there is, as cultural reflexes and memories fade, substantial risk that mere Rortyian socialization will no longer suffice.[39]

The basic problem is that while Rorty's utopia may begin with a fervent consensus on liberal values, that consensus will really amount largely to inertia or to a cultural remnant, its force dependent solely upon accumulated cultural momentum. Liberalism in Rorty's utopia is in practice parasitic upon discarded notions of moral objectivity. In Rorty's utopia, liberalism's continuing, if temporary, efficacy is crucially attributable to the fact that changes in a limited number of conscious beliefs do not immediately radiate out to instantaneously modify all of our other logically implicated beliefs so as to achieve immediate cognitive consonance. Nor do changes in beliefs immediately generate all of the changes in our motivations and preferences necessary to bring the latter into congruence with our revised beliefs.[40] As Ivan Karamazov recognizes, "I may still even admire an act of heroism with my whole heart, perhaps out of habit, although I may have long since stopped believing in heroism."[41]

Socializing succeeding generations into consistent self-restraint or self-sacrificial behavior on the basis of no reason transcending short or long-term prudence or mere aesthetic taste is a daunting task, especially in the absence of illiberal coercion. It is possible that self-sacrifice beyond mere prudence may, for a time, have some vaguely romantic appeal, as some sort of aesthetic pose, perhaps. But after a time, such self-sacrifice may be seen as tiresome and boring. Rebelling against parental injunctions of liberal self-sacrifice may itself come to seem romantic, or an attractive pose.

But any special motivation toward selfishness is unnecessary. Since self-restraint or self-sacrifice beyond the dictates of objective morality and prudence is almost by definition in some sense unpleasant, succeeding generations will tend to notice the absence of any binding reason for such sacrifice. Worse, it may well tend to be that the better educated, more privileged groups notice this first. This is not a matter of some grimly pessimistic, atomistic psychology. It is simply a matter of the unmetaphysical appeal of doing what would seem to be gratifying or broadly pleasurable in the absence of any serious reason to refrain.

Consider what we would say to someone, or to some fraction of an entire generation, contemplating plugging in permanently to one of Robert Nozick's famous experience or pleasure machines.[42] Compare that with what Rorty can say and mean. Metaphysically objective liberalism can make non-empty claims as to human dignity, the realization of one's highest possibilities, and the infinite and equal value of each human personality, as well as to binding obligations to take steps toward relieving suffering or oppression among all persons. Rorty, in this respect no better placed than the noncognitivists, can recur to only the desiccated husks of these ideas. That is unnecessarily risky at best.[43] And it is risky not only for the communicants of Rorty's utopia itself, but for oppressed, stricken, and despairing people everywhere whose well-being predictably would eventually cease to count significantly among the general pragmatic concerns of the well-off.[44]

While there can be no Rortyian claim to one's metaphysical superiority over others, neither can there be binding reasons to take the ways in which people are empirically equal more seriously than the ways in which they are empirically unequal, such as being born into a rich or poor society. In Rorty's utopia, a person's remoteness, or their difference, or even their bare affective separateness, licenses our indifference. A Rortyian liberal can, with suitable gravity of bearing and tone of voice, tell stories about the respects in which the values of some repressive regime differ from the values merely pragmatically instantiated in Rorty's utopia.[45] But that is unlikely to long suffice for any serious purpose.

Rorty is certainly not alone as a distinguished contemporary philosopher who seeks to defend liberal tolerance and pluralism through an impoverished pragmatism. Hilary Putnam, dismayed by the ability of any social oppressor to sincerely reject all moral criticism, abandons any objectivity of morals. Putnam endorses pragmatism through a three step argument to the effect that the choice of pragmatism is neither mandated nor precluded on rational grounds, that the choice for or against pragmatism is somehow "vital" to Putnam, and that a choice for or against pragmatism is unavoidable.[46]

While our primary concern is with the practical consequences of pragmatism rather than the logic of its adoption, we might note parenthetically a curious element of Putnam's schema for arriving at pragmatism. A crucial step, as noted above, is taken when Putnam somehow determines that choosing for or against pragmatism is "vital." If Putnam's grounds for deeming the choice vital are not objective, Putnam would appear to be building arbitrariness, subjectivity, or pragmatism into an intermediate stage of an argument the conclusion of which is not much more interesting than this intermediate stage. But if Putnam claims to have objectively reasonable grounds for considering the choice concerning pragmatism to be vital, those objective grounds might hold promise as a possible partial source of one or more objective moral principles.

On a purely pragmatic basis, Putnam wishes to condemn as "fanatics" those who oppose tolerance and pluralism. The problem, though, is that given the moral insubstantiality and sheer voluntarism of pragmatism, a pragmatist's accusation of fanaticism necessarily carries absolutely no objective moral sting. Putnam can hardly say that it is objectively worse to be a fanatic than to not be a fanatic. On Putnam's logic, Martin Luther King, Jr., the Mahatma Gandhi, Bishop Tutu, Florence Nightingale, Malcolm X, Corazon Aquino, and Vaclav Havel are also blatantly metaethically overambitious. Putnam cannot objectively commend them any more than he can objectively condemn fanatics. Whatever force may be carried by Putnam's accusation of fanaticism is illicitly, if predictably, borrowed from the familiar negative connotations of the term as used by moral objectivists opposing fanaticism.

The desire on the part of moral pragmatists to take advantage, at least for a time, of what might be called 'scarecrow' moral language and moral symbolism is explicit in the writings of Jeffrey Stout.[47] Stout is driven to moral pragmatism by the apparent vicious interminability of contemporary metaethical debate, with no particular approach being currently widely accepted. Interminable conflict among different sorts of moral realists has tended to promote moral relativism and skepticism. Moral pragmatism is thought to become appealing once it is appreciated that moral systems can be judged only subject to the resource limitations of particular languages. We may assume this to be true. One might wonder why this should be thought crucial, if, for example, a physicist who writes only in English can cogently criticize a physics paper written in German, or in mathematical language.

Stout wishes to continue having selective, episodic recourse to the vocabulary traditionally associated with moral objectivity. The locutions of moral objectivity have, Stout recognizes, on occasion worked tellingly against putatively unjust practices. The language of Dr. Martin Luther King, Jr. is an obvious such example. Stout therefore approves of pragmatic use of Dr. King's rhetoric shorn, of course, of its now problematic and controversial objectivist metaphysics.

The problem, again, is that given time, even crows can distinguish between real challenges and mere scarecrows. Dr. King's words, deprived of their ambitiously metaphysical substance, provide no logically forceful or compelling reason to do anything to which, consistently and on the basis of the relevant known factual evidence, we are disinclined. If Dr. King's moral objectivism is abandoned, so ultimately is any reasoned hope of uplifting, shaming, or inspiring, through Dr. King's language. For a further example, the reader is invited to consider a thought experiment involving Cesar Chavez, the champion of the dignity of farmworkers. Consider what the likely reception of Chavez by ordinary people would have been had Chavez repudiated the objectivity of morality, and carefully offered a relativist, noncognitivist, or pragmatist account of his moral language instead. Would any diminished enthusiasm for Chavez as their champion have reflected lack of sophistication on the part of ordinary people? Could or should a non-objectivist Chavez have embraced moral objectivism only for purposes of public statements?

Let us consider one final response to moral objectivism which might be called romantically pragmatist. Roberto Unger has argued that the idea of a recognizably objectively true moral principle trivializes and devalues human choice as the expression of human personality.[48] There is certainly something to this. However difficult or exciting the process of actually detecting an objective moral principle might be, once such a principle is discovered, the decision whether to accept it seems anticlimactic. Acceptance seems to involve mainly passive acknowledgment; rejection seems wilful and capricious, whatever its romantic appeal as an act of arbitrary self-assertion.

One could therefore seek to protect human dignity by denying all moral objectivity. But human dignity is not only compatible with moral objectivity, it presupposes moral objectivity. The human personality is of infinite value because this is so on some objectively true moral theory, not because we may or may not, on whatever grounds, wish it to be so. We need not feel humiliated because we may be confronted with moral truth, or with effort can learn something true about morality. If a principle is objectively sound, it does not ordinarily cease to be objectively sound just because recognizing its objectivity leaves us feeling humiliated, whether our humiliation is rational or not. Moral objectivism need not claim that it is simply impossible for anyone to feel humiliated by the objectivity of morals. A moral objectivist might even argue, though, that an objectively true morality by definition cannot be something that genuinely trivializes the choosing human personality. A genuinely humiliating morality on this view, simply cannot be true. Surely this further metaethical truth need not rationally be itself viewed as humiliating.

Unger's challenge can also be satisfactorily responded to on other grounds. First, as John Finnis has pointed out,[49] it is the often rich diversity of rationally appealing but mutually incompatible available choices that gives morality much of its point. Many such choices may be morally permissible, others not. If we think of moral objectivity as permitting a highly intricate network of streets, avenues, and back alleys through which to constrainedly move about town, we see the potential vitality of human choice under an objective moral system.

A second response to Unger is also possible, one that highlights the remarkably common ambivalence about objective moral principles among those who on occasion deny the existence of any such principles. Let us simply ask about the status of the expression of the human personality through choice. Is this expression an objective moral good in at least some circumstances, or not? If it is, it is hardly in order for Unger to deny that there are any genuinely objective moral truths. But if it is not, why should we necessarily feel devastated and devalued when we run up against some implacable, take-it-or-leave-it objective moral truth? If this is not an objectively devaluing experience, why should we necessarily take it to be somehow devaluing at all?

No doubt alternative conceptions of dignified activity are possible. Imprinting our own arbitrary subjectivity upon allegedly more or less formless world-material is one. But there is dignity, arguably, in the often long and tedious process of finding out the deepest truths about a world we do not in its entirety simply invent. Certainly, working scientists tend to be motivated more by the possibility of seeking or obtaining genuine or at least approximate answers, as opposed to an image of their painting unconstrainedly on a blank world-canvas. Ultimately, it seems backwards to suppose that any confrontation with moral objectivity must be demoralizing. It is only the existence of at least some minimal objective rational constraints on our choices that endows those choices with any real meaningfulness, weight, and seriousness.

We have some reason, then, to believe that the choice between more and less metaphysically ambitious alternatives is likely to make a practical difference. But a recent argument by Jeremy Waldron casts doubt on this conclusion. Waldron has argued that if we all recognized moral objectivism to be false, politics and the law would be merely the arena for the conflict of views none of which would be certifiably more reasonable than any other. But Waldron goes on to argue that the situation is essentially parallel even if we were all to recognize moral objectivism to be true.[50] The mere existence of objective moral truth does not in itself provide a means of limiting arbitrariness in law and politics. This is because the mere existence of a truth does not ensure its ready ascertainability or its demonstrability to doubters.[51]

Waldron's point is that objectivists have not established, objectively or by consensus, an epistemology adequate to cash out their claims as to the existence of particular moral truths. As it turns out, we witness politically and legally dominant beliefs being defended and attacked in the name of objective moral principles, apparently interminably. Waldron follows Simon Blackburn in pointing out, as well, that noncognitivist metaethics need not be confined to the crude models of A.J. Ayer or C.L. Stevenson. A noncognitivist need not reject gratuitous torment of innocent victims simply on the grounds that such stimuli generate adverse visceral or cognitive reactions within the noncognitivist, or on the bare grounds that the noncognitivist finds such conduct inexplicably evocative of an attitude of disapproval.

But can we conclude on the basis of Waldron's argument that there is no morally significant difference between a morally objectivist society and a society that denies moral objectivity? We have defended the possibility of gradual moral progress above in responding to relativist arguments based upon the rich diversity of moral practice. We will confront the problem of the alleged interminability of objectivist moral debate below. Both of these arguments may perhaps make some indirect headway against the claim that an objective moral truth cannot cash itself out so as to lead to a politics significantly different than an overtly noncognitivist politics.

But it is important to recognize and admit that the mere existence of objective moral truth, whether conceived of naturalistically or theistically, does not guarantee the knowledge of such truth. Suppose that the visible constellations were tomorrow rearranged across the heavens so as to spell out, in flawless typography, the Esperanto translation for "Be Kind to Everyone." However impressive some might find this celestial phenomenon, it would certainly be subject to dismissal as involving secret retinal surgeries, technically advanced but morally deluded alien civilizations, mass hypnosis, chemically drugged drinking water, crowd delusion, hysteria, CIA laser technology, etc. And on some theologies, particularly those emphasizing the value and dignity of human freedom of choice, this is as it should be.

Even a theistic assumption of God's knowledgeable benevolence toward humans cannot by itself bridge the gap between what is true and what is knowable or can be shown. It is logically possible for someone to say that even if a knowledgeable God wishes each of us well, God might wish us as individuals to act nonbenevolently toward some or all of our fellows. This logic has, undeniably, led historically to many instances of religiously-based oppression of the relatively weak. At most, the assumption that a knowledgeable God is benevolent toward us might set up some sort of presumption that we ought to be benevolent toward one another, rebuttable by any allegedly sufficient reason.

On a theistic approach, the gulf between knowing that there is at least some objective moral truth and knowing concretely what that truth is can only be reasonably bridged at the level of particular theologies teaching particular moral principles.[52] It might be argued that this is a damaging admission, in that it appears to equally license all sorts of cognitivist and noncognitivists to announce their secular faith that all objections to each of their views will eventually be dissipated. But this would ignore the fact that crucial elements of some theologies can be tested, in principle and in practice, in the court of publicly accessible fact, evidence, and reason. Often, crucial claims are made by particular theologies that particular events factually occurred in nature or history. These claims can be subject to empirical evidentiary support and rebuttal. The case for such claims can, based on the evidence, be stronger or weaker, and can be supported or rebutted in surprisingly interesting and important ways. It should be borne in mind that the fact that a theology is particular does not imply that it is narrow, sectarian, intolerant, repressive, or non-pluralist. In general, there is no reason to suppose that no single theology can solve outstanding problems in metaethics, be very widely attractive in its moral substance, and also be subject to empirical support or rejection.

The question of evidentiary support and rebuttal is discussed below. But in the meantime, it can be asked what particular facts, or what further factual evidence, would reasonably establish the truth of moral claims made by Rawls, or Ackerman, or Gewirth, or Kant, or Bentham, and so on, to the exclusion of the others? David Hume, as typically interpreted on the logical gap between fact and moral value, seems generally on target in his skepticism, as we have seen above.

Ultimately, the most decisive response to the claim that moral objectivity makes no difference would involve carrying out an actual or hypothetical test. Such a test would compare a number of morally objectivist societies—equipped with as little or as much as can reasonably be known about what we ought morally to do—with a number of non-objectivist societies. Obviously, we would expect substantial diversity within each of the two societal test categories. It might be that some moral objectivist societies would more closely resemble, say, some emotivist societies than some other objectivist societies. It is possible as well that many of us might find the worst morally objectivist societies to be more loathsome than even the least attractive noncognitivist societies. Someone who believes this, and who also believes that morality requires avoiding the morally worst possibilities, however unlikely they may be, might then opt for noncognitivism over objectivism. Arguably, tapping into pleasure machines for a lifetime, even if it involves a repudiation of the possibility of human dignity, and of morality in any familiar sense, is better than life under the objectively moralized Third Reich.

But none of this changes the likely results of the sorts of admittedly speculative thought experiments referred to above. The typical non-objectivist society will, over time, likely tend toward a condition that most of us, objectivist and nonobjectivist alike, would not now find appealing, let alone inspiring or dignified. And there is no reason to suppose that relatively attractive morally objectivist societies will tend to degenerate, beyond a mere statistical regression toward the mean, to a level of unattractiveness characteristic of most noncognitivist or pragmatic societies over the long term.

In sum, the emotivist, or other noncognitivist, again has no overarching reason not to give full sway to the recognition that individual or group self-restraint and self-sacrifice that does not significantly contribute to one's immediate or perhaps future gratifications is gratuitous. It is true that members of oppressed or subordinated groups have little or no reason, logically or morally, for such restraint. But not all persons are, in all respects, members of such groups. Nor should ascription of such status itself be made arbitrarily, or merely as a further assertion of group interest.

The appeal of mere sensory pleasure and the avoidance of sensory pain requires no recourse to moral objectivity. It is metaphysically unproblematic. The typical emotivist society would presumably reach an equilibrium emphasizing avoidance of subjectively painful conflicts and the experience of gratifying sensations. Notions such as the infinite dignity of each human personality would have been metaphysically punctured. They would be available for embrace only as an arbitrary pose, or for merely aesthetic sorts of reasons. The typical emotivist society is therefore unlikely to be terribly fastidious in the long term as to how its pleasurable and metaphysically unambitious sensations are to be derived. If each of us can permanently tap into a machine in which we are convinced that we are vividly experiencing what it is like to be all sorts of sensorily pleasurable things,[53] what would logically hold us back? This is not to suggest that all, or even most, such citizens would literally plug into such a machine. There are many viable social roles in the emotivist society. Mischievously unplugging people from the machines against their wishes is only one such alternative role. Admittedly, it is certainly possible to criticize morally objectivist societies for being unduly hedonistic or selfish. But such societies can be, and are, powerfully criticized on these grounds in morally objectivist terms.

Now, we may assume that the typical emotivist would care to some degree about the welfare of at least some other people. It would be surprising if our brains were not hard-wired this way to some degree. But for the emotivist, there are no reasoned grounds transcending one or more of one's own attitudes why any sacrifice should be made on behalf of any others. Undetected theft from even one's closest relatives need not, in the emotivist society, be somehow inherently self-punishing, in the absence of objective moral guilt. Our non-moral identifications with others carries us only so far. Strangers are of course even worse placed. Natural selection in favor of cooperation and altruism similarly can be reasonably expected to carry us only so far.

It may even suffice for the typical emotivist to sincerely believe, though perhaps falsely, through vivid perceptions induced by the experience machine, that other persons are prospering. If not, there is no metaphysically more exalted way of caring for others in the emotivist society than ensuring that those we care for can be permanently hooked up to the gratifying experience machine as well. Even if an emotivist society can inexplicably retain some sort of qualitative distinction between the pleasures of delusory experience and those of genuine experience, without invoking genuine human dignity or any such abandoned metaphysics, the appeal of such a society to most of us now, emotivist and non-emotivist alike, is limited.

NOTES TO *DOES MORAL OBJECTIVISM MATTER?*: *SOME PRELIMINARY RESPONSES*

1. See Stephen Darwall, Allan Gibbard & Peter Railton, Toward *Fin de siècle* Ethics: Some Trends, 101 Phil. Rev. 115, 183 (1992). One might incidentally compare the increasing diversity of approaches to metaethics with Derek Parfit's belief that the historical demise of theistic ethics catalyzes progress in normative ethics, if not in metaethics. See Derek Parfit, Reasons and Persons 453 (Oxford: Clarendon Press 1984). It would seem to be too soon since the general decline of theistic normative ethics to tell whether recent progress in normative ethics is truly independent of the legacy of theistic ethics.

2. See, e.g., John L. Mackie, Ethics: Inventing Right and Wrong 15-49 (New York: Penguin 1977); Jonathan Dancy, Two Conceptions of Moral Realism, 60 Proc. Aristotelian Society 167, 167 (Supp. 1986); Allan Gibbard, Normative Objectivity, 19 Nous 41, 41 (1985); Michael S. Moore, Moral Reality, 1982 Wis. L. Rev. 1061, 1086-88, 1117-24.

3. See, e.g., Michael S. Moore, The Interpretive Turn in Modern Theory: A Turn for the Worse?, 41 Stan. L. Rev. 871, 878 (1989); Mark Timmons, Putnam's Moral Objectivism, 34 Erkenntnis 371, 372 (1991).

4. See David Papineau, Reality and Representation 159-61 (Oxford: Basil Blackwell 1987). The reader is invited, though, to recall the last time they heard it said that a certain decision, for example, had the property of being right. Things such as chemical elements, or metals, are said to have properties. We do say that a certain decision "is" right. But this locution should not necessarily import all of our concepts of a property.

5. Those influenced by accounts of some versions of quantum theory may be reluctant to assert that anything at all is generally mind-independent. See, at an admitted extreme, John Archibald Wheeler, Law Without Law, in Quantum Theory and Measurement 182, 196-210 (John Archibald Wheeler & Wojciech Hubert Zurek eds.) (Princeton: Princeton Univ. Press 1983). Even if we can in some respects alter or even constitute the world merely by observing it, it remains true that our powers in this respect are not limitless. We cannot, for example, assign a hugely different value to Planck's Constant, and still tell a convincing story about how computers and other electronic devices operate.

6. These approaches are intended to hold open the compatibility of even theistic moral objectivity with non-foundationalist epistemologies such as coherentism. See, e.g., David O. Brink, Moral Realism and the Foundations of Ethics 141 (Cambridge: Cambridge Univ. Press 1989); Brian Hebblethwaite, The Ocean of Truth 87 (Cambridge: Cambridge Univ. Press 1987); Michael Perry, Love and Power 62 (New York: Oxford Univ. Press 1991); Ralph Walker, The Coherence Theory of Truth 4 (London: Routledge 1989); Norman Daniels, Wide Reflective Equilibrium and Theory Acceptance in Ethics, 76 J. Phil. 256, 277 (1979); Michael S. Moore, The Interpretive Turn in Modern Theory: A Turn for the Worse?, 41 Stan. L. Rev. 871, 880 (1989). But see, for criticism in this regard, David Papineau, Reality and Representation 150 (Oxford: Basil Blackwell 1987); Joseph Boyle, Natural Law and the Ethics of Traditions, in Natural Law Theory: Contemporary Essays 3, 27 (Robert P. George ed.) (Oxford: Oxford Univ. Press 1992); Alvin Plantinga, Coherentism and the Evidentialist Objection to Belief in God, in Rationality, Religious Belief, and Moral Commitment 109 (Robert Audi & William Wainwright eds.) (Ithaca: Cornell Univ. Press 1986); Brian Bix, Michael Moore's Realist Approach to Law, 140 U. Pa. L. Rev. 1293, 1309 (1992); David Copp, Moral Realism: Facts and Norms, 101 Ethics 610 (1991). See also Joseph Raz, The Relevance of Coherence, 72 B.U. L. Rev. 273 (1992).

7. See, e.g., Geoffrey Sayre-McCord, Being a Realist About Relativism (in Ethics), 61 Phil. Stud. 155, 156 (1991); David B. Wong, Commentary on Sayre-McCord's "Being a Realist About Relativism," 61 Phil. Stud. 177, 177 (1991). See also Geoffrey Sayre-McCord, The Many Moral Realisms, 24 S.J. Phil. 1, 13 (1986) (moral relativism as a non-objectively based moral realism).

8. This seems to characterize the subjectivism referred to in Robert M. Stewart & Lynn L. Thomas, Recent Work on Ethical Relativism, 28 Am. Phil. Q. 85, 94 (1991) (discussing David Wong's moral relativism). Stewart and Thomas conclude that "an interesting case can be made that some form of subjectivism is the correct metaethical theory for a divided, liberal, and individualistic society such as ours."

9. See, e.g., Steve F. Sapontzis, Groundwork for a Subjective Theory of Ethics, 27 Am. Phil. Q. 27, 30 (1990) (noting the frequent linkage between subjectivism and emotivism, a form of noncognitivism). Sapontzis's basic "subjectivist" thesis is that "the existence of valuers is a necessary condition for things having value." Id. at 27. This proposition can be conceded by any objectivist, including theistic objectivists. For examples of a variety of noncognitivist metaethics, see, e.g., A.J. Ayer, Language, Truth and Logic (New York: Dover 1952); Charles L. Stevenson, Ethics and Language (New Haven: Yale Univ. Press 1944). For contemporary such efforts, see, e.g.,

Allan Gibbard, Wise Choices, Apt Feelings (Cambridge: Harvard Univ. Press 1990); Simon Blackburn, Errors and the Phenomenology of Value, in Morality and Objectivity 1 (Ted Honderich ed.) (London: Routledge 1985) (developing what Blackburn refers to as "quasi-realism"); Allan Gibbard, Normative Objectivity, 19 Nous 41 (1985).

10. See, e.g., Brenda Almond, Seven Moral Myths, 65 Phil. 129, 131 (1990) ("It is no exaggeration to say that relativism is the prevailing ideology of our schools and colleges at the present time"); Richard B. Brandt, Relativism Refuted?, 67 Monist 297, 301 (1984) (referring to "how widespread moral relativism is today").

11. See, e.g., David Wong, Moral Relativity 9 (Berkeley: Univ. of California Press 1984); Richard B. Brandt, Relativism Refuted?, 67 Monist 297, 301, 305-06 (1984); Philippa Foot, Moral Relativism, in Relativism: Cognitive and Moral 164 (Michael Krausz & Jack W. Meiland eds.) (Notre Dame: Notre Dame Univ. Press 1982); Gilbert Harman, Moral Relativism Defended, in id. at 189, 190; Bernard Williams, The Truth in Relativism, in id. at 175, 183-84; David Wong, On Moral Realism Without Foundations, 26 S.J. Phil. 95, 95 (1986). For a critique of Foot, Harman, and Williams, see Mark de Bretton Platts, Moral Realities 163-85 (London: Routledge 1991). For a critique of Williams and of relativist elements in the work of Alasdair MacIntyre and of Sabina Lovibond, see E.J. Bond, Could There Be a Rationally Grounded Universal Morality?, 15 J. Phil. Res. 15 (1989). See also E.J. Bond, Reason and Value (Cambridge: Cambridge Univ. Press 1983). Ernest Gellner has argued, exaggeratedly, that relativism would commit us, as a matter of logical inference, to nihilism. See Ernest Gellner, Postmodernism, Reason and Religion chs. 3-4 (London: Routledge 1992). This claim of relationship is too strong. For relevant work by MacIntyre, see Alasdair MacIntyre, Whose Justice? Which Rationality? (Notre Dame: Univ. of Notre Dame Press 1988). For the work of Lovibond, see Sabina Lovibond, Realism and Imagination in Ethics (Oxford: Basil Blackwell 1983).

12. See Gilbert Harman, Moral Relativism Defended, in Relativism: Cognitive and Moral 190 (Michael Krausz & Jack W. Meiland eds.) (Notre Dame: Notre Dame Univ. Press 1982). See also David Copp, Harman on Internalism, Relativism, and Logical Form, 92 Ethics 227, 228 (1982); Anne M. Wiles, Harman and Others on Moral Relativism, 42 Rev. Metaphysics 783 (1989).

13. For a reference to the linkage between moral objectivity and the practical outcome of such cases, see Thomas L. Carson, Relativism and Nihilism, 15 Philosophia 1, 17 (1985).

14. See David Lyons, Ethical Relativism and the Problem of Incoherence, 86 Ethics 107, 110 (1976).

15. Advocates and critics of moral objectivism often agree that competing metaethical theories should be tested on the basis of which theory can provide the best explanation of various features of common patterns of moral thought and language. For the best compilation of views on this issue, see generally Essays on Moral Realism (Geoffrey Sayre-McCord ed.) (Ithaca: Cornell Univ. Press 1988). See also Simon Blackburn, Wise Feelings, Apt Reading, 102 Ethics 342, 351 (1992) (describing the test endorsed by Allan Gibbard); David Copp, Moral Realism: Facts and Norms, 101 Ethics 610 (1992); David Wiggins, Moral Cognitivism, Moral Relativism and Motivating Moral Beliefs, 91 Proc. Aristotelian Society (n.s.) 61, 65 (1991); David Wong, Commentary on Sayre-McCord's "Being a Realist About Relativism," 61 Phil. Stud. 177, 184 (1991). While such tests seem generally useful, they should not be considered decisive, by definition or otherwise. See Stephen Darwall, Allan Gibbard & Peter Railton, Toward *Fin de siècle* Ethics, 101 Phil. Rev. 115, 129 n.31 (1992) (referring to arguments by others that such explanatory tests are too narrow). The assumptions and perceptions embodied in ordinary moral language and in language about morality are susceptible of error.

16. See, e.g., Frank Snare, The Diversity of Morals, 89 Mind 353, 354-55 (1980); David Wong, Commentary on Sayre-McCord's "Being a Realist About Relativism," 61 Phil. Stud. 177, 184 (1991).

17. For relevant discussion, see Richard Swinburne, The Existence of God 185-87, 199 (Oxford: Oxford Univ. Press 1979); Russell Hittinger, Review of Jean Porter, The Recovery of Virtue, 8 Faith & Phil. 549, 551 (1991); Michael S. Moore, The Interpretive Turn in Modern Theory: A Turn for the Worse?, 41 Stan. L. Rev. 871, 879 (1989) (citing the work of John Finnis). See also David Wiggins, Moral Cognitivism, Moral Relativism and Motivating Moral Beliefs, 91 Proc. Aristotelian Society (n.s.) 61, 77 (1991) (discussing limited scope moral cognitivism in general). In general, neither the possibility of equally legitimate rival approaches to a moral problem, nor the inescapable cultural embededness, cultural conditioning, and cultural contextuality of our moral beliefs implies any familiar form of moral relativism. For an analogous argument in a broader context, see Nancey Murphy, Truth, Relativism, and Crossword Puzzles, 24 Zygon 299, 312-13 (1989) (rejecting both familiar "correspondence" and "coherence" theories of truth in favor of an amalgamated, "crossword puzzle-inspired" theory of truth). But see Michael Dummett, The Logical Basis of Metaphysics 9 (Cambridge: Harvard Univ. Press 1991) (seeking to link realism and bivalence). Interestingly, though, Dummett goes on to argue that "there is no reason why God, in creating the Universe, should

have filled in all the details, have provided answers to all conceivable questions, any more so than a human artist—a painter or novelist—is constrained to do so. The conception of a created but partially indeterminate universe is easier to grasp than that of an uncreated and partially indeterminate one." Id. at 319.

18. For useful responses, see, e.g., Peter Railton, Moral Realism, 95 Phil. Rev. 163 (1986); Carl Wellman, Ethical Disagreement and Objective Truth, 12 Am. Phil. Q. 211, 211-14 (1975).

19. See Peter Berger, The Capitalist Revolution 32-33 (New York: Basic Books 1986).

20. Note, for example, the unresolved, long-standing issues involved in genuinely understanding and interpreting the results of quantum mechanics. This is a matter not only of a correct philosophy of quantum mechanics, but of what actually happens in the world. See, e.g., Nick Herbert, Quantum Reality (New York: Anchor Books 1987).

21. Note that Thomas Aquinas, for example, appreciated that "all men are not agreed as to their ultimate end" and that tastes vary considerably. Thomas Aquinas, Treatise on Happiness qu. 1, art. 7 (John A. Oesterle trans.) (Notre Dame: Univ. Notre Dame Press 1983). Aquinas observed as well that sometimes even "a universal principle known by understanding or through some science, is perverted in a particular case by some passion." Thomas Aquinas, Treatise on the Virtues qu. 58, art. 5 (John A. Oesterle trans.) (Notre Dame: Univ. Notre Dame Press 1984). Aquinas explicitly recognizes that even natural law changes over time in several respects. The Political Ideas of St. Thomas Aquinas qu. 94, art. 5 (Dino Bigongiari ed.) (New York: Hafner 1953). Aquinas concludes that "the general principles of the natural law cannot be applied to all men in the same way, on account of the great variety of human affairs, and hence arises the diversity of positive laws among various people." Id. at qu. 95, art. 2, reply to objection 3. See also id. at art. 3. Each of these citations is ultimately to the Summa Theologica, and to the First Part of the Second Part thereof.

22. See in particular Simon Blackburn, Errors and the Phenomenology of Value, in Morality and Objectivity 1 (Ted Honderich ed.) (London: Routledge 1985), and more generally Simon Blackburn, Spreading the Word (Oxford: Clarendon Press 1984). For one brief critique of Blackburn among many, see David McNaughton, Moral Vision 182-89 (Oxford: Basil Blackwell 1988).

23. See Simon Blackburn, Errors and the Phenomenology of Value, in Morality and Objectivity 1, 10-11 (Ted Honderich ed.) (London: Routledge 1985). A similar argument was recently made by a well-known scientist. See Peter W. Atkins, Will Science Ever Fail?, 135 New Scientist 32, 32 (1992). Before conceding the claim of "defect," though, we may want to consider the argument that "[t]he alternative to objectivity is arbitrariness; and this rules out responsibility as we normally understand it." Judith Lichtenberg, Subjectivism as Moral Weakness Projected, 33 Phil. Q. 378, 384 (1983).

24. See Allan Gibbard, Normative Objectivity, 19 Nous 41, 41 (1985). More broadly, see Allan Gibbard, Wise Choices, Apt Feelings (Cambridge: Harvard Univ. Press 1990). See also Jonathan Bennett, The Necessity of Moral Judgments, 103 Ethics 458, 459 (1993). On Bennett's view moral judgments cannot be true or false, and instead either express attitudes or amount to injunctions of some sort. See id.

25. See, e.g., John Beckstrom, The Potential Dangers and Benefits of Introducing Sociobiology to Lawyers, 79 Nw. U.L. Rev. 1279, 1280 (1985).

26. Again, this is not to deny that the noncognitivist, or other opponents of moral objectivism, can "be in sympathy with some people, dislike others, approve of some actions, and disapprove of others. . . ." Torbjorn Tannsjo, Moral Realism 125 (Savage, Md: Rowman & Littlefield 1990). For relevant discussion, see Simon Blackburn, Wise Feelings, Apt Readings, 102 Ethics 342, 355-56 (1992); Paul Boghossian, The Status of Content, 99 Phil. Rev. 157 (1990); Daniel Stoljar, Emotivism and Truth Conditions, 70 Phil. Stud. 81 (1993). Blackburn, however, goes on, in interpreting Gibbard, to verge upon reintroducing a sort of genuine objectivity of morals in which one's assertion of moral norms commits one to accord equal right to assert moral norms to other persons, in light of our presumed mutual need to coordinate. Such a view would hardly qualify as noncognitivist. For further commentary on some of Gibbard's argument, see David Gauthier, Review Essay: The Roots and Roles of Normative Governance, 91 Synthese 319, 330 (1992). See also Stephen Darwall, Allan Gibbard & Peter Railton, Toward *Fin de siècle* Ethics: Some Trends, 101 Phil. Rev. 115, 146-47 (1992); Richard T. Garner, On the Genuine Queerness of Moral Properties and Facts, 68 Australasian J. Phil. 137 (1990). Garner argues, interestingly, that "[i]t is hard to believe in objective prescriptivity because it is hard to make sense of a demand without a demander. . . ." Id. at 143. For a further defense of noncognitivism as viable in social practice, see Nicholas Unwin, Can Emotivism Sustain a Social Ethics?, 3 Ratio (n.s.) 64 (1990). Unwin focuses on what would seem to be the secondary problem of social coordination or agreement under noncognitivism, rather than the problem of either coerced agreement, or agreement to

live lives that most of us would now view as lacking human dignity. Unwin appears to cope with the problem of tyrannical brainwashing or mind control by simply defining autonomy in terms of acting in accordance with one's deepest internalized beliefs, whether such beliefs were implanted by tyrannical brainwashing or not, on the grounds that all belief formation is social. Thus freedom and autonomy are reduced to merely feeling free and autonomous. See id. at 74. For what amounts to an implicit rebuttal to Unwin's general claims, see Paul Eidelberg, The Malaise of Modern Psychology, 126 J. Psychology 109 (1992).

27. Richard Rorty, Contingency, Irony, and Solidarity 173 (Cambridge: Cambridge Univ. Press 1989). See also Hilary Putnam, The Many Faces of Realism 77-78 (La Salle: Open Court 1987) ("our moral beliefs, in my view, are not approximations to The Universe's Own Moral Truths. . . ."). For a sense of the seriousness with which modern scientists, on the other hand, still take the universe's own scientific truths, see, e.g., Subrahmanyan Chandrasekhar, Truth and Beauty 52-53 (Chicago: Univ. of Chicago Press 1987).

28. Richard Rorty, Philosophy and the Mirror of Nature 373 (Princeton: Princeton Univ. Press 1979).

29. Id. at 379.

30. Richard Rorty, Contingency, Irony, and Solidarity 7 (Cambridge: Cambridge Univ. Press 1989).

31. See Richard Rorty, Consequences of Pragmatism 166 (Minneapolis: Univ. of Minn. Press 1982).

32. See Richard Rorty, Contingency, Irony, and Solidarity 44 (Cambridge: Cambridge Univ. Press 1989).

33. See id. at 83 n.4.

34. See id. at 59. Cf. Crispin Wright, Truth and Objectivity 200-01 (Cambridge: Harvard Univ. Press 1992) ("the immediate price of minimalism about morals is that the gravity of moral judgment will lack an external sanction. No discourse-neutral notion of objectivity will give value to moral truth").

35. See Richard Rorty, Postmodernist Bourgeoise Liberalism, 80 J. Phil. 583 (1983); Richard Rorty, Thugs and Theorists: A Reply to Bernstein, 15 Pol. Theory 564 (1987) (replying to Richard J. Bernstein, One Step Forward, Two Steps Backward: Richard Rorty on Liberal Democracy and Philosophy, in id.

at 38). See also Richard Rorty, The Priority of Democracy to Philosophy, in The Virginia Statute for Religious Freedom 257 (Merrill D. Peterson & Robert C. Vaughn eds.) (Cambridge: Cambridge Univ. Press 1988).

36. See Richard Rorty, What Can You Expect from Antifoundationalist Philosophers?: A Reply to Lynn Baker, 78 Va. L. Rev. 719, 721-22 (1992) (replying to Lynn A. Baker, "Just Do It": Pragmatism and Progressive Social Change, 78 Va. L. Rev. 697 (1992)). The title of Rorty's piece should not be thought to imply that Rorty's basic objection is only to foundationalist, as opposed to, say, coherentist epistemologies. See also Richard Rorty, Consequences of Pragmatism 174 (Minneapolis: Univ. of Minn. Press 1982). For an intriguing, broadranging debate over the merits of Rortyian politics, contrast Sanford Levinson, Constitutional Faith (Princeton: Princeton Univ. Press 1988) with Thomas L. Pangle, The Ennobling of Democracy: The Challenge of the Postmodern Era (Baltimore: Johns Hopkins Univ. Press 1992).

37. Cf. Michael S. Moore, The Interpretive Turn in Modern Theory: A Turn for the Worse?, 41 Stan. L. Rev. 871, 904 (1989).

38. See Richard Rorty, Contingency, Irony, and Solidarity 85 (Cambridge: Cambridge Univ. Press 1989).

39. See Timothy P. Jackson, The Theory and Practice of Discomfort: Richard Rorty and Pragmatism, 51 Thomist 270, 289 (1987) ("Such a society may live for a time on past cultural capital embodied in liberal institutions and traditions, but a purely conventional virtue will not last long"). For a lively, more informal response to Rorty, see Jay Rosenberg, Raiders of the Lost Distinction: Richard Rorty and the Search for the Last Dichotomy, 53 Phil. & Phenomenological Res. 195 (1993). For a defense of something like Rortyian conversationalism, see Fred D'Agostino, Transcendence and Conversation: Two Conceptions of Objectivity, 30 Am. Phil. Q. 87 (1993). For a more radical argument that straightforwardly abandoning all concern for ethical concepts and ethical language will actually tend to be the best way of avoiding personal quietism and "nihilism," see Mark Douglas Mercer, On a Pragmatic Argument Against Pragmatism in Ethics, 30 Am. Phil. Q. 163 (1993).

40. Consider the large literature on cognitive dissonance and attribution theory. See also Gilbert Harman, Change in View (Cambridge: Bradford Press 1986); Judgment Under Uncertainty: Heuristics and Biases (Daniel Kahneman, Amos Tversky & Paul Slovic eds.) (Cambridge: Cambridge Univ. Press 1982).

41. Fyodor Dostoevsky, The Brothers Karamazov 276 (Andrew H. MacAndrew trans.) (New York: Bantam 1970).

42. See Robert Nozick, Anarchy, State and Utopia 42-45 (New York: Basic Books 1974).

43. See Timothy P. Jackson, The Theory and Practice of Discomfort: Richard Rorty and Pragmatism, 51 Thomist 270, 293 (1987) ("I fear that modern pragmatists such as Rorty are incapable of supporting the liberal values on which genuine respect for individual rights and the common good is founded").

44. Compare the response of Jeffrey Goldsworthy to John L. Mackie's moral skepticism: "By unsettling peoples' beliefs about their reasons for action, this kind of moral scepticism may threaten others likely to be affected by their actions. It may threaten not just our concepts or beliefs—it may threaten us." Jeffrey Goldsworthy, Externalism, Internalism and Moral Scepticism, 70 Australasian J. Phil. 40, 60 (1992) (citations omitted).

45. Compare the impoverished criticism of Nazism available on the subjectivist metaethics of, for example, Steve Sapontzis. See Steven F. Sapontzis, Groundwork For a Subjective Theory of Ethics, 27 Am. Phil. Q. 27, 35 (1990) ("something like Nazism can be both historically true, because its principles continue to define contexts of ethical discussion and determination, and contextually false, because its principles are inconsistent with those of our ethical tradition").

46. See Hilary Putnam, A Reconsideration of Deweyan Democracy, 63 S. Cal. L. Rev. 1671, 1690-91 (1990). For an attempted systematization of Putnam's metaethics based mainly on Putnam's writings in the early to mid-1980s, see Mark Timmons, Putnam's Moral Objectivism, 34 Erkenntnis 371 (1991).

47. See, e.g., Jeffrey Stout, Ethics After Babel (Boston: Beacon Press 1988); Jeffrey Stout, Truth, Natural Law, and Ethical Theory, in Natural Law Theory: Contemporary Essays 71 (Robert P. George ed.) (Oxford: Clarendon Press 1992).

48. See Roberto M. Unger, Knowledge and Politics 77 (New York: Free Press 1975). For a relevant, if implicit, response to Unger, see Charles Taylor, The Ethics of Authenticity 39 (Cambridge: Harvard Univ. Press 1991). See also Stephen R.L. Clark, God's Law and Morality, 32 Phil. Q. 339, 341 (1982). Pico della Mirandola shows how it is possible to combine Unger's belief in the enormous plasticity of human nature with a belief in the objectivity of

morals. See Giovanni Pico della Mirandola, Oration on the Dignity of Man, in The Renaissance Philosophy of Man 223, 225-27 (Ernst Cassirer, Paul Oskar Kristeller & John Herman Randall, Jr. eds. and trans.) (Chicago: Univ. Chicago Press 1948).

49. See John Finnis, Natural Law and Legal Reasoning, in Natural Law Theory: Contemporary Essays 134, 136 (Robert P. George ed.) (Oxford: Clarendon Press 1992). See also Charles Taylor, The Ethics of Authenticity 39 (Cambridge: Harvard Univ. Press 1991).

50. See Jeremy Waldron, The Irrelevance of Moral Objectivity, in Natural Law Theory: Contemporary Essays 158 (Robert P. George ed.) (Oxford: Clarendon Press 1992). See also Brian Bix, Michael Moore's Realist Approach to Law, 140 U. Pa. L. Rev. 1293, 1309-10 (1992); Stanley Fish, Dennis Martinez and the Uses of Theory, 96 Yale L.J. 1773, 1782-85 (1987); Bernard Williams, Subjectivism and Toleration, in Royal Institute of Philosophy Studies no. 30: A.J. Ayer Memorial Essays 197, 197 (A. Phillips Griffiths ed.) (Cambridge: Cambridge Univ. Press 1992) (discussing the views of A.J. Ayer).

51. See Philip E. Devine, Relativism, Nihilism, and God 88 (Notre Dame: Notre Dame Univ. Press 1989); Joel J. Kupperman, Ethical Fallibility, 1 Ratio (n.s.) 33, 33 (1988).

52. Technically, a theist might support her belief in a particular moral principle with the combined consistent factual evidence in favor of all of the theologies that logically support the particular moral principle in question. The principle might be opposed in an analogous way.

53. Ironically, a typical emotivist might, without reason or the need for reason beyond the subjective satisfaction expected, prefer to experience, or believe vividly that she is experiencing, sensations of what it would feel like to undertake various roles logically dependent upon moral objectivism. Thus an emotivist might choose to hook up to a machine that allowed her to feel, or seem to feel, what it was like to be Gandhi when Gandhi was inducing the British to leave India, or Dr. King, Jr. during the March on Washington.

6

Polyphony, Dissonance, and Moral Objectivity

Suppose for a moment that we were engaged in a doubtless chimerical search for the objectively best kind of musical composition. How likely is it that we would settle upon the view that the objectively best music must involve the least scope for polyphony or for dissonance? It would certainly be possible to make such a claim. But that claim would have to be supported by argument sufficiently cogent to overcome our initial deep suspicion. Certainly, it would be impossible to show that the very concept of objective value in music, if we could find such a concept, somehow implies or leads inevitably to anything like the minimization of polyphony and dissonance.[1]

This seems obvious enough. But analogous arguments in the field of morality tend to be more controversial. It has not escaped notice that pretensions to moral objectivity, and to theistic moral objectivity in particular, underlie a long historical legacy of at least apparently religious wars, crusades and jihads, systematic persecutions, torture, chronic sectarian strife, inquisitions, massacres, pogroms, bigotry, and literal and figurative witch hunts.[2] For this among other reasons, authoritative justification of legal outcomes in our society must not depend upon theistic reasoning. And even if one were to argue that these phenomena have really been driven more by economics and power politics than by religious belief, the responsibility of religion would remain. As Bernard Williams has argued, "[s]ome cognitivist views certainly provide added motives to bigotry, for instance by holding out hopes of divine reward, suggesting divine encouragement of zeal, offering assurances that the benighted are being assisted and so on."[3]

If one were to respond by claiming that the frequency of the most grievous sorts of religiously-based depredations had been abating historically, two objections seem obvious. First, any abatement in the frenzy of religious depredations may be explained by the historical fading, at least in the West, of religious belief. And second, it may still be argued that even contemporary religious belief is directly linked to an extended litany of various depredations: repression, terrorism and massacre, conformism, enforced uniformity, false universality, discrimination, narrow-mindedness, social distrust, intolerance, alienation, monism, rigidity, anti-inclusiveness, judgmentalism, fear of ambiguity or complexity, lack of empathy, coldness, xenophobia, bigotry, prejudice, ethnocentrism, various inegalitarianisms, and so forth.

Let us admit in response that no general approach to metaethics can guarantee that in practice, just the right[4] attitude is taken toward pluralism, diversity, dissent, and tolerance. Restricting the discussion to the general level of, say, adherence to or denial of any form of moral objectivism is unhelpful. Torquemada and Stalin were moral objectivists. But then, so were Gandhi and Dr. King, along with some of the major historical theorists of tolerance, including Milton, Locke, and John Stuart Mill. To make analytical progress, we must descend from this level of abstraction. Some forms of moral objectivism are benevolent, and others are not. Objectivism as a metaethic can encompass both benevolent and non-benevolent substantive or normative ethics. In general, no approach to metaethics is specially conducive to tolerance at the normative ethical level.

This claim itself is often denied, though. It is often supposed in particular that metaethical relativism, in general, perhaps along with other unambitious forms of metaethics, offers a short cut to tolerance, pluralism, and diversity, or to the kinds or degrees of these things that most generous-minded persons would for one reason or another prefer. But this is not so. Generally, there is no determinate relation between moral relativism and tolerance, or between moral relativism and any form of pluralism and diversity as moral values or as valued states of affairs.

The error of thinking that relativism in general has some advantage in this regard is understandable. It may be, as David Brink has argued, that a relativist cannot view normative moral attitudes different from her own "as mistaken, provided those attitudes reflect the moral beliefs of those who hold them or perhaps, the moral beliefs of the group of which those who hold them are members."[5] This logically limits the grounds upon which a relativist might be intolerant. Intolerance on the part of relativists thus logically cannot be due to their belief that the contrasting moral beliefs of members of other groups are mistaken, at least if those latter beliefs are consistently held and are not inconsistent with the factual evidence.

But intolerance on the part of relativists need not involve disbelief of any moral claim not accepted by the relativist. Intolerance can instead be motivated by the metaethically unambitious belief that it suits one's individual or group interests, or one's mere preferences, to be intolerant. For the relativist, intolerance of others is not wrong unless, roughly, that intolerance is condemned by one's own group. And there is no obvious reason for one's group to condemn their being intolerant of other groups, at least beyond the dictates of mere prudence. In fact, one might imagine that the very construction of a group-based morality, built upon the distinction between we and they, potentiates a feeling of moral separateness and difference that may lead to intolerance. Even if not, there need be no reason to refrain from any apparently prudent intolerance the relativist finds gratifying. Why not simply be group-selfish? Of course, even a moral objectivist might agree that a specially high degree of "selfishness" is appropriate for oppressed groups. But moral relativism is not confined especially to oppressed groups.

The possibility should be noted as well of what might be referred to as "nightmare" moral relativism: a relativist society might well follow a moral code that allows oppressing weak societies—if the weak society wishes to resist, that may be right for them, but we as the oppressing society are not bound by their belief that we should desist—while barring intervention in the affairs of strong societies such as South Africa, or Nazi Germany in the 1930s. The relativist group morality may say that what is right in one society may not be right for Nazi Germany, especially if intervening in the affairs of Nazi Germany is likely to be at least minimally dangerous and costly. It is thus readily possible for a relativist society to be exactly morally backward, from the standpoint of standard objectivist humanitarianism.

Thus it is impossible to claim some general advantage for moral relativism as such in the matter of tolerance. And without tediously rehearsing the parallel arguments, the same conclusion can be reached with regard to moral noncognitivism and pragmatism as well. As Professor Brink has noted, "[i]f no one moral judgment is any more correct than another, how can it be that I should be tolerant?"[6] There is simply no obvious relationship between relativism, noncognitivism, or pragmatism, and supposedly kindred notions such as the value of living-and-letting-live or generally being respectful of neighboring groups. While even stronger criticisms somehow linking relativism to violent struggle[7] or to ethnocentrism[8] are possible, they are not necessary for our argument.

None of this is to deny the sanguinary history of moral objectivism in general. But there are any number of obvious, historically recognized reasons for the moral objectivist to embrace tolerance, pluralism, and diversity as vital substantive moral principles. Some objectivists do so. Many of these reasons can be shared by various sorts of relativists, noncognitivists, and pragmatists. But for some such arguments, this is less clearly so. There may be important reasons to be tolerant and benevolent toward diversity, the substance of which is most clearly at home under objectivism.

Consider, for example, Will Kymlicka's argument that tolerance and respect for the liberty of others should be based not upon any inability to reasonably criticize basic moral judgments, but precisely upon the belief that freedom and tolerance is most conducive to rationally making and revising such judgments.[9] On such a view, discovering a moral truth, or best understanding a moral truth, may require that we take seriously, on their own terms, all those persons who might even indirectly contribute to that process. And as John Stuart Mill classically observed, it will in some respect be those most unlike us who can most valuably so contribute. For some objectivists, of course, as in the cases of Gandhi and Dr. King, intolerance is straightforwardly forbidden by basic, allegedly objective moral principle. Anyone who wishes to behave intolerantly under, say, a Gandhian regime will have to confront whatever difference there is between allegedly objective moral principles of tolerance, and whatever sort of justification is provided for tolerance in non-objectivist societies.

More broadly, objectivist moral arguments based on ideas such as of the equality of persons, the value of universal individual freedom, personal autonomy, or human dignity can easily issue in injunctions to pluralism and tolerance.[10] Recognition of the many legitimate dimensions of difference among persons and cultures can similarly lead the objectivist naturally to value pluralism and diversity, instrumentally or for their own sake.[11] There are thus any number of obvious reasons for at least some objectivists to deny that one size fits all.

As noted above, though, not all arguments for tolerance and pluralism are naturally associated only with moral objectivism. Objectivists and non-objectivists of all sorts may see tolerance, pluralism, and diversity as linked to some version of freedom and justice, to social productivity, to peace and stability, or even to survival.[12] Objectivists and nonobjectivists alike might argue by analogy that just as genetic diversity serves the overall survival interests of a population, so cultural diversity serves similar interests at a broad social level. Encouraging diversity can be a risk-reduction strategy. Less exaltedly, there is the Madisonian Federalist argument for controlling the adverse effects of political factions precisely through multiplying and diversifying factions, as opposed to suppressing them.[13] As well, there is the calculation that intolerant policies would be likely to backfire or otherwise fail, a fear of being or appearing to be morally smug or complacent, as well as analogous fears of being perceived as morally dictatorial or imperialist.[14]

Each of these rationales seems equally available to moral objectivists and non-objectivists alike.

It is important, though, to remember that for the moral objectivist, the value of tolerance and pluralism may flow as much from what the objectivist does not know, or may falsely imagine she knows, as from any genuinely objective moral insight. This is a legacy of the undeniable fallibility, bias, and finitude of human beings, and it is central to the classic fallibilism of John Stuart Mill. More recently, the implications of human fallibility for all sorts of moral objectivists have been admirably traced by Professor Michael J. Perry.[15]

The compatibility of objectivist morality and fallibilist-based tolerance should not be surprising. It is in part merely the obverse of the important and undeniable gap, noted in the preceding chapter, between the bare existence of some moral truth and our limited, unreliable capacity to ascertain and interpret that truth. Thus while it is perfectly possible for a moral objectivist to embrace intolerance and conformism, such an approach is hardly dictated by the logic of moral objectivism itself. It is admittedly also possible for moral relativists, at least, to admit that on some occasions, they took a considered moral stand which turned out, on deeper reflection, to really be inconsistent with the group's moral code. Moral objectivists, though, can admit not only the analogous error, but the possibility, if not the strong likelihood, that the best current understanding of what morality objectively requires may itself be wrong in crucial respects.

Now, it may be objected that we are here judging moral objectivism by laxer standards than those employed in the preceding chapter to judge relativism, noncognitivism, and pragmatism. The latter approaches were indeed criticized above. But moral objectivism can obviously be put in the service of the worst sorts of intolerance, exclusionism, and regimentation. Moral objectivism can offer no guarantees either.

But there is really no double standard at work here. This is so even if we assume that most contemporary varieties of moral objectivism are just as disposed toward intolerance as the fighting faiths of several hundred years ago, and even if we further assume that any recent increase in tolerance is due to the decline of either theistic or other objectivist metaethics.[16] The point of the preceding chapter was not that moral objectivism can offer guarantees where its rivals cannot. The point, instead, was the admittedly contingent, speculative claim that based upon what we know of psychology, motivation, and culture, only some form of moral objectivism can help a society escape a reasonably predictable long-term transition into moral circumstances that most persons today would now view as decidedly unattractive.

This advantage of moral objectivism is not undermined in those forms of objectivism that pretend only to a limited scope of applicability,[17] or which place special emphasis on the difficulties of converting a moral truth into a demonstrable or reasonably well known moral truth. But another problem seems to be lurking here. Whether an objectivist morality presumes to answer all apparently moral questions or to leave answers to some such questions open or indeterminate, the potential for divisiveness, sectarianism, authoritarianism, and alienation seems real. Will not one tend reasonably to feel like an outsider if one cannot accept any official, but logically undemonstrated, answer to some question in which one has an important interest?

There is something to this, in that only where there is some pretension to objectivity can there be a literal orthodoxy, and therefore a literal heterodoxy. But we know enough of relativism, noncognitivism, and pragmatism to know that they too are compatible with unfortunate social divisiveness and a sense of separation. In fact, it is hardly clear why relativists and multiple-conversational pragmatists should view a sense of mutual separation and mutual emotional indifference, at least along group lines, as somehow regrettable. Relativists, noncognitivists, and pragmatists ultimately may tend to feel as a matter of principle that it is better, all things considered, if they distance themselves from anyone who wants to tell any sort of meta-narrative, including any story about the genuinely objective value of tolerance and inclusion.

In contrast, objectivism, including some varieties of theism, will have good moral reasons to avoid sectarianism, divisive arguments, exclusion, or authoritarianism.[18] Each of the possible reasons for tolerance, pluralism, diversity, and inclusion cited briefly above remains potentially fully applicable for the moral objectivist. To the extent that the objectivist realistically appreciates that not all moral, or apparently moral, questions have unique best answers even in principle, the objectivist has further reason to recognize the logic of pluralism and diversity. Defenses of objectivism in various theistic and nontheistic forms need not be dogmatic, divisive, or exclusionary, as the argument thus far and in the following chapter indicate. For at least some moral objectivists, disrespectfully abandoning the conscientious dissenter may well be morally worse than foregoing whatever objective moral value might flow from universal adherence to some objective moral principle.

There may still be some uneasiness, though, regarding the nature and potential of moral objectivism. It might be asked whether moral objectivism itself does not somehow privilege reason over desire, or tend to underemphasize the moral dimensions of love, relatedness, and responsibility.[19] Now, there are technical, merely point-scoring responses to these concerns. For example, one can ask whether the claim that reason should not be privileged over desire amounts to a claim that it is irrational, somehow unreasonable, or arbitrary to do so. If so, even the critic of excessive reliance on reason still relies ultimately on reason when it comes to assessing the proper roles of reason and emotion.

We can respond more seriously, though, by observing that the sensitive exercise of reason may offer the ultimately surest path to recognizing and carrying into effect the moral importance of care and relatedness.[20] Even if reason is not invariably the slave of the passions, reason is often driven and steered by desire and by the passions. Nor is reason, when exercised correctly on its own narrow standards, by itself capable of morally horrifying results in the absence of objectionable desires. While reason obviously cannot neutrally arbitrate between desire and reason itself, reason can certainly suggest a balance between reason and desire. Reason can also recognize the unreasonableness and undesirability of excessive planning, lack of spontaneity, undue calculativeness, or a constricted role for emotion and desire. As well, reason properly exercised can adjudicate between worthy and unworthy passions. And some of the most powerful, moving discussions of the importance of care and relatedness among persons may owe more to reason or speculation than to emotion unguided by reason.

Admittedly, all this is at the level of abstract argument, and abstract argument may provide little genuine reassurance to those who fear the potential for coldness, excessive abstraction, atomism, narrow rationalism, sectarianism, divisiveness, and exclusionism of any sort of objective metaethics. An ounce of concrete example may therefore be worth a pound of abstract argument. So it may be useful to recur to the imperfect but concrete example of Gandhian objectivist, indeed theistic, metaethics. This is certainly not to hold up Gandhian thinking as invariably sound and progressive. That is not the point. We need merely note the cross-cultural appeal of crucial elements of Gandhian social thought,[21] and the reassuring character of a few basic themes emphasized by Gandhi.

Certainly, Gandhi talks of self-discipline, self-control, self-sacrifice, self-purification, and the possibility of joy in certain kinds of suffering, particularly on the part of those working for basic political change for the sake of the ostracized and excluded.[22] Doubtless this may have a certain puritanical or Victorian quality. But the Gandhian emphasis on love for one's political antagonists cannot be casually psychoanalyzed or otherwise dismissed. Gandhi urges, for example, that "the silent and undemonstrative action of truth and love produces far more permanent and abiding results than speeches or such other showy performances."[23]

The moral objectivism of those such as Gandhi, or any number of others, amounts to an eloquent testimonial to love, to caring, to relatedness, and to the likely ultimate moral insignificance of political change that marginalizes such concerns. By virtue of the nature of love itself as understood by Gandhi, including especially genuine love for one's political opponents, no regime could be less threatening, less sectarian, less divisive, and less exclusionary than one consistently based on such love. Moral objectivism as a whole should therefore not be especially suspect in this regard. Our opposition to the authoritarian abuse of reason need not lead us to abandon the potential authoritativeness of moral objectivity based in reason.[24]

NOTES TO *POLYPHONY, DISSONANCE, AND MORAL OBJECTIVITY*

1. The musicological analogy is suggested by Amelie Oksenberg Rorty, Varieties of Pluralism in a Polyphonic Society, 44 Rev. Metaphysics 3 (1990). Rorty in turn cites Michael M. Bakhtin, The Dialogic Imagination (Austin: Univ. of Texas Press 1981).

2. See, e.g., Renford Bambrough, Fools and Heretics, in Royal Institute of Philosophy Supplement no. 29: Wittgenstein Centenary Essays 239, 239 (A. Phillips Griffiths ed.) (Cambridge: Cambridge Univ. Press 1991); Gordon Graham, Religion, Secularization and Modernity, 67 Phil. 183, 192 (1992); Hilary Putnam, A Reconsideration of Deweyan Democracy, 63 S. Cal. L. Rev. 1671, 1680 (1990).

3. Bernard Williams, Subjectivism and Toleration, in Royal Institute of Philosophy Supplement no. 30: A.J. Ayer Memorial Essays 197, 202 (A. Phillips Griffiths ed.) (Cambridge: Cambridge Univ. Press 1992). For the proverbial other side of the story, in which objectivism and theism are alleged to be necessary to motivate any great moral sacrifice needed for a suitably worthy cause, see Mohandas K. Gandhi, Non-Violent Resistance 364 (Bharatan Kumarappa ed.) (New York: Schocken Books 1961).

4. This use of 'right' is not intended to beg the question in favor of some form of moral objectivism; it may be read in any way one wishes. It is also worth noting that the literature is a bit unclear on whether intolerance is by definition morally wrong, or else wrong merely in most cases. Compare, e.g., Jeremy Waldron, Locke: Toleration and the Rationality of Persecution, in John Locke, A Letter Concerning Toleration: In Focus 98, 98 (John Horton & Susan Mendus eds.) (London: Routledge 1991) with Maurice Cranston, John Locke and the Case for Toleration in id. at 78, 79. Whether in opposing the rise of, say, some neo-Nazi party one is being intolerant, if justifiably intolerant, or not intolerant at all is not crucial to our argument. Nor is it crucial that while the concept of tolerance normally refers only to beliefs or practices the tolerator disfavors, see id. at 78, we could certainly use the concept of tolerance in a broader sense, without this restriction.

5. David O. Brink, Moral Realism and the Foundations of Ethics 92 (Cambridge: Cambridge Univ. Press 1989).

6. Id. at 93. See David McNaughton, Moral Vision 159-60 (Oxford: Basil Blackwell 1988); Michael J. Perry, Love and Power 130 (New York: Oxford

Univ. Press 1991); Jeremy Waldron, Locke: Toleration and the Rationality of Persecution, in John Locke, A Letter Concerning Toleration: In Focus 98, 105 (John Horton & Susan Mendus eds.) (London: Routledge 1991). See also Max Hocutt, Must Relativists Tolerate Evil?, 17 Phil. Forum 188, 197 (1986); Bernard Williams, An Inconsistent Form of Relativism, in Relativism: Cognitive and Moral 171, 173 (Michael Krausz & Jack W. Meiland eds.) (Notre Dame: Notre Dame Univ. Press 1982).

7. See Phillip E. Devine, Relativism, Nihilism, and God xii (Notre Dame: Notre Dame Univ. Press 1989).

8. See Allison Dundes Renteln, Relativism and the Search for Human Rights, 90 Am. Anthropologist 56, 63 (1988).

9. See Will Kymlicka, Liberalism, Community, and Culture 9-10 (Oxford: Clarendon Press 1989). For the classic linkage of tolerance, fallibilism, discovery, knowledge, progress, and self-realization, see John Stuart Mill, On Liberty (Currin V. Shields ed.) (New York: Library of Liberal Arts 1956). See also Michael J. Perry, Love and Power 132-33 (New York: Oxford Univ. Press 1991); Amelie Oksenberg Rorty, Varieties of Pluralism in a Polyphonic Society, 44 Rev. Metaphysics 3, 11 (1990) (plurality of perspectives as forcing each position toward reduced ambiguity and greater precision). This is not to suggest, though, that a quasi-realist, for example, could not modestly take the attitude that her own (other) attitudes are, in some unspecified, attenuated way, "improvable," and that the best way to engage in the process of attitude-improvement is to be respectful of the attitudes of others.

10. Thus the cognitivist might argue that as a general rule it is objectively best to allow competent adults, at least, to find things out for themselves. See Bernard Williams, Subjectivism and Tolerance, in Royal Institute of Philosophy Supplement no. 30: A.J. Ayer Memorial Essays 197, 205 (A. Phillips Griffiths ed.) (Cambridge: Cambridge Univ. Press 1992).

11. See, e.g., David McNaughton, Moral Vision 160-61 (Oxford: Basil Blackwell 1988); E.J. Bond, Could There Be a Rationally Grounded Universal Morality?, 15 J. Phil. Res. 15, 41 (1989); Susan Wolf, Two Levels of Pluralism, 102 Ethics 785, 788-89 (1992). Of course, one hardly need be a moral objectivist to arrive at moral diversity, or to simply take delight in diversity. See, e.g., Mark Timmons, Putnam's Moral Objectivism, 34 Erkenntnis 371, 386 (1991); Allan Gibbard, Communities of Judgment, in Foundations of Moral and Political Philosophy 185-86 (Ellen Frankel Paul, Fred D. Miller, Jr. & Jeffrey Paul eds.) (Oxford: Basil Blackwell 1990).

12. See, e.g., Michael S. Moore, Moral Reality Revisited, 90 Mich. L. Rev. 2424, 2533 (1992) ("[a]moral realist might well think that democracy, . . . tolerance, autonomy, and pluralism are real values too. . . ."); Amelie Oksenberg Rorty, Varieties of Pluralism in a Polyphonic Society, 44 Rev. Metaphysics 3, 3, 6, 17 (1990); Steven D. Smith, The Restoration of Tolerance, 78 Calif. L. Rev. 305, 334-35 (1990). Consider also the intriguing possibility that intolerance may often be practiced not by groups that perceive themselves as politically dominant, or even as reasonably strong, but by groups that do not perceive themselves as free to express themselves. See James L. Gibson, The Political Consequences of Intolerance: Cultural Conformity and Political Freedom, 86 Am. Pol. Sci. Rev. 338 (1992).

13. For general commentary, see David F. Epstein, The Political Theory of the Federalist (Chicago: Univ. of Chicago Press 1984); Morton White, Philosophy, The Federalist, and the Constitution (New York: Oxford Univ. Press 1987).

14. See Mark de Bretton Platts, Moral Realities 166 (London: Routledge 1991). See also Steven L. Ross, A Real Defense of Tolerance, 22 J. Value Inquiry 127, 138 (1988) (citing several possible policy-based justifications for legal tolerance generally or in particular circumstances).

15. See Michael J. Perry, Love and Power 100-01, 132 (New York: Oxford Univ. Press 1991) ("[a]uthentic religious faith and the virtue of fallibilism are intimately connected").

16. If we assume that theistic or other objectivist metaethics have been in decline, and that tolerance has generally expanded in the same period or in lagged fashion, we have certainly established a correlation. But two observations should be made in response. First, it is technically difficult to be sure that expanded tolerance is not at all logically or causally dependent upon the considerable residues of theistic or objectivist metaethics, particularly of relatively humane sorts. As we saw in the previous chapter, very few non-objectivist metaethicists can resist the temptation to consciously or inadvertently trade upon the residual logical and moral clout of objectivist language. How much tolerance we would observe if moral objectivism were entirely wrung out of our culture is doubtful. The moral objectivist can argue that tolerance and diversity are morally right, and that over a long period of time, more and more people will tend to recognize this and its implications in more contexts. This in itself would be a simple explanation of any general increase in tolerance or the acceptance of diversity as a moral value. Second, to the extent that any purported increased tolerance and diversity can be ascribed to less ambitious metaethics, this may in some measure be only the

positive side of, for example, feelings of indifference, passivity, or futility regarding other groups of people. If one simply does not care about other groups of people, it will often seem inexpedient either to oppress them, unless they are weak, or to assist them. Tolerance, or apparent tolerance, may reflect merely an increasing absorption with our own individual or group concerns. For an interesting possible theoretical linkage between the rejection of the idea of objective moral truth and some decidedly unattractive, anti-progressive political trends, see Dean MacCannell, Empty Meeting Grounds: The Tourist Papers 183, 187 (London: Routledge 1992).

17. See, e.g., John Finnis, Natural Law and Natural Rights 284-86 (Oxford: Clarendon Press 1980); Michael S. Moore, The Interpretive Turn in Modern Theory: A Turn for the Worse?, 41 Stan. L. Rev. 871, 879 (1989) (discussing Finnis's approach); John J. Tilley, Moral Relativism and Hume, 69 Modern Schoolman 81, 96-97 (1992); David Wiggins, Moral Cognitivism, Moral Relativism and Motivating Moral Beliefs, 91 Proc. Aristotelian Society (n.s.) 61, 63 (1991). See also Thomas Nagel, Equality and Partiality 50 (New York: Oxford Univ. Press 1991) ("in a substantial intermediate range, the quest for a universalizable principle that accommodates both personal and impersonal reasons seems to me to have no solution").

18. See Michael J. Perry, Love and Power 106 (New York: Oxford Univ. Press 1991). Glenn Tinder has concisely and suggestively observed that "[t]olerance may be regarded as a kind of hospitality—toward persons (attentiveness) and toward truth (openness)." Glenn Tinder, Tolerance: Toward a New Civility 182 (Amherst: Univ. of Mass. Press 1976).

19. See, e.g., Lynne Henderson, Whose Nature? Practical Reason and Patriarchy, 38 Clev. St. L. Rev. 169, 169-71 (1990). Professor Henderson's concerns are raised here in the context of a critique of John Finnis's work, but her arguments raise issues of broader concern. See also Lynne Henderson, Authoritarianism and the Rule of Law, 66 Ind. L.J. 379 (1991).

20. See R. George Wright, Should the Law Reflect the World?: Lessons for Legal Theory From Quantum Mechanics, 18 Fla. St. L. Rev. 855, 864-70, 879-81 (1991). See also Owen Fiss, The Other Goldberg, in The Constitution of Rights 229 (Michael J. Mayer & W.A. Parent eds.) (Ithaca: Cornell Univ. Press 1992).

21. See Michael J. Perry, Love and Power 108-09 (New York: Oxford Univ. Press 1991).

22. See Mohandas K. Gandhi, Non-Violent Resistance 77, 78, 237, 365, 383 (Bharatan Kumarappa ed.) (New York: Schocken Books 1961).

23. Id. at 77. See also The Brihadaranyaka Upanisad 602 (Rai Bahudur Sris Chandra Vasu trans.) (New York: AMS Press reprint ed. 1974) ("let everyone learn these three (virtues), humility, charity and mercy"); The Laws of Manu ch. 4, para. 238 at 96 (Wendy Doniger & Brian K. Smith trans.) (New York: Penguin 1992) (enjoining "refraining from oppressing any living being"). Note as well that the theistic objectivist Thomas More has King Utopus promulgating a strict rule barring even vehement and unpleasant defenses of one's religious beliefs. See Thomas More, Utopia 155 (Mildred Campbell ed.) (Toronto: D. Van Nostrand Co. 1947).

24. Cf. Michael Devitt, Realism and Truth 257 n.11 (Oxford: Basil Blackwell 2d ed. 1991) ("In opposing the illegitimate imposition of, say, one culture or class upon another, [constructivists] come to oppose the imposition of *any* authority whatsoever, even the legitimate authority that might come from actually *knowing* something about an independent world.") (emphasis in the original).

7

Can Debate Over Justice Be Progressive?

Contemporary ethical debate is sometimes thought to be pathologically interminable.[1] This chapter seeks, on the contrary, to show how it is possible for some forms of even a theistic approach to revivify, rather than paralyze, ethical debate, and the debate over obligation in particular. If ethical debate can be progressive here, it can surely be progressive elsewhere.

Crucially, theistic approaches to obligation need not depend exclusively upon dogmatic claims not susceptible of reasoned examination. The rational case for theistic views can in some important respects be strengthened or weakened by the marshalling of publicly accessible evidence and reasoned argument. In particular, claims that strengthen or weaken the rational case for theistic approaches to obligation can be subjected to the kinds of critical scrutiny successfully employed by scientists to improve their understanding of nature.[2] As a matter of terminology, to the extent that a theistic approach to obligation seeks to accord with public reason, we may speak generally of theistic natural law.

This does not mean that all versions of theistic natural law are subject to empirical disconfirmation, that there can be a rationally overwhelming case for theistic natural law,[3] that the best way to theism is through an examination of nature,[4] or that public authorities should justify their decisions by relying on any theistic premiss. We can justify public policy choices on purely secular grounds, even if some believe that a deeper, theistic layer of justification is also possible. Our focus on those elements of a possible theistic natural law approach that allow for their own discursive vulnerability is intended simply to avoid the problem of pathologically interminable debate.

Consider the apparently crucial theistic claim that a Being intended that intelligent life exist, and accordingly created, influenced, or allowed the creation of all that exists.[5] Without intending to beg any interesting theological issues, we will for the sake of convenience refer to this Being as God. Of course, we must bear in mind that we have referred in previous chapters to Beings with at least slightly different attributes as God as well.

Now, it is perfectly possible and quite common to deny the existence of God thus defined. But it is wrong to assume that the assertion and the denial of this God must inevitably descend into a non-progressive, stalemated, question-begging debate. Admittedly, much of the relevant scientific evidence currently "rests on highly uncertain foundations."[6] Admittedly as well, certain varieties of dogmatic theism would survive any sort of evidence against the existence of a God thus defined.[7] But it is not beyond the current and future capacities of natural science to reach consensual conclusions that significantly count for or against a non-dogmatic argument for this sort of God.[8]

It is important to avoid undue skepticism concerning the inherent limitations of science. The physicist Joe Rosen has argued that

> Unique phenomena, being inherently irreproducible and unpredictable, are outside the domain of concern of physics and are food for metaphysics. The universe as a whole, along with its big bang, . . . kinds of elementary particles, fundamental interactions, etc. is a unique phenomenon. Thus considerations concerning these matters are considerations of metaphysics, not of physics, and personal taste and inclination dominate the scene.[9]

Setting aside the issue of the relation between metaphysics and personal taste, and the observation *ad hominem* that Rosen himself has contributed to the physics of exactly such problems,[10] let us simply examine the evidence.

As a result of the recent progress of modern science, for example, there are apparently well-grounded reasons for concluding that anyone who denies the existence of God as defined above should, in reason, accept at least one highly controversial and rarely held proposition about the natural world. John Leslie has recently argued at length, more specifically, that one cannot, on the evidence, reasonably deny the existence of God while still accepting the common sense view that there is only one universe.[11]

Certainly, not every writer accepts the force of this putative dilemma. There are, as Leslie recognizes, other possible, if controversial, views one might take that might reconcile the denial of God and the existence of only one universe. Or one might claim that Leslie's scientific evidence, when properly understood, can be explained away. The point, though, is that if Leslie is right, that would inescapably put a certain amount of rational pressure on the nontheist to respond to Leslie with better science. Leslie's argument itself is strengthened or weakened by scientific theory and investigation.

As we will see momentarily, Leslie's argument is a modern, more sophisticated variant of what is often pejoratively, if not dismissively, referred to as a "God of the Gaps" approach. This kind of argument concludes that positing God accounts more satisfactorily for the existence of some natural phenomenon than does science, where science, at least for the moment, can offer no convincing explanation of the phenomenon in question. Theologies based on a "God of the Gaps" have, historically, fared poorly.[12] But that is precisely the point. This chapter aims, again, not at developing and adequately defending a sound theology, but at showing that crucial theistic claims need not be purely dogmatic, and can be reasonably promoted or undermined through discussion and investigation.

It seems clear that if Leslie's scientific and logic-based argument could reasonably establish that the nontheist should believe in an enormous number of crucially varied and perhaps in principle unobservable universes, that would be a rationally progressive step in an ongoing discussion. It is of course open to the nontheist to simply swallow this consequence. But some nontheists would find such a conclusion surprising and to some degree troubling. Depending upon what a belief in such universes involved, some nontheists might reasonably come to find theism more attractive, given the alternatives, than formerly. On the other hand, many theists would be equally disturbed by apparently well-grounded scientific evidence that there is nothing surprising about the existence of conscious life, or that the universe, whether multiple or single, can be entirely self-explanatory, and can properly be said to be capable of arising entirely causelessly.

The scientific evidence for Leslie's conclusion begins with a large number of varied and apparently independent states of affairs, numerical constants, ratios, and quantitative relationships that have been referred to as "anthropic coincidences." Metaphors such as "fine tuning" or "knife-edge balancing" have been invoked. The idea, roughly, is that if any of a large number of diverse, apparently variable and independent features of the universe had in fact varied by even a slight amount in either direction, no reasonably imaginable form of intelligent life, among other things, would have been likely, or even physically possible, anywhere in the universe. The existence of intelligent life is therefore thought to be, on the scientific evidence, staggeringly improbable. A call for the best explanation of our existence understandably ensues.

Even before we specify a few of the alleged anthropic coincidences or consider the scientific evidence, several lines of criticism arise. First, it may be thought improper to apply the logic of probability to allegedly unique events such as the creation or development of the universe. Second, a more precise and satisfying account of just what the anthropic coincidences are supposed to make unlikely or impossible may be demanded. Third, it may be urged that there is really no puzzle to solve, and no explanation to seek: since intelligent life exists, all the necessary numbers must have come out right. We would otherwise not be around to observe the situation. Each of these criticisms, arguably, can be satisfactorily answered, and they will be treated briefly, along with other less preliminary objections, at various points in the text below. The interested reader is encouraged to examine the endnotes following, and the sources cited therein, for more substantive and detailed further discussion.

The literature on the cosmology and philosophy associated with the idea of the anthropic coincidences is large.[13] The most influential discussion of the anthropic coincidences is contained in John Barrow and Frank Tipler's monumental work, *The Anthropic Cosmological Principle*.[14] Probably the most philosophically sophisticated discussion of the anthropic coincidences is contained in John Leslie's *Universes*.[15]

For a taste of merely a few of the alleged anthropic coincidences, though, we might turn to an earlier formulation by John Leslie. Leslie refers to claims that

> if the cosmic expansion rate at an early stage of the Big Bang had been different by as little as one part in a million then this would have led to lifelessness (since the cosmos would then fall to bits too fast or recollapse too soon); that tiny increases in turbulence would have multiplied the primeval heat billions of times, disastrously, yet that great turbulence is what one would expect when regions causally disconnected at the start of the Bang first appeared on one another's horizons; that increasing or decreasing the strength of the strong nuclear force by one or two per cent would have prevented carbon forming in any quantity, while a two per cent increase would have stopped quarks forming protons, essential constituents of atoms; that chemistry and biology depend on the mass of the neutron's being greater than that of the proton by just about one part in a thousand; and so on.[16]

Thus it is amazing that we, or perhaps anyone remotely like us, have existed. One obvious way of accounting for this would be to conclude that it was affirmatively intended that we exist. If, by analogy, we were to come across a number of stones on the ground spelling out our full name in flawless Palmer script, our most reasonable reaction would be to infer intent behind the arrangement, even though no particular arrangement of stones is any more likely than any other, and any particular arrangement of the stones can be said to be in a sense unlikely.

Another way of avoiding the intentional, and ultimately theistic, implication is through a protracted war of attrition. Even if we assume that the various anthropic coincidences are mutually independent, each is potentially vulnerable, in that it may somehow be shown to involve no fine tuning at all. Any given "coincidence" may turn out, on the scientific evidence, to be much more probable than at first appears, or to in fact be inevitable, given other physical laws.

This is obviously a long route to undermining the anthropic coincidences as a whole, and no theist imagines that each and every putative anthropic coincidence will remain forever unexplained on natural grounds.[17] But for a start, at least the first alleged anthropic coincidence quoted above from John Leslie is already suspect. The rate or rates at which the universe expanded may involve no precarious avoidance of opposing disastrous outcomes at all.[18] Whether this is genuinely the case or not is subject to non-dogmatic investigation.

As Leslie recognizes, another way of avoiding the theistic implications of the anthropic coincidences would be to show that the universe we observe is, in fact, merely one of an enormous number of independent "trials," or relevantly separate universes.[19] That we have at some unspecified point won a Las Vegas slot machine jackpot becomes less remarkable if we have been feeding coins into the slot night and day for months. Just as most pulls of the handle do not result in a payoff, most universes are assumed to be devoid of life, and the surprisingness of our existence is thereby negated.[20]

The best known version of the idea that there are many universes is the so-called "many worlds" interpretation of quantum mechanics. This interpretation, or family of interpretations,[21] has the virtue of arguably solving a difficult basic problem in the interpretation of quantum mechanics,[22] and seems necessary for much of mainstream quantum cosmology.[23] But the "many worlds" interpretation has been objected to on a number of grounds.

The many worlds interpretation has, perhaps forgivably, been characterized as "rather bizarre."[24] The unobservability in principle of all but one of the many universes,[25] coupled with the arguable profligacy of universes,[26] leads some to find an extravagant and contrived metaphysics at work.[27] It is sometimes thought that the interpretation involves a massive violation of the principle, embodied in Ockham's Razor,[28] that one should not postulate entities unnecessarily.[29] This criticism, though, is controversial.[30] The genuine explanatory scope of the many worlds interpretation has also been called into question.[31] The interpretation itself is not clear on precisely when and how, assumedly without violating conservation laws,[32] the constant splitting of the universe takes place.[33]

It has been suggested that the many worlds interpretation, which is often relied upon to avoid theistic conclusions, itself ironically reverses in part the Copernican Revolution that denies the centrality of conscious beings in the universe,[34] on the assumption that universe-splitting occurs through the activity of conscious observers. However, it is apparently possible that universe-splitting occurs via what are referred to as "measurement-like interactions" requiring no observation.[35] If so, however, it is incumbent upon the nontheist, according to one writer's calculations, to believe in roughly ten to the tenth power, to the twelfth power, unobservable universes.[36] The choice, apparently, is not between theism on the one hand and a lean and mean empirical ontology on the other.

Finally, anyone who subscribes to a many worlds interpretation, or to any of the other means discussed below of avoiding the apparent force of the anthropic coincidences, should bear in mind one additional, admittedly quite speculative possibility. It may be that such theories commit us to rather dramatic and widely unattractive revisions of commonly held notions of moral responsibility and of the production of good and evil by human acts.[37] As well, if the many universes are in principle unobservable, empiricists are faced with a serious problem. The unobservability of God becomes no longer an argument against the existence of God if the empiricist, like the rest of us, is faced with a forced choice between an unobservable God and many unobservable universes.

In any event, it seems clear thus far that investigation and debate over matters vital to even a theistic natural law need not be sterile, futile, or otherwise unproductive. Doubtless the debate is technical, quantitative, complex, and multi-faceted,[38] but this hardly implies pathological interminability.

Additional complexity enters when we recognize that other responses to the challenge of the anthropic coincidences are possible. As our point is not to settle any of these debates here, we can again afford to be brief. But it should at least be mentioned that one might also account for the anthropic coincidences by arguing not that there are many universes, but that only one internally consistent universe—ours—is even possible.[39] It is hardly surprising that conscious life exists if no universe without conscious life is physically or logically possible:[40] if the slot machine is capable of only one outcome, there need be no surprise when that outcome occurs, even if it is a payoff.

While there is some interest in this approach,[41] leading cosmologists seem less than enthusiastic.[42] One basic problem is that there seems to be no detectable reason why there could not be relatively simple universes consisting, say, of just photons and electrons.[43] Or there might be less simple universes, perhaps differing only trivially from ours, describable with enough ad hoc epicycles to accommodate all the necessary physical constraints. But we again do not need to settle the matter. The point is simply that nontheists, and particularly those nontheists who subscribe to any familiar notion of morality or moral responsibility, ordinarily do not rush to embrace the idea that only one internally consistent universe is possible.[44]

In general, the strengths and weaknesses of the several ways of negating the potential theistic implications of the anthropic coincidences seem susceptible to reasoned investigation. This is not to deny, though, that some possible developments of the anthropic coincidences argument threaten to plunge us into apparently perpetual murkiness. For example, it might be asked how we can be sure that intelligent life could not exist within, or associated with, say, gamma rays.[45] Science can shed some light on the possibility of diverse forms of intelligent life, but at some point we may simply have to rely upon informed judgments as to the relative contrivedness of alternative approaches. In the meantime, most nontheists do not ordinarily assert not only the potentiality, but the actuality, of intelligent life in such apparently rugged ecological niches.

Some may object as well to the apparent anthropomorphism of the "anthropic" coincidences. Why assume that the thing to be explained by the appeal to the anthropic coincidences is, precisely, intelligent life, or conscious life?[46] After all, if most of the putative "knife-edge balances" alluded to thus far had not held, there would have been no snail darters, spotted owls, or garden slugs either. It would seem, unfortunately, that a genuinely full and complete answer to this question can be found only at the level of some particular theology.[47] This is because no merely factual description of an anthropic coincidence can pin down the intention or "aim" allegedly underlying that apparent coincidence beyond a certain point.

Consider the case of someone who wakes up with dozens of fresh bullet holes completely tracing that person in a precise, form-fitting outline. That person would reasonably reject explanations relying solely upon natural phenomena, as well as the possibility that one or more agents tried to kill or injure that person with those bullets, but, luckily, happened to miss. The most reasonable conclusion would instead be that at least one person intended that the apparent target survive. But we could not necessarily provide a precise account of the intention in question. Perhaps the intention was that the apparent target not be injured, or not be killed, or not be killed only for the sake of the apparent target's feeling some emotional response or carrying out some task. Without further information, we cannot be sure. Similarly, given only some of the most basic anthropic coincidences, we cannot tell by examination whether the existence of humans is, for example, an inevitable or accidental byproduct of the intended creation of amoebas, or vice versa, or whether both were intended, perhaps for particular purposes.

The crucial point, though, is that regardless of which of these accounts is most accurate, there is still some difficult-to-specify overall state of affairs that is impossible to account for unless we posit some intention on the part of at least one other person, above and beyond the intention that shots be fired in the victim's direction or that just some universe exist. The anthropic coincidences are still genuinely startling even if we assume that the various anthropic coincidences permit, say, amoebas on up. A more definitive response at a scientific level would be possible if one could establish or preclude anthropic coincidences that by their nature precisely fit only conscious minds or intelligent life.[48] There may well be some parameter or circumstance that opens the door wide to life in general, but which makes conscious or intelligent life highly improbable.

Finally, and most broadly, it might be argued that the logic of the anthropic coincidences argument improperly relies upon a priori probabilities for a unique, nonrecurring event,[49] or that there is really nothing about our existence that is genuinely surprising,[50] or that theistic arguments do not offer a better combination of simplicity and explanatory power in this context than their nontheistic rivals.[51] But again, responses to each of these claims need not take the form of dogmatic assertion, as opposed to reasoned, progressive examination and judgment.[52] Scientific claims that are admittedly highly speculative or practically impossible to test today may well become subject to actual empirical testing, and to support or disconfirmation, tomorrow.

To further illustrate this general point, let us shift the focus away from the debate over the alleged anthropic coincidences. It has been thought that modern cosmology establishes that with respect to the onset of the universe itself, a nontheistic approach is available which is logically simpler than any possible theistic approach. It is sometimes believed in particular that our universe could well have arisen "from nothing," or on its own, without any interesting preconditions or logically prior requisites or constraints, and with no need for divine intent or intervention. Doubtless the most widely known such model is the Hartle-Hawking "no boundary" proposal,[53] though other, even more ambitious models are possible.[54]

Relatedly, it seems clear from well-established quantum theory and experiment that a quantum "vacuum" spontaneously generates brief-lived particles, and it may well be that a vacuum fluctuation, well-balanced as to "negative" and "positive" energy, with a net energy of nearly zero, could persist, flourish and multiply for an apparently long time, subject to conservation laws and the Heisenberg Uncertainty Principle, precisely by taking advantage of laxities built into the latter.[55] It is sometimes said that this would amount to a universe that creates itself from nothing.[56] But this "nothing," it has been replied, is neither absolutely nothing, nor free of non-self-explanatory preconditions and presuppositions.[57] Nor is it appropriate to infer that the Hartle-Hawking universe or a vacuum fluctuation universe has no cause in the relevant philosophical sense.[58]

Each of these points is of course to be taken as tentative. The overall point, indeed, is linked to their reasonable tentativeness. Arguments that bear on the most crucial constituents of a theistic natural law view can be criticized and defended in ways no more pathologically interminable than those characteristic of "normal" debate in physical science. This simply reflects a genuine and historically increasing substantive overlap between theistic debate and scientific debate. The mood even among those who disagree is one of genuine intellectual excitement, rather than ennui and a fear of protracted trench warfare or scholastic posturing. This is so even in light of the obvious difficulties involved in acquiring even indirect evidence of the earliest stages of the universe's development.

There can again be no guarantee that any state of the cumulative evidence will rationally dictate the universal acceptance of any position on the viability of any form of theistic natural law. But this is neither surprising nor discouraging. Debate in even the physical sciences is not necessarily susceptible of any decisive, knockout resolution.[59] Yet we do not despair of gradual progress in the physical sciences, or regard debate in the physical sciences as pathologically interminable.[60] Any fear that debate over all forms of even theistic natural law must sink into interminability is thus unreasonable.

The crucial inference to be drawn, then, is this. If a surprising degree of progress is possible even in areas least subject to rigorous investigation, evidentiary scrutiny, testing and comparison, and direct observation, it is reasonable to expect that in more readily accessible areas, including that of the morally relevant consequences of particular forms of political government, at least as much progress can be made. And more particularly, the waxing or waning of theistic and non-theistic approaches to matters as abstruse, but as fundamental, as cosmology may well tend to have some impact, at least indirectly, on how private citizens come to conceive of legitimate government or the just society. This is so even if we stipulate, as we should, that no democratic society should seek to justify its laws on theistic grounds. In fact, it is difficult to think of any examples of a stable society whose conception of just and legitimate government was uninfluenced by its broader understanding of nature and the place of humanity in nature.

NOTES TO *CAN DEBATE OVER JUSTICE BE PROGRESSIVE?*

1. See, e.g., Alasdair MacIntyre, After Virtue 7-9 (Notre Dame: Univ. Notre Dame Press 2d ed. 1984). See also Jeffrey Stout, Ethics After Babel 1-3 (Boston: Beacon Press 1988).

2. The kinds of critical scrutiny that have historically proved their worth in the natural sciences may range, at least in an ideal case, from something close to falsification of a theory's key predictions all the way, arguably, to a trained sense that a theory is simply too contrived and ad hoc to be sound, or, even more ineffably, to the intrinsic elegance or mathematical beauty of the theory. See, e.g., Subrahmanyan Chandrasekhar, Truth and Beauty (Chicago: Univ. of Chicago Press 1987); John Polkinghorne, Reason and Reality (Philadelphia: Trinity International Press 1991). For a relevant and useful distinction between reason and faith, see Anthony Kenny, What Is Faith? 64 (Oxford: Oxford Univ. Press 1992).

3. Of course, on some theologies, we should not expect evidence for the existence of God to, at any historical period, become so overwhelming as to virtually dictate assent, leaving choice and faith as impossible or irrelevant. This has the interesting implication that we can be most confident of the existence of God when we seem to have substantial, but not overpowering, evidence to that effect. It is possible that some persons might accept this logic, find substantial but not overwhelming evidence for theism, and on that very basis find that they have no rational choice but to accept a theistic view. In practice, though, this paradox should have little effect. It is always easy to interpret moderately strong evidence as only moderately supportive of a case, and as not precluding any alternative hypothesis. See Russell Stannard, Grounds For Reasonable Belief 176 (Edinburgh: Scottish Academic Press 1989). The best probabalistic, cumulative-weight-of-the-evidence case for theism is worked out by Richard Swinburne, The Existence of God (Oxford: Oxford Univ. Press 1979). See also L. Stafford Betty & Bruce Cordell, God and Modern Science, 27 Int. Phil. Q. 409, 433 (1987). For criticism, see John L. Mackie, The Miracle of Theism (Oxford: Clarendon Press 1982); Robert Prevost, Probability and Theistic Explanation (Oxford: Clarendon Press 1990); Willem B. Drees, Quantum Cosmologies and the "Beginning," 26 Zygon 373, 387 (1992); Michael Martin, Swinburne's Inductive Cosmological Argument, 27 Heythrop J. 151 (1987). For a response, see Richard Swinburne, Mackie, Induction, and God, 19 Religious Stud. 385 (1983). See also Richard Swinburne, The Limits of Explanation, in Royal Institute of Philosophy Lecture Series no. 24: Key Themes in Philosophy 177 (Supplement to

Philosophy (1988)) (A. Phillips Griffiths ed.) (Cambridge: Cambridge Univ. Press 1989); George N. Schlesinger, New Perspectives on Old-Time Religion ch. 5 (Oxford: Clarendon Press 1988).

4. See, e.g., Willem B. Drees, Beyond the Big Bang: Quantum Cosmologies and God (La Salle: Open Court 1990); Errol E. Harris, Cosmos and Anthropos 60, 172 (Atlantic Highlands: Humanities Press 1991).

5. A Being thus described might reasonably be called God, or one might insist upon further description before employing that term. Reference to "intention" would be at worst analogical. The attributes of God relied upon in this chapter differ from those relied upon earlier in discussing the possible attractiveness of theistic natural law in resolving crucial metaethical and normative ethical problems. The notion of God minimally relied upon by this book, then, is the joint mutually consistent set of all attributes necessary for all of the book's arguments to go through. These attributes will strike many as being theologically "weak." Unavoidably, though, there is some tradeoff between specifying God's attributes well enough to make each of the arguments work, while leaving God's attributes unspecified enough to be compatible with all sorts of diverse theologies. However, the bare conception of a relevantly knowledgeable God, benevolent toward conscious life, suffices to do much of the work in establishing the objective superiority of some answers to some moral problems, the logic of a tolerant, non-divisive, egalitarian, inclusive, non-oppressive theistic natural law, and on some cosmologies, perhaps even in accounting for the phenomena examined in this chapter.

6. Don Page, An Enthusiasm in Cosmology: Review of S. Coleman, J.B. Hartle, T. Piran & S. Weinberg eds., Quantum Cosmology and Baby Universes, 256 Science 864, 865 (1992).

7. See T.D. Sullivan, Coming To Be Without a Cause, 65 Phil. 261, 261 n.1 (1990).

8. See, despite their dramatic differences in other respects, Ernan McMullin, Is Philosophy Relevant to Cosmology?, 18 Am. Phil. Q. 177, 187 (1981); Quentin Smith, The Uncaused Beginning of the Universe, 55 Phil. Sci. 39, 39 (1988).

9. Joe Rosen, No Rumors of Transcendence in Physics, 54 Am. J. Physics 700, 700 (1986).

10. See, e.g., Joe Rosen, Self-Generating Universe and Many Worlds, 21 Foundations of Physics 977 (1991) (presenting a mathematical framework, with testable implications, for the origin of the universe). See also Joe Rosen, The Capricious Universe 53 (New York: MacMillan 1991) (recognizing the possibility that even the most ambitious cosmological schemes may be subject to falsification).

11. See John Leslie, Universes 198 (London: Routledge 1989) ("fine tuning is evidence, genuine evidence, of the following fact: *that God is real and/or there are many and varied universes*") (emphasis in the original). Again, there may be logical slippage here, in that the term 'God' for Leslie need not correspond to our definition in this chapter, or the consistent conjunction of the attributes of God relied upon in this book. For Leslie's philosophical theology, see John Leslie, Value and Existence (Totowa: Rowman & Littlefield 1979).

12. See, e.g., Hugo Meynell, More Gaps for God?, in Origin and Evolution of the Universe: Evidence for Design 247 (Alan Batten & John Robson eds.) (Kingston: McGill-Queen's Univ. Press 1987).

13. A bibliographical review as of 1991 referred to over 400 contributions to the broadly related literature concerning various anthropic principles. See Yuri Balashov, Resource Letter AP-1: The Anthropic Principle, 59 Am. J. Physics 1069, 1070 (1991).

14. See John D. Barrow & Frank J. Tipler, The Anthropic Cosmological Principle 288-570 (New York: Oxford Univ. Press 1986). See also the various brief essays, written from various conflicting perspectives, in The Anthropic Principle: Proceedings of the Second Venice Conference on Cosmology and Philosophy (F. Bertola & U. Curi eds.) (Cambridge: Cambridge Univ. Press 1989). For an early popular treatment, see Reinhard Breuer, The Anthropic Principle (Harry Newman & Mark Lowery trans.) (Boston: Birkhäuser 1991). See also, in the popular vein, M.A. Corey, God and the New Cosmology: The Anthropic Design Argument (Lanham, Md: Rowman & Littlefield 1993). For a brief introduction to some relevant philosophical issues, see Jeffrey L. Johnson, Inference to the Best Explanation and the New Teleological Argument, 31 S.J. Phil. 193 (1993).

15. See generally John Leslie, Universes (London: Routledge 1989).

16. John Leslie, Observership in Cosmology: The Anthropic Principle, 92 Mind 573, 575 (1983). For a sampling of further analyses along similar lines, see, e.g., Robert K. Adair, The Great Design 366 (New York: Oxford Univ. Press

1987) ("It appears that the universe must be exquisitely fine-tuned to accommodate us"); Paul Davies, The Accidental Universe (Cambridge: Cambridge Univ. Press 1982); George F.R. Ellis, Before the Beginning 89-91 (London: Boyars/Bowerdean 1993); John Gribbin & Martin Rees, Cosmic Coincidences 269 (New York: Bantam 1989); Errol E. Harris, Cosmos and Anthropos 48 (Atlantic Highlands: Humanities Press 1991); Stephen W. Hawking, A Brief History of Time 125 (New York: Bantam 1988); Bernard Lovell, Emerging Cosmology 196 (New York: Columbia Univ. Press 1981) ("If the forces of attraction between the fundamental particles had been slightly stronger, helium would have been dominant. In this event no stars of the type we observe with sufficiently long-term stability to facilitate evolution would have existed"); Roger Penrose, The Emperor's New Mind 344 (New York: Oxford Univ. Press 1989); John Polkinghorne, Reason and Reality 77 (Philadelphia: Trinity International Press 1991) ("Significant 'coincidences' in given law and circumstance appear to be necessary at every stage of the world's development if that history is to prove capable of fertility"); Quantum Cosmology and the Laws of Nature (Robert John Russell, Nancey Murphy, and Chris J. Isham eds.) (forthcoming); Ernan McMullin, Is Philosophy Relevant to Cosmology?, 18 Am. Phil. Q. 177, 186 (1981); George Wald, Consciousness and Cosmology: Their Interrelations, in Bergson and Modern Thought 344 (Andrew C. Papanicolaou & Peter A.Y. Gunter eds.) (London: Harwood Academic 1987) ("If any one of a considerable number of the physical properties of the universe (some of them seem quite trivial) were different, that life which is now so prevalent would become impossible, here or anywhere"); Joseph M. Zycinski, The Anthropic Principle and Teleological Interpretations of Nature, 41 Rev. Metaphysics 317, 318-19 (1987). For the argument that at least some of the universe's basic constants seem arbitrary rather than necessitated by any broader law, see George Gale, Some Metaphysical Perplexities in Contemporary Physics, 26 Int. Phil. Q. 393, 396 (1986). Robert John Russell has observed that for certain fixed values, such as Planck's constant, some degree of fine tuning may be needed at vastly different scales, as for stellar evolution and, apparently separately, for the development of life in familiar forms. See Robert John Russell, Theological Lessons from Cosmology: Two Case Studies, 41 Cross Currents 308, 318-20 (1991).

17. See, e.g., John Leslie, Observership in Cosmology: The Anthropic Principle, 92 Mind 573, 575 (1983). As well, the anthropic approach may itself generate testable implications. This claim is made in Dennis Temple, Hume's Logical Objection to the Argument From Design Based on the Uniqueness of the Universe, 28 Religious Stud. 19, 30 (1992).

18. See, e.g., John Polkinghorne, Reason and Reality 80 (Philadelphia: Trinity International Press 1991). Polkinghorne refers here to the postulated brief early stage or stages of the universe featuring extremely rapid expansion, known as "inflation." See Alan H. Guth & Paul J. Steinhardt, The Inflationary Universe, 250 Sci. Am. 116, 127 (1984). See also Sergio del Campo, Initial Conditions for Anisotropic Extended-Type Inflationary Universes, 45 Physical Review D 3386 (3d series) (1992). But see P.D.B. Collins & R.F. Langbein, Thermodynamics of Inflation, 45 Physical Review D 3429 (3d series) (1992) (certain currently popular inflation scenarios apparently nonviable). More generally, see John Earman, The SAP Also Rises: A Critical Examination of the Anthropic Principle, 24 Am. Phil. Q. 307, 314-15 (1987) (perhaps the various anthropic "coincidences" can be derived from some more basic law); B.J. Carr & M.J. Rees, The Anthropic Principle and the Structure of the Physical World, 278 Nature 605, 612 (1979) (same). See also George Greenstein & Allen Kropf, Cognizable Worlds: The Anthropic Principle and the Fundamental Constants of Nature, 57 Am. J. Physics 746 (1989) (contending that at least some "anthropic coincidences" are far from delicate balances, and set only very crude, broad constraints on universes in which life could appear). But see Joseph M. Zycinski, The Anthropic Principle and Teleological Interpretations of Nature, 41 Rev. Metaphysics 317, 323 (1987) (arguing for the independence of several of the most basic features of the universe, despite "inflation").

19. The universes had better be separate in the sense of having different basic physical laws, even if they stem from the same parent universe, lest the conditions of conscious life remain improbable. See Robert K. Clifton, Review of John Leslie's Universes, 41 Phil. Q. 339, 342-43 (1991). To neutralize the anthropic coincidences, the number of universes need not be infinite, despite the fact that the discussion is often conducted in those terms. See, e.g., Richard Swinburne, Argument from the Fine-Tuning of the Universe, in Physical Cosmology and Philosophy 154, 170 (John Leslie ed.) (New York: MacMillan 1990); Joseph M. Zycinski, The Anthropic Principle and Teleological Interpretations of Nature, 41 Rev. Metaphysics 317, 327 (1987).

20. See, e.g., Quentin Smith, The Anthropic Principle and Many-Worlds Cosmologies, 63 Australasian J. Phil. 336, 341 (1985) ("If worlds with life and without life are both actual, then it is not surprising that *this* world is actual but is something to be expected") (emphasis in the original). But see Errol E. Harris, Cosmos and Anthropos 13 (Atlantic Highlands: Humanities Press 1991) (unobservability in principle of the other worlds allegedly vitiates their potential explanatory power).

21. See Richard Healey, How Many Worlds?, 18 Nous 591, 591 (1984). On some interpretations, what results is not so much many worlds as many minds associated, somehow, with each observer. See David Albert, Quantum Mechanics and Experience ch. 6 (Cambridge: Harvard Univ. Press 1992); David Albert & Barry Loewer, Interpreting the Many Worlds Interpretation, 77 Synthese 195, 207 (1988); David Albert & Barry Loewer, The Measurement Problem: Some Solutions, 86 Synthese 87 (1991). Such a view is developed philosophically at some length in Michael Lockwood, Mind, Brain and the Quantum chs. 12-13 (Oxford: Basil Blackwell 1989). For a philosophical response to Lockwood, see David Hodgson, Mind Matters: Consciousness and Choice in a Quantum World 337-42 (Oxford: Clarendon Press 1991).

22. The basic problem is, roughly, that we would otherwise need some sort of transition mechanism or process that transforms an entity existing in a probabalistic "superposition" or combination of different, apparently incompatible quantum states into the single determinate, unequivocal state in which the object is normally observed. The many worlds view avoids the necessity of this mysterious "collapse of the wave packet" by assuming that no particular quantum outcome is privileged, and that all possible quantum outcomes are realized. See, e.g., Hugh Everett, III, The Theory of the Universal Wave Function, in The Many-Worlds Interpretation of Quantum Mechanics 3, 116-17 (Bryce S. DeWitt & Neill Graham eds.) (Princeton: Princeton Univ. Press 1973); Howard Stein, The Everett Interpretation of Quantum Mechanics: Many Worlds or None?, 18 Nous 635, 647 (1984). Whether Everett's theory itself really requires the splitting of the universe, or the production of large numbers of worlds or minds is open to doubt. See, e.g., Yoav Ben-Dov, Everett's Theory and the "Many-Worlds" Interpretation, 58 Am. J. Physics 829 (1990). We will simply assume that there can be an attractive interpretation of quantum mechanics that posits many worlds or otherwise challenges the force of the anthropic coincidences.

23. See Frank J. Tipler, The Omega Point as Eschaton: Answers to Pannenberg's Questions for Scientists, 24 Zygon 217, 235 (1989).

24. B.J. Carr, On the Origin, Evolution and Purpose of the Physical Universe, in Physical Cosmology and Philosophy 134, 153 (John Leslie ed.) (New York: MacMillan 1990).

25. See, e.g., Russell Stannard, Grounds for Reasonable Belief 20 (Edinburgh: Scottish Academic Press 1989); L. Stafford Betty & Bruce Cordell, God and Modern Science, 27 Int. Phil. Q. 409, 417 (1987).

26. See, e.g., John Polkinghorne, Science and Creation 24 (Boston: New Science Library 1989); John Leslie, Observership in Cosmology: The Anthropic Principle, 92 Mind 573, 579 (1983); Holmes Rolston, III, Review of John Leslie's Universes, 26 Zygon 317, 323 (1991) (many universes interpretation as "messy" and "complicated" in comparison to theistic accounts); Dennis Temple, Hume's Logical Objection to the Argument From Design Based on the Uniqueness of the Universe, 27 Religious Stud. 19, 29 (1992). But see Quentin Smith, A Natural Explanation of the Existence and Laws of Our Universe, 68 Australasian J. Phil. 22 (1990); William Stoeger, The Origin of the Universe in Science and Religion, in Cosmos, Bios, Theos 254, 267 (Henry Margenau & Roy Abraham Varghese eds.) (La Salle: Open Court 1992). Professor Stoeger wishes to combine theism with some version of a multiple universe scenario which, despite its positing many unobservable entities, Stoeger "strongly" suspects may be correct. Id.

27. See, e.g., Paul Davies, The Mind of God 220 (New York: Simon & Schuster 1992); Brian Hebblethwaite, The Ocean of Truth 91 (Cambridge: Cambridge Univ. Press 1988). See also Dennis Dieks, On Some Alleged Difficulties in the Interpretation of Quantum Mechanics, 86 Synthese 77 (1991) (worldsplitting theoretically unnecessary).

28. See, e.g., 1 Marilyn M. Adams, William Ockham 156-60 (Notre Dame: Notre Dame Univ. Press 1987).

29. See, e.g., Russell Stannard, Grounds for Reasonable Belief 20 (Edinburgh: Scottish Academic Press 1989); Joseph M. Zycinski, The Anthropic Principle and Teleological Interpretations of Nature, 41 Rev. Metaphysics 317, 328 (1987).

30. See, e.g., Paul Davies, God and the New Physics 173 (New York: Simon & Schuster 1983) (noting that while the many worlds interpretation does require enormous numbers of unobservable, mainly defunct universes, it arguably offers a simpler solution to at least one basic problem in quantum epistemology). For further discussion, see, e.g., Robert Geroch, The Everett Interpretation, 18 Nous 617, 626 (1984); Richard Healey, How Many Worlds?, 18 Nous 591, 599 (1984). See also Andrei Linde & Arthur Mezhlumian, Stationary Universe, 307 Physics Letters B 25 (1993) (describing a separate process of effusive "bubbling" into being of many universes).

31. See, e.g., Paul Davies, The Mind of God 229 (New York: Simon & Schuster 1992). See also Errol E. Harris, Cosmos and Anthropos 13-15 (Atlantic Highlands: Humanities Press 1991) (arguing that the many worlds interpretation cannot make the anthropic coincidences any less surprising).

32. Presumably, no violation occurs because the familiar conservation laws apply only to individual universes. We do not notice the splitting, presumably, because each of us is separately and entirely present on each path, before and after each foliation of separate universes. The image of splitting is in this respect less apt than that of multiplication.

33. See, e.g., John Earman, The SAP Also Rises: A Critical Examination of the Anthropic Principle, 24 Am. Phil. Q. 307, 312 (1987); Adrian Kent, Against Many-Worlds Interpretations, 5 Int. J. Modern Physics 1745, 1746 (1990) ("the literature neither contains nor suggests a plausible set of axioms for an MWI that describes known physics"). Kent goes on to conclude that "the defining axioms of such a theory would have to be extremely ugly and arbitrary." Id. at 1760.

34. See John Polkinghorne, Reason and Reality 78 (Philadelphia: Trinity International Press 1991); Joseph M. Zycinski, The Anthropic Principle and Teleological Interpretations of Nature, 41 Rev. Metaphysics 317, 328 (1987).

35. See, e.g., John Leslie, Observership in Cosmology: The Anthropic Principle, 92 Mind 573, 577 (1983).

36. See Alastair Rae, Quantum Physics: Illusion or Reality 79 (Cambridge: Cambridge Univ. Press 1986).

37. For some speculation on this point, see R. George Wright, Should the Law Reflect the World?: Lessons For Legal Theory From Quantum Mechanics, 18 Fla. St. L. Rev. 855, 872-74 (1991).

38. We have omitted mention of an interesting but controversial variant of the many universes approach, the "successive universes" view developed originally by John Wheeler, who has also developed the "participatory" model discussed briefly below. For a brief account of the "successive universes" approach, in which the separate and independent universes follow upon the "random shuffle" birth, expansion, and (it is assumed) the inescapable contraction of their predecessor universe, see, e.g., Quentin Smith, The Anthropic Principle and Many-Worlds Cosmologies, 63 Australasian J. Phil. 336, 345-46 (1985). There may be unsolved technical problems associated with this approach, see id., and it may not successfully resolve the basic issues in quantum metaphysics. But despite some controversy, the successive cycles view does not seem unsuited in principle to explain the apparent anthropic coincidences. For all we know, ours could be the trillionth cycle, following an enormous number of sterile universes, so it becomes less astonishing that conscious life exists. This view is also evidently open to

empirical evidentiary support or challenge, at least in some respects. For criticism of the logic of the successive universes view in this respect, see Ian Hacking, The Inverse Gambler's Fallacy: The Argument from Design. The Anthropic Principle Applied to Wheeler Universes, 96 Mind 331 (1987); Dennis Temple, Hume's Logical Objection to the Argument From Design Based on the Uniqueness of the Universe, 28 Relig. Stud. 19, 29 n.36 (1992). For defenses of the logic of the successive universes view in this respect, see M.A.B. Whitaker, On Hacking's Criticism of the Wheeler Anthropic Principle, 97 Mind 259 (1988); P.J. McGrath, The Inverse Gambler's Fallacy and Cosmology: A Reply to Hacking, 97 Mind 265 (1988); John Leslie, No Inverse Gambler's Fallacy in Cosmology, 97 Mind 269 (1988).

39. Part of the overall complexity is reflected in the fact that some arguments seeking to avoid the theistic implications of the anthropic coincidences affirmatively deny that only one universe is logically possible. See, e.g., Quentin Smith, Atheism, Theism, and Big Bang Cosmology, 69 Australasian J. Phil. 48, 53 (1991). For a response to Smith's general argument, see William Lane Craig, Theism and Big Bang Cosmology, 69 Australasian J. Phil. 492 (1991). Smith and Craig divide over whether the evidence suggests that God had to awkwardly intervene in the ongoing process of creation in order to insure that life arose. For further general discussion, see Quentin Smith & William Lane Craig, Atheism, Theism, and Big Bang Cosmology (Oxford: Oxford Univ. Press forthcoming).

40. Of course, the theist can still argue, following Stephen Hawking, that there is a logical gap between our universe's being the only possible universe, and the further claim that our universe is somehow necessary and noncontingent. See Stanley L. Jaki, God and the New Cosmologists 93 (Washington, D.C.: Regnery Gateway 1989) (per Hawking, not even a uniquely descriptive set of equations for the universe can breathe fire into itself, thereby actualizing the universe). Or one might wonder why only one universe is self-consistent, or even why the only self-consistent universe contains conscious life. See B.J. Carr & M.J. Rees, The Anthropic Principle and the Structure of the Physical World, 278 Nature 605, 612 (1979) ("even if all apparently anthropic coincidences could be explained [as a consequence of a broader physical theory], it would still be remarkable that the relationships dictated by physical theory happened also to be those propitious for life"). But cf. Chris Mortensen, Explaining Existence, 16 Can. J. Phil. 713, 720 (1986) (laws of physics as not requiring explanation, on the grounds that even if many other sets of laws seem to have been possible, there can be nothing remarkable to explain, as laws are not existent things, and perhaps not even particular things). These questions, however, may not be readily resolvable even in principle.

41. See, e.g., John D. Barrow & Frank J. Tipler, The Anthropic Cosmological Principle 105 (New York: Oxford Univ. Press 1986).

42. Barrow and Tipler rely on James Hartle and Stephen Hawking in this regard, but apparently neither Hartle nor Hawking endorses the idea that our universe is the sole logical possibility. See Paul Davies, The Mind of God 91, 159, 168-69 (New York: Simon & Schuster 1992) (discussing and endorsing Hartle's demurrer) and Stephen Hawking, A Brief History of Time 137 (New York: Bantam 1988) (apparently assuming that possible universes differ in their probability under his "no boundary" proposal for the universe). See also Don Page, Review of The Anthropic Cosmological Principle, 18 Foundations of Physics 479, 480 (1988).

43. See John Polkinghorne, Reason and Reality 78-79 (Philadelphia: Trinity International Press 1991).

44. One might weaken the claim at issue by arguing, for example, that "[i]t is possible that there exists only one logically consistent set of laws which also allows for the existence of structures sufficiently complex to have self-consciousness." W.G. Unruh, Is the Universe Natural?, in Origin and Evolution of the Universe: Evidence for Design 109, 117 (Allen Batten & John Robson eds.) (Kingston: McGill-Queen's Univ. Press 1987). While this view may be more plausible, it leaves the anthropic coincidences unaccounted for. Why didn't one of the many possible simpler, lifeless worlds result? In a different context, one might note parenthetically that if only one set of laws and initial conditions is consistent with life, this might help resolve what has been called the "problem of evil." See Murdith McLean, Residual Natural Evil and Anthropic Reasoning, 27 Religious Stud. 173 (1991).

It bears mention that John Wheeler's "Participatory Anthropic Principle," or participatory universe view, can be considered a variant of the "single possible universe" view. See, e.g., John Archibald Wheeler, Law Without Law, in Quantum Theory and Measurement 182, 196-210 (John Archibald Wheeler & Wojciech Hubert Zurek eds.) (Princeton: Princeton Univ. Press 1983). On this view, which has at the very least an interesting basis in quantum theory and in actual experiments, the universe remains in a murky superposition of various possibilities until its being measured or observed, perhaps on billions of occasions by billions of conscious minds, snaps the universal wave function out of its indeterminacy and into a single state, compatible, of course, with the existence of life. This notion, which seems to resurrect both the Platonic idea of degrees of reality and the pre-Copernican idea of mind at the center of the universe, relies upon what is in a sense backward causation. The idea has not been worked out in detail, and has been greeted with skepticism on a number of grounds. See, e.g., L. Stafford Betty

& Bruce Cordell, God and Modern Science, 27 Int. Phil. Q. 409, 417-18 (1987) (participatory universe as "solipsistic"); John Earman, The SAP Also Rises: A Critical Examination of the Anthropic Principle, 24 Am. Phil. Q. 307, 312-13 (1987) (Wheeler's thesis as self-admittedly "a frail reed"); Fred W. Hallberg, Barrow and Tipler's Anthropic Cosmological Principle, 23 Zygon 139, 143-45 (1987) (Wheeler's thesis as either inconsistent or insufficiently developed for assessment); John Leslie, Observership in Cosmology: The Anthropic Principle, 92 Mind 573, 576-77 (1983) (Wheeler approach as self-contradictory). See also Anthony J.M. Garrett & Peter Coles, Bayesian Inductive Inference and the Anthropic Cosmological Principle, 17 Comments on Astrophysics 23, 39 (1993).

45. See Quentin Smith, The Anthropic Principle and Many-Worlds Cosmologies, 63 Australasian J. Phil. 336, 347 (1985). For a response, see John Polkinghorne, Reason and Reality 79-80 (Philadelphia: Trinity International Press 1991).

46. See Patrick A. Wilson, What Is the Explanandum of the Anthropic Principle?, 28 Am. Phil. Q. 167 (1991).

47. Richard Swinburne argues, for example, that "intelligent life is something which a creator God would have the power and abundant reason for bringing about." Richard Swinburne, Argument from the Fine-Tuning of the Universe, in Physical Cosmology and Philosophy 154, 154 (John Leslie ed.) (New York: MacMillan 1990).

48. It is often argued that science has so far not persuasively accounted for the phenomenon of consciousness or self-consciousness, for the association of particular conscious states with particular brain states, or for the intelligibility of the atomic and intergalactic world, which has been linked with an allegedly unexplained effectiveness of the language of mathematics. For general discussion, see, e.g., Paul Davies, The Mind of God 24 (New York: Simon & Schuster 1992); Philip E. Devine, Relativism, Nihilism and God 90 (Notre Dame: Notre Dame Univ. Press 1989); Brian Hebblethwaite, The Ocean of Truth 111 (Cambridge: Cambridge Univ. Press 1988); Hugo Meynell, More Gaps For God?, in Origin and Evolution of the Universe: Evidence for Design 248-49 (Alan Batten & John Robson eds.) (Kingston: McGill-Queen's Univ. Press 1987); John Polkinghorne, Reason and Reality 76 (Philadelphia: Trinity International Press 1991); William G. Pollard, Rumors of Transcendence in Physics, 52 Am. J. Physics 877, 880 (1984); Richard Swinburne, The Origin of Consciousness, in Origin and Evolution of the Universe: Evidence for Design 211-25 (Kingston: McGill-Queen's Univ. Press 1987); George Wald, Consciousness and Cosmology: Their Interrelations, in Bergson and Modern

Thought 344 (Andrew C. Papanicolaou & Peter A.Y. Gunter eds.) (London: Harwood Academic 1987); Eugene P. Wigner, The Unreasonable Effectiveness of Mathematics in the Natural Sciences, 13 Communications On Pure and Applied Mathematics 227 (1960). Of course, none of these arguments needs be accepted, and the historical track record of this general form of argument, again, has been poor. For a response, see, e.g., Willem B. Drees, Beyond the Big Bang: Quantum Cosmologies and God 107-08 (La Salle: Open Court 1990).

49. See, e.g., Joe Rosen, No Rumors of Transcendence in Physics, 54 Am. J. Physics 700, 701 (1986). But see Anthony J.M. Garrett & Peter Coles, Bayesian Inductive Inference and the Anthropic Cosmological Principle, 17 Comments on Astrophysics 23 (1993).

50. See Jonathan Katz, Why There Is Something: The Anthropic Principle and Improbable Events, 27 Dialogue 111, 116 (1988).

51. See, e.g., J.J.C. Smart, Laws of Nature and Cosmic Coincidences, 35 Phil. Q. 272, 275-76 (1985).

52. Probably the best responses to the above critiques are embodied, at length, in John Leslie, Universes (London: Routledge 1989) and Richard Swinburne, The Existence of God (Oxford: Oxford Univ. Press 1979). See also William Lane Craig, Barrow and Tipler on the Anthropic Principle vs. Divine Design, 38 Brit. J. Phil. Sci. 389-95 (1988); George N. Schlesinger, The Anthropic Principle, 23 Tradition 1 (1988). At its most abstruse, the debate might compare the appeal of an explanatory but in many respects mysterious God, along with the view that God necessarily or by definition cannot have an external cause or any preconditions, with a less fully complete, but simpler, nontheistic account of causation in and of the universe. Of course, explanations in terms of intention do not occupy the same "space" as explanations in terms of causal mechanisms, so we may want to add in some complexity on the theistic side to cover any logically necessary account of how, causally, God effectuated the relevant intentions.

53. The best-known account of this proposal is contained in Stephen Hawking, A Brief History of Time 134-40 (New York: Bantam 1988). The original proposal is contained in James Hartle & Stephen Hawking, Wave Function of the Universe, 28 Physical Review D 2960-75 (3d series) (1983).

54. For an allegedly improved model, see, e.g., P.D. Mannheim, Conformal Gravity and the Flatness Problem, 391 Astrophysical J. 429 (1992).

55. See, e.g., Jonathan J. Halliwell, Quantum Cosmology and the Creation of the Universe, 265 Sci. Am. 76 (1991).

56. See, e.g., Fang Li Zhi & Li Shu Xian, Creation of the Universe 146 (T. Kiang trans.) (Singapore: World Scientific Publishing 1989); Hokee Minn, Creation From "Anything or Nothing," 105 Il Nuovo Cimento B 901, 901-03 (1990); Chris J. Isham, Creation of the Universe as a Quantum Process, in Physics, Philosophy and Theology 401 (Robert John Russell, William R. Stoeger & George V. Coyne eds.) (Vatican City: Vatican Observatory 1988). Isham himself then goes on to provide a discussion of certain implicit assumptions of, and problems associated with, the Hartle-Hawking proposal. For technical criticism of the Hartle-Hawking proposal not raising the question of its presupposed, but not self-explanatory, conditions, see, e.g., L.P. Grishchuk & L.V. Rozhansky, Does the Hartle-Hawking Wavefunction Predict the Universe We Live In?, 234 Physics Letters B 9, 9 (1990).

57. See, e.g., Willem B. Drees, Beyond the Big Bang: Quantum Cosmologies and God 72-73 (La Salle: Open Court 1990); John Leslie, Universes 81 (London: Routledge 1989); Milton K. Munitz, Cosmic Understanding 136-37 (Princeton: Princeton Univ. Press 1987); John Polkinghorne, Science and Creation 59-60 (Boston: New Science Library 1989) (because of the complexity of our world, more than one quantum field must be presupposed); Michael Redhead, Physics For Pedestrians: An Inaugural Lecture 18 (Cambridge: Cambridge Univ. Press 1989); William Lane Craig, God, Creation and Mr. Davies, 37 Brit. J. Phil. Sci. 163, 167 (1986); Victor Weiskopf, The Origin of the Universe, 36 N.Y. Rev. Books 10, 13 (1989).

58. See, e.g., L. Stafford Betty & Bruce Cordell, God and Modern Science, 27 Int. Phil. Q. 409, 412 (1987); T.D. Sullivan, Coming to Be Without a Cause, 65 Phil. 261, 270 (1990) (while quantum causation is in a sense indeterminate or undefined, it can still be sensibly asked what caused or explains the onset of the universe); Jack C. Carloye, The Existence of God and the Creation of the Universe, 27 Zygon 167, 177 (1992) (universe as contingent, not self-explanatory, and requiring a transcendent cause); Charles W. Misner, Cosmology and Theology, in Cosmology, History, and Theology 96 (Wolfgang Yourgrau & Allen D. Breck eds.) (New York: Plenum Press 1977) ("[p]hysics does not even appear to be approaching an understanding of the Universe that would make its existence necessary").

Significantly, even those who advance "no boundary" or vacuum fluctuation accounts of the onset of the universe sometimes raise the possibility of a state of affairs logically, if not temporally, prior to the vacuum field, and giving rise to the vacuum field. See John Polkinghorne, Science and Creation 60 (Boston: New Science Library 1989). But see

Quentin Smith, The Uncaused Beginning of the Universe, 55 Phil. Sci. 39 (1988) (arguing that quantum fluctuations do not require philosophical causes). Smith has argued as well that it may be possible to explain both the observable universe and its basic laws naturalistically, without, however, being able to similarly account for Smith's hypothesized infinite series of universes and the "metalaws" governing that series. See Quentin Smith, A Natural Explanation of the Existence and Laws of Our Universe, 68 Australasian J. Phil. 22, 35 (1990). See also Paul Davies & John Gribbin, The Matter Myth 163 (New York: Simon & Schuster 1992) (referring briefly to the spontaneous, uncaused coming into being of spacetime itself). Note, finally, that the onset of the universe via a vacuum fluctuation or other mechanism is not "everything," such that it would be absurd to seek for something outside "everything" in order to causally explain "everything." Thus while physicists such as Victor Stenger, for example, have described processes of universe-creation that emphasize spontaneity, independence of any "external" influence, and the absence of law violation, such models typically presuppose something like "a vacuum of negative spacetime curvature" with "positive energy density but *negative* pressure." Victor J. Stenger, The Universe: The Ultimate Free Lunch, 11 Eur. J. Physics 236, 240 (1990) (emphasis in the original). Merely not presupposing matter does not mean that one has not relied on any interesting presuppositions.

Confusion in this regard may stem from the fact that in the Hartle-Hawking proposal, it becomes impossible to ask some basic questions about causation in time, as the idea of time is ordinarily used. As we regress toward the onset of the universe, the Hartle-Hawking proposal begins to depend, beyond a certain logical stage, upon mathematical "imaginary" time. The term "imaginary" time is not intended to carry any metaphysical prejudice; 'imaginary' is not to be contrasted with 'real' in the sense of 'genuine.' Imaginary time, on the Hartle-Hawking proposal, becomes indistinguishable from space, and directionality in time therefore becomes less constrained than in our ordinary experience. As a result, it becomes impossible in principle to specify uniquely any first instant of the universe. See Stephen Hawking, A Brief History of Time 134-35 (New York: Bantam 1988). It seems exaggerated, though, to claim that this "no boundary" proposal does away with the need for non-self-explanatory initial conditions, or collapses the distinction between laws and initial conditions in such a way as to make further philosophical probing inappropriate. On this point, see Jonathan J. Halliwell, Quantum Cosmology and the Creation of the Universe, 265 Sci. Am. 76, 83 (1991). But see Adolf Grünbaum, Creation as a Pseudo-Explanation in Current Physical Cosmology, 35 Erkenntnis 233, 250 (1991); Adolf Grünbaum, The Pseudo-Problem of Creation in Physical Cosmology, 56 Phil. Sci. 373, 393 (1989). While Grünbaum recognizes that Hartle and Hawking's universe does not arise from nothing, he apparently considers it dispositive that their universe does not arise in or at a specifiable first moment of time.

For further brief discussion of the Hartle-Hawking "no boundary" proposal, see John D. Barrow, Theories of Everything 67-69 (Oxford: Clarendon 1991); William Lane Craig, 'What place, then, for a creator?': Hawking on God and Creation, 41 Brit. J. Phil. Sci. 473 (1990). For one writer's critique of particular interpretations of the Hartle-Hawking proposal, see Robin Le Poidevin, Creation in a Closed Universe, Or, Have Physicists Disproved the Existence of God?, 27 Religious Stud. 39 (1991). See also T.D. Sullivan, Coming To Be Without a Cause, 65 Phil. 261 (1990); Alexander Vilenkin, Did the Universe Have a Beginning?, 46 Physical Review D 2355 (3d series) (1992).

59. Consider, for example, the consistent denial of some of the most basic elements of the most widely held interpretations of quantum theory expressed in David Bohm, Wholeness and the Implicate Order 65-110 (London: Routledge & Kegan Paul 1980).

60. Even if the ultimate results of further scientific and logical inquiry are mixed, that would not necessarily mean that the debate was stagnating. For the theist, for example, it would be intellectually exciting if the anthropic coincidences held up, even if science definitively established as well that the onset of the universe could be explained in completely naturalistic terms.

8

Conclusion: What Would a Sound Theory of Obligation Look Like?

This book has not identified a uniquely best theory of legal and political obligation. We have, at least by implication, identified some plausible constraints on any such theory. These constraints can be briefly recapitulated. A sound theory of obligation should certainly avoid the particular weaknesses associated with the various approaches surveyed in chapters 1-4 above. It should not surprise us if a sound theory of legal and political obligation makes very direct, crucial reference to broad issues of justice and morality. This may be inevitable.

Any sound theory of obligation, as well, should be persuasive in the way in which it links 'is' and 'ought,' or facts and values. We cannot, for example, simply hand the prize of legitimacy to the regime that offers the largest net balance of pleasure over pain. Even assuming such an approach to be coherent, we need to know why maximizing net pleasure ought morally to be valued above other arrangements.

A further constraint was suggested in chapter 5. Specifically, a sound theory of obligation must allow its own basic moral vocabulary to be interpreted in a metaethically objective way. The ideas of right, justice, and moral good should be understood in an ambitious, full-blooded sense. Of course, the full or partial objectivity of a particular theory of obligation must be satisfactorily shown, and not just asserted. Political history is largely a matter of partially or entirely false pretensions to moral objectivity. But we have seen some reason to believe that in practice, over the long term, aiming for anything less than metaethical objectivism will tend to lead to results that would today be found very widely unattractive.

As well, no satisfactory approach to obligation can be intolerant, inegalitarian, repressive, exclusionary, or divisive. Nor, finally, can such a theory amount to a closed, dogmatic system insusceptible of any serious logical or empirical challenge. A sound theory of obligation must come to terms with potential objections, and not merely talk past them. These constraints flow from chapters 6 and 7 respectively.

It seems reasonable to conclude that a sound theory of legal and political obligation must meet each of these constraints. There seem to be no convincing reasons for either ignoring any of the constraints noted above, or for concluding that no theory of obligation could possibly meet them all.

Beyond the various constraints discussed above, though, can we say anything further about a potentially legitimate government? This book has not heavily emphasized matters of substantive or "normative" justice. What a just government looks like is controversial in ways unlikely to be dissolved by the argument of this book. But at least speculatively, a brief word or two may be essayed along these lines.

If and when we reach a rationally and freely arrived at consensus upon the general outlines or nature of a legitimate government, the content of that consensual view is unlikely to be stunning in its novelty. If some government is morally legitimate, it is likely to be so for reasons at least roughly now familiar to us after thousands of years of active discussion.

There are doubtless many ways of characterizing such a government. One such way seems unduly neglected in contemporary legal and political debate, even though it obviously owes much to the work of Aristotle and Kant, among others.[1] This view focuses upon a government's effectiveness in promoting the fullest development of the capacity of all persons for actions and choices for which they reasonably may be held fully morally responsible. Of course, the importance of human dignity and the capacity for responsibility is trans-historical and cross-cultural in its origin and development.

It is quite common to think of very young children, the insane, or people being subjected to overwhelming physical force, as not fully responsible for what they do. Governments and legal institutions tend to fail to realize, however, that these and similar easy cases do not exhaust the range of circumstances under which it is unreasonable to hold people less than fully responsible for what they do.

In our own society, many persons eke out their daily existence under physical circumstances undreamt of by Hobbes, or perhaps even by Dante. The informational constraints and the real or reasonably perceived constraints on their opportunities are severe. They live this way through no responsible fault of their own, or at least no proportionate fault. They do not perceive, and have no reasonable grounds to believe in, any genuinely practical and realistic means of avoiding such circumstances through individual or group effort. If one has always lived under this sort of realistically inescapable regime of obstacles, privation, and threat, with few resources, one has lived a severely constrained life. Now, it is undeniably possible for some persons to triumph over the most horrifyingly adverse circumstances. But this is a kind of heroism, or a kind of luck, and neither heroism nor luck of this sort can reasonably be required of individuals. No doubt almost everyone, including the most desperately addicted, can avoid committing any particular criminal or non-criminal act on any particular occasion. But this is not enough for moral responsibility to attach. For many who have known only the most dire circumstances, the constraints under which they labor cannot but diminish, if not completely annul, the moral responsibility they bear for many of their actions. If the rest of us labored under the same ratio of resources to constraints, we would fare no better, and be no more blameworthy. Yet often enough, governments and societies impose moral blame upon, and impute moral responsibility to, persons who do not bear such responsibility according to the society's own most basic understanding of the requisites of such responsibility. Instead, governments attempt to compress the logic of moral responsibility into narrow categories such as insanity or duress, ignoring the role of some degree of relevant knowledge, freedom, and control as logical prerequisites to moral responsibility for one's actions.

This is not to deny the remarkable human capacity for resourcefulness and adaptation, or the infinite value of each human personality. Far from it. Instead, a crucial task of government and the legal system is to respect and promote human dignity by doing all it can, perhaps subject to other conceivably overriding moral constraints, to reduce obstacles to universal full moral responsibility. Doubtless this requires substantial redistribution of opportunities, resources, and wealth broadly conceived, in favor of those least advantaged. To the extent that any government or legal system neglects this task, it ignores what is of distinctive moral value in the human personality, and thereby jeopardizes its legitimacy and its moral authority. This conclusion, one suspects, would follow from the best forms of metaethical moral objectivism upon which we are likely to be able to lay our hands.

There are two reasons to be tentative in pressing a substantive theory of legal and political obligation much further. First, few writers on obligation have been clear about the degree to which a regime may depart from the best that is morally attainable, while still retaining a legitimate claim to our allegiance. In our terms, the best regime would do all it could, and would do more than viable alternative regimes, to promote human dignity and the associated capacity for moral responsibility, especially among the most severely oppressed. But deciding at what point a regime's failure in this respect would imply the forfeiture of its legitimacy is not easy.

Clearly, in such cases, we will want to know about the capabilities and likely performance of alternative regimes, the probability of their achieving power, and the likely risks and costs of transition, including violence. The answers we arrive at may well depend upon the length of the time perspective employed. Few transitions of authority will seem worthwhile if we insist upon a very prompt net social payoff. On the other hand, if we adopt a longer time perspective, the uncertainties and unintended consequences, good and bad, of all actions are multiplied.

Where a utilitarian calculation may counsel against revolution, though, a non-utilitarian approach may not. Surely one of the highest priorities of any rational tyrant would be to raise as high as possible the social costs of peacefully or violently adopting any alternative order. But just as surely, there must be limits to the extent that citizens are morally required to obey, where the social costs of disobedience are high largely because the current regime has engineered this to be so. Paradoxically, the more a tyrannical government calculatedly raises the costs of disobedience, the greater the dignitary gains from resisting the government and freely incurring those costs.

Now, a utilitarian might presume to reach a similar result, on the grounds that social quiescence in the face of deliberately engineered high costs of rebellion sets a bad, utility-diminishing precedent. It is doubtful, though, that a society engaged in a long, painful transition from a prior regime imagines that it is helping to deter future tyrants not from tyranny itself, but from the tyrant's strategic decision to make any rebellion as socially painful as possible.

The second reason to be modest about any substantive theory of obligation reflects the proper tentativeness, fallibilism, incompleteness, and approximation of even the best sorts of objectivist morality. We have seen something above of the depredations and false universalization committed in the name of objectivity. Historically, political privilege has sought to present itself as a reflection of neutral, objective moral truth. Along these lines, Janet Martin Soskice has observed that we are unavoidably "embedded in a language which privileges certain perspectives and powers and which, without thinking, hears only the dominant voice as 'true' voice. 'Voicelessness' in this sense is so substantially documented as to be no longer regarded as a contested hypothesis."[2]

As we have suggested above, listening to the previously voiceless is not an ultimately more or less arbitrary choice. This is precisely because exclusion of the voiceless is wrong according to such elements of an objective view of human dignity as we are able to attain. It is precisely the ideal of objectivity itself, as Sandra Harding has suggested, that requires us to carefully and sympathetically adopt, as fully as possible, all relevant "alien" perspectives, and that bars us from minimizing or depreciating the importance of those "alien" perspectives.[3]

But while only the moral objectivist can condemn such exclusion or depreciation of the voiceless with the fullest and most stable argument available, the need to make such a condemnation itself shows how readily subject to political misuse the idea of moral objectivity has been. It must be said that not all misuse of, or failure to live up to the ideal standards of, moral objectivity has involved conscious, cynical manipulation. But, in turn, precisely because not all misuse of the ideal of objectivity has been conscious, those who value the ideal of moral objectivity must let a strong sense of their own situatedness and fallibility be reflected in the tentativeness of their recommendations.

Fallibilism is taken too far, though, if it leads us to view objectivity as invariably so murky as to make plausible whatever moral claims dominant political groups may care to make.[4] We have enough current insight into what morality requires to make continued progress in blocking and reversing the ideological abuse by the powerful of the idea of objectivity. Our grasp of the objective requirements of human dignity and responsibility is not so tentative as to have impaired our relying on the idea of moral objectivity in progressively undermining various historical forms of repression. Nor is there any reason to suppose that our understanding of the objective nature of human dignity and its practical implications cannot be further enhanced.

We have speculated that the best morally objectivist approach to basic issue of law and government will turn out to emphasize matters of human dignity and the capacity for responsibility. We have speculated further that such an approach will turn out to be substantially redistributionist in its practical implications.

At least vaguely similar results would be welcome in a number of philosophical quarters, but it is worth mentioning the theory of Alan Gewirth in particular, because Gewirth believes that he can actually logically demonstrate the objective and nearly universal moral rightness of particular political arrangements that emphasize individual freedom, equality, and well-being. If Gewirth is right, only matters of secondary importance would remain to be resolved in political philosophy.

Gewirth's argument is too extended, complex, and by now too well-known, or at least too readily accessible elsewhere,[5] to be set forth here. Perhaps the crucial element of Gewirth's argument is that being an actual or at least prospective actor, or a genuinely free agent pursuing freely chosen purposes, logically commits that actor to claims to freedom and well-being for herself, and ultimately for all other such actual or prospective actors as well. While we may be unequal in certain respects, perhaps including the ability to achieve our purposes, we are presumably equal in having at least some capacity to actually or prospectively pursue freely chosen purposes, which triggers the rest of Gewirth's argument for freedom, equality, and well-being.

Gewirth is a leading defender of the objectivity of morality. His substantive principles are appealing. But it is reasonable to entertain certain reservations as to whether his broader argument for the logical necessity of his results is successful. As it turns out, even given Gewirth's contribution, there is still much very basic work to be done in political philosophy.

Perhaps the best way to illustrate this is by reference not to any of the interesting and controversial later steps in Gewirth's argument, but to Gewirth's initial step, in which he discusses what he conceives acting or agency to involve. As our brief exposition above indicates, Gewirth begins with the idea of an action, or an actor. Gewirth's critics have often gone technically astray by failing to notice how much of importance for his argument is already built in at this first stage.

For Gewirth, action is not merely doing, or attempting to do, what one wishes to do. If this were how Gewirth thought of action, many of his critics would be more literally right in their criticisms. Instead, Gewirth relies, as he must, on a narrower and more stringent view of what action involves. Action is not just voluntary, purposive or goal-directed behavior, but only such behavior when it is undertaken to achieve purposes or goals that are genuinely freely chosen by the actor. Thus someone who seeks to achieve some goal, where that goal was not chosen freely, but as a result of a choice process skewed by socialization, indoctrination, peer pressure, mass advertising, the sheer force of cultural tradition, propaganda, or direct coercion in any form, is in Gewirth's sense not in this respect an actual or prospective actor. What that person does, in response to the above sorts of promptings, is not an action.

Gewirth thus builds freedom into the very idea of an action. Now, this is not to suggest that there is anything amiss in doing so. But Gewirth's argument, on this basis, cannot then be as categorical, universal, or necessary as he suggests. This is because there is nothing necessary or universal about Gewirth's stringent concept of action. Persons who single-mindedly pursue certain goods only because they were somehow told to do so are not actors in Gewirth's sense. We might instead call them need-fulfillment-pursuers. Such persons might be said to act, in a looser, non-Gewirthian sense, to satisfy their real or perceived needs, perhaps including their real or perceived moral obligations, regardless of the origin or development of those needs.

Gewirth recognizes that some of us may not value life, choice, freedom, or even our own well-being. In some cases, even the decision to surrender one's freedom may have been freely made, or an actor may want to renounce freedom only as a result of her own free decision. But Gewirth's argument does not recognize the possibility of living a recognizable, and on some views, a worthy and desirable life, without once ever acting, or seeking to act, in Gewirth's narrow sense. One way of seeing this is by noticing that someone who wants, for example, to be happy is not thereby committed to wanting any freedom at all with regard to being happy. Someone who merely wishes to be happy need not object if there is some person or group overseeing her activities who will ensure her happiness, regardless of her own efforts, miscalculations, second thoughts, or potential changes of mind.

What is even more crucial is that someone who wishes only to be happy, or more magnanimously, to spread happiness throughout the world, need not care in the slightest about the origin of that wish. Someone can value a desire, or deem it worthy of pursuit, even if that desire was, for example, calculatedly inculcated deep into that person's psyche, and even if the person knows that the desire in question arose thus unfreely, and would otherwise not have arisen. Persons can strongly identify with aspects of their character or belief system that they realize they did not freely adopt. Of course, it is open to argue that one's happiness, or the happiness of other people, depends upon our freely adopting such pursuits. But this is a large empirical question, on which students of, for example, traditional societies may have something, convincing or unconvincing, to say. In any case, the supposed necessity and universality of Gewirth's argument is difficult to defend.

Gewirth recognizes that persons may, reasonably or unreasonably, wish to allow others to limit their freedom, as in the case of Ulysses and the Sirens, or even to entirely bring their own agency to an end. Gewirth's error lies in supposing that such persons are logically committed to wishing to have or preserve their own freedom at least in regard to the choice to limit or terminate their own freedom.

Let us suppose that Person A wishes to utterly submit his fate to Person B. Why must Person A, as a matter of logical necessity, care whether that wish arose as a result of free deliberation, or instead as the nearly inevitable result of some sort of cultural pressure? Of course, it is hardly unreasonable to be suspicious of external pressures to surrender one's freedom, but one does not somehow necessarily land oneself in a contradiction by not insisting that one only freely surrender one's freedom. One might decide, freely or unfreely, either that the risks of being coerced into surrendering one's freedom to one's eventual detriment are low, or that others are better at assessing such a risk. And, most definitely, no one is bound in logic to want the latter decision itself to be made only on the basis of one's free choice. Of course, some persons may be born and remain unfree, with no choice in the matter, yet lead at least arguably worthwhile lives pursuing their own happiness, or the happiness of the poor, whether they themselves are rich or poor.

It follows, then, that if we need not in logic claim even an original or a residual sort of freedom in decisionmaking we need not be logically committed, in the ordinary goal-pursuits of our lives, to recognizing any extensive degree of freedom on the part of other persons. Merely acquiescing in the authority of cultural traditions, or more clearly, not even at any point considering the possibility of failing to acquiesce in such authority, hardly commits us logically to the liberal polity Gewirth envisions.

This is of course not in the slightest to detract from the appeal and attractiveness of the substance of the political principles Gewirth endorses. What is at issue is not the obvious appeal of Gewirth's results, but whether he has derived those results with the claimed degree of rigor. And to that question, our answer must be in the negative.

It should be borne in mind, though, that even if Gewirth's argument is not strictly successful on its own terms, it may still be of great value. We might be inspired, for example, to carefully compare the moral attractiveness of a society of Gewirthian agents with a society devoid of such agents. While such a comparison might not lead us to an inescapable conclusion, it might strengthen the argument for particular sets of political arrangements. It seems fair to say, for example, that Gerwith's argument strengthens the appeal of the arguments made above for the primacy of dignity and for providing for all citizens the material and social requisites of the capacity for responsible action. Gewirth's argument thus lends further support for a general focus on universal dignity and the developed capacity for responsibility as central to a satisfactory theory of legal and political obligation.

NOTES TO *CONCLUSION:*
WHAT WOULD A SOUND THEORY OF OBLIGATION LOOK LIKE?

1. See also, for example, Giovanni Pico Della Mirandola, Oration on the Dignity of Man, in The Renaissance Philosophy of Man 223 (Ernst Cassirer, Paul Oskar Kristeller & John Herman Randall, Jr. eds. and trans.) (Chicago: Univ. of Chicago Press 1948). Pico, whose actual reference is to *hominis* rather than to "man," closely linked the dignity of human persons with their freedom of will and their ability to become what they wished, in accordance with their choice.

2. Janet Martin Soskice, The Truth Looks Different From Here, 73 New Blackfriars 528, 536 (1992).

3. See Sandra Harding, After the Neutrality Ideal: Science, Politics, and "Strong Objectivity," 59 Social Res. 567, 571, 579, 583-85 (1992).

4. For a thoughtful discussion of the status of the ethical indeterminacy of broad principles in the concrete circumstances of a pluralistic world, see Onora O'Neill, Ethical Reasoning and Ideological Pluralism, 98 Ethics 705 (1988).

5. The fullest statement by Gewirth of his theory is contained in Alan Gewirth, Reason and Morality (Chicago: Univ. of Chicago Press 1978). See also Alan Gewirth, The Ontological Basis of Natural Law: A Critique and an Alternative, 29 Am. J. Juris. 95 (1984). Gewirth's approach is endorsed in Deryck Beyleveld & Roger Brownsword, Law as Moral Judgment (London: Sweet & Maxwell 1986). Beyleveld has more recently produced a remarkably thorough and detailed defense of Gewirth's argument against numerous objections. See Deryck Beyleveld, The Dialectical Necessity of Morality (Chicago: Univ. of Chicago Press 1991). For a sample of some of the objections, see, e.g., Gewirth's Ethical Rationalism (Edward Regis ed.) (Chicago: Univ. of Chicago Press 1984); Alasdair MacIntyre, After Virtue 66-67 (Notre Dame: Univ. of Notre Dame 2d ed. 1984); Seyla Benhabib, Afterword: Communicative Ethics and Current Controversies in Practical Philosophy, in The Communicative Ethics Controversy 330, 336 (Seyla Benhabib & Fred Dallmayr eds.) (Cambridge: MIT Press 1990); Jurgen Habermas, Discourse Ethics: Notes on a Program of Philosophical Justification, in id. at 60, 98.

BIBLIOGRAPHY

Abbott, Philip. The Shotgun Behind the Door: Liberalism and the Problem of Political Obligation (Athens: Univ. of Georgia Press 1976)

Adair, Robert K. The Great Design (New York: Oxford Univ. Press 1987)

Adams, Marilyn M. William Ockham (Notre Dame: Notre Dame Univ. Press 1987)

Adams, Robert M. The Virtue of Faith (New York: Oxford Univ. Press 1987)

Albert, David. Quantum Mechanics and Experience (Cambridge: Harvard Univ. Press 1992)

Albert, David and Barry Loewer. Interpreting the Many Worlds Interpretation, 77 Synthese 195 (1988)

_____. The Measurement Problem: Some Solutions, 86 Synthese 87 (1991)

Alexander, Larry. Law and Exclusionary Reasons, 18 Phil. Topics 5 (1990)

Almond, Brenda. Seven Moral Myths, 65 Phil. 129 (1990)

The Anthropic Cosmological Principle: Proceedings of the Second Venice Conference on Cosmology and Philosophy (F. Bertola & U. Curi eds.) (Cambridge: Cambridge Univ. Press 1989)

Aquinas, Thomas. The Political Ideas of St. Thomas Aquinas (Dino Bigongiari ed.) (New York: Hafner 1953)

_____. Summa Theologica (Fathers of the English Dominican Province trans.) (London: Burns Oates & Washbourne Ltd. reprint ed. 1935)

_____. Treatise on Happiness (John A. Oesterle trans.) (Notre Dame: Univ. Notre Dame Press 1983)

_____. Treatise on the Virtues (John A. Oesterle trans.) (Notre Dame: Notre Dame Univ. Press 1984)

Arneson, Richard J. The Principle of Fairness and Free Rider Problems, 92 Ethics 616 (1982)

Atiyah, Patrick S. Promises, Morals and Law (Oxford: Clarendon Press 1981)

Atkins, Peter W. Will Science Ever Fail?, 135 New Scientist 32 (1992)

Ayer, A.J. Language, Truth and Logic (New York: Dover 1952)

Baker, Lynn A. "Just Do It": Pragmatism and Progressive Social Change, 78 Va. L. Rev. 697 (1992)

Bakhtin, Michael M. The Dialogic Imagination (Austin: Univ. of Texas Press 1981)

Balashov, Yuri. Resource Letter AP-1: The Anthropic Principle, 59 Am. J. Physics 1069 (1991)

Ball, Steven W. Facts, Values, and Normative Supervenience, 55 Phil. Stud. 143 (1987)

Bambrough, Renford. Fools and Heretics, in Royal Institute of Philosophy Supplement no. 29: Wittgenstein Centenary Essays (A. Phillips Griffiths ed.) (Cambridge: Cambridge Univ. Press 1991)

Barnett, Randy. A Consent Theory of Contract, 86 Colum. L. Rev. 269 (1986)

Barrow, John D. Theories of Everything (Oxford: Clarendon Press 1991)

Barrow, John D. and Frank J. Tipler. The Anthropic Cosmological Principle (New York: Oxford Univ. Press 1986)

Beckstrom, John. The Potential Dangers and Benefits of Introducing Sociobiology to Lawyers, 79 Nw. U.L. Rev. 1279 (1985)

Ben-Dov, Yoav. Everett's Theory and the "Many-Worlds" Interpretation, 58 Am. J. Physics 829 (1990)

Benhabib, Seyla. Afterword: Communicative Ethics and Current Controversies in Practical Philosophy, in The Communicative Ethics Controversy (Seyla Benhabib & Fred Dallmayr eds.) (Cambridge: MIT Press 1990)

Bennett, Jonathan. The Necessity of Moral Judgments, 103 Ethics 458 (1993)

Beran, Harry. The Consent Theory of Political Obligation (London: Croon Helm 1987)

Berger, Fred R. Gratitude, 85 Ethics 298 (1985)

Berger, Peter. The Capitalist Revolution (New York: Basic Books 1986)

Bernstein, Richard J. One Step Forward, Two Steps Backward: Richard Rorty on Liberal Democracy and Philosophy, 15 Pol. Theory 38 (1987)

Betty, L. Stafford and Bruce Cordell. God and Modern Science, 27 Int. Phil. Q. 409 (1987)

Beyleveld, Deryck. The Dialectical Necessity of Morality (Chicago: Univ. of Chicago Press 1991)

Beyleveld, Deryck and Roger Brownsword. Law as Moral Judgment (London: Sweet and Maxwell 1986)

Bix, Brian. Michael Moore's Realist Approach to Law, 140 U. Pa. L. Rev. 1293 (1992)

Blackburn, Simon. Spreading the Word (Oxford: Clarendon Press 1984)

_____. Errors and the Phenomenology of Value, in Morality and Objectivity (Ted Honderich ed.) (London: Routledge 1985)

_____. Wise Feelings, Apt Readings, 102 Ethics 342 (1992)

Boghossian, Paul. The Status of Content, 99 Phil. Rev. 157 (1990)

Bohm, David. Wholeness and the Implicate Order (London: Routledge & Kegan Paul 1980)

Bond, E.J. Reason and Value (Cambridge: Cambridge Univ. Press 1983)

_____. Could There Be a Rationally Grounded Universal Morality?, 15 J. Phil. Res. 15 (1989)

Bourke, Vernon. Review of John Finnis' Natural Law and Natural Rights, 26 Am. J. Juris. 243 (1981)

Boxill, Bernard R. On Some Criticisms of Consent Theory, 24 J. Social Phil. 81 (1993)

Boyle, Joseph. Natural Law and the Ethics of Traditions, in Natural Law Theory: Contemporary Essays (Robert P. George ed.) (Oxford: Oxford Univ. Press 1992)

Brandt, Richard B. Relativism Refuted?, 67 Monist 297 (1984)

Breuer, Reinhard. The Anthropic Principle (Harry Newman & Mark Lowery trans.) (Boston: Birkhäuser 1991)

The Brihadaranyaka Upanisad (Rai Bahudur Sris Chadra Vasu trans.) (New York: AMS Press Reprint ed. 1974)

Brilmayer, Lea. Consent, Contract and Territory, 74 Minn. L. Rev. 1 (1989)

Brink, David O. Moral Realism and the Foundations of Ethics (Cambridge: Cambridge Univ. Press 1989)

Camenisch, Paul F. Gift and Gratitude in Ethics, 9 J. Religious Ethics 1 (1981)

Card, Claudia. Gratitude and Obligation, 25 Am. Phil. Q. 115 (1988)

Carloye, Jack C. The Existence of God and the Creation of the Universe, 27 Zygon 167 (1992)

Carr, B.J. On the Origin, Evolution and Purpose of the Physical Universe, in Physical Cosmology and Philosophy (John Leslie ed.) (New York: MacMillan 1990)

Carr, B.J. and M.J. Rees. The Anthropic Principle and the Structure of the Physical World, 278 Nature 605 (1979)

Carson, Thomas L. Relativism and Nihilism, 15 Philosophia 1 (1985)

Chandrasekhar, Subramanyan. Truth and Beauty (Chicago: Univ. of Chicago Press 1987)

Clark, Stephen R.L. God's Law and Morality, 32 Phil. Q. 339 (1982)

Clifton, Robert K. Review of John Leslie's Universes, 41 Phil. Q. 339 (1991)

Collins, P.D.B. and R.F. Langbein. Thermodynamics of Inflation, 45 Physical Review D 3429 (3d series) (1992)

Contractarianism and Rational Choice: Essays on David Gauthier's Morals By Agreement (Peter Vallentyne ed.) (Cambridge: Cambridge Univ. Press 1991)

Cooke, Vincent M. Moral Obligation and Metaphysics, 66 Thought 65 (1991)

Copp, David. Harman on Internalism, Relativism, and Logical Form, 92 Ethics 227 (1982)

_____. Moral Realism: Facts and Norms, 101 Ethics 610 (1991)

_____. Book Review of Morals By Agreement, 98 Phil. Rev. 411 (1989)

Corey, M.A. God and the New Cosmology: The Anthropic Design Argument (Lanham, Md.: Rowman & Littlefield 1993)

Craig, William Lane. Barrow and Tipler on the Anthropic Principle vs. Divine Design, 38 Brit. J. Phil. Sci. 389 (1988)

_____. God, Creation and Mr. Davies, 37 Brit. J. Phil. Sci. 163 (1986)

_____. Theism and Big Bang Cosmology, 69 Australasian J. Phil. 492 (1991)

_____. 'What place, then, for a creator?': Hawking on God and Creation, 41 Brit. J. Phil. Sci. 473 (1990)

Cranston, Maurice. John Locke and the Case for Toleration, in John Locke, A Letter Concerning Toleration: In Focus (John Horton & Susan Mendus eds.) (London: Routledge 1991)

D'Agostino, Fred. Transcendence and Conversation: Two Conceptions of Objectivity, 30 Am. Phil. Q. 87 (1993)

D'Amato, Anthony. The Obligation to Obey the Law: A Study of the Death of Socrates, 49 S. Cal. L. Rev. 1079 (1976)

Dancy, Jonathan. Two Conceptions of Moral Realism, 60 Proc. Aristotelian Society 167 (Supp. 1986)

Daniels, Norman. Wide Reflective Equilibrium and Theory Acceptance in Ethics, 76 J. Phil. 256 (1979)

Darwall, Stephen, Allan Gibbard and Peter Railton. Toward *Fin de Siècle* Ethics: Some Trends, 101 Phil. Rev. 115 (1992)

Davies, Paul. God and the New Physics (New York: Simon & Schuster 1983)

_____. The Accidental Universe (Cambridge: Cambridge Univ. Press 1982)

_____. The Mind of God (New York: Simon & Schuster 1992)

Davies, Paul and John Gribbin. The Matter Myth (New York: Simon & Schuster 1992)

Day, J.P. Threats, Offers, Law, Opinion, and Liberty, 14 Am. Phil. Q. 265 (1977)

del Campo, Sergio. Initial Conditions for Anisotropic Extended-Type Inflationary Universes, 45 Physical Review D 3386 (3d series) (1992)

Devitt, Michael. Realism and Truth (Oxford: Basil Blackwell 2d ed. 1991)

Devine, Philip E. Relativism, Nihilism and God (Notre Dame: Notre Dame Univ. Press 1989)

Dieks, Dennis. On Some Alleged Difficulties in the Interpretation of Quantum Mechanics, 86 Synthese 77 (1991)

Doppelt, Gerald. Is Rawls's Kantian Liberalism Coherent and Defensible?, 99 Ethics 815 (1989)

Dostoevsky, Fyodor. The Brothers Karamazov (Andrew H. MacAndrew trans.) (New York: Bantam 1970)

Double, Richard. The Non-Reality of Free Will (New York: Oxford Univ. Press 1991)

Drees, Willem B. Beyond the Big Bang: Quantum Cosmologies and God (La Salle: Open Court 1990)

_____. Quantum Cosmologies and the "Beginning," 26 Zygon 373 (1992)

Dummett, Michael. The Logical Basis of Metaphysics (Cambridge: Harvard Univ. Press 1991)

Dworkin, Ronald. Law's Empire (Cambridge: Harvard Univ. Press 1986)

Earman, John. The SAP Also Rises: A Critical Examination of the Anthropic Principle, 24 Am. Phil. Q. 307 (1987)

Eidelberg, Paul. The Malaise of Modern Psychology, 126 J. Psychology 109 (1992)

Ellis, George F.R. Before the Beginning (London: Boyars/Bowerdean 1993)

Epstein, David F. The Political Theory of the Federalist (Chicago: Univ. of Chicago Press 1984)

Essays on Moral Realism (Geoffrey Sayre-McCord ed.) (Ithaca: Cornell Univ. Press 1988)

Everett, Hugh. The Theory of the Universal Wave Function, in The Many-Worlds Interpretation of Quantum Mechanics 3 (Bryce S. DeWitt & Neill Graham eds.) (Princeton: Princeton Univ. Press 1973)

Fallon, Richard H. Reflections on Dworkin and the Two Faces of Law, 67 Notre Dame L. Rev. 553 (1992)

Fang Li Zhi and Li Shu Xian. Creation of the Universe (T. Kiang trans.) (Singapore: World Scientific Publishing 1989)

Finnis, John. Fundamentals of Ethics (Washington, D.C.: Georgetown Univ. Press 1983)

_____. Moral Absolutes: Tradition, Revision, and Truth (Washington, D.C.: Catholic Univ. of America Press 1991)

_____. Natural Law and Natural Rights (Oxford: Clarendon Press 1980)

_____. Natural Law and Legal Reasoning, in Natural Law Theory: Contemporary Essays (Robert P. George ed.) (Oxford: Clarendon Press 1992)

_____. Natural Law and the "Is"—"Ought" Question: An Invitation to Professor Veatch, 26 Catholic Lawyer 266 (1981)

_____. The Authority of Law in the Predicament of Contemporary Social Theory, 1 Notre Dame J.L. & Pub. Pol'y 115 (1984)

Finnis, John and Germain Grisez. The Basic Principles of Natural Law: A Reply to Ralph McInerney, 26 Am. J. Juris. 21 (1981)

Finnis, John, Joseph Boyle and Germain Grisez. Nuclear Deterrence, Morality and Realism (Oxford: Clarendon Press 1987)

Fish, Stanley. Dennis Martinez and the Uses of Theory, 96 Yale L.J. 1773 (1987)

Fiss, Owen. The Other Goldberg, in The Constitution of Rights (Michael J. Mayer & W.A. Parent eds.) (Ithaca: Cornell Univ. Press 1992)

Flathman, Richard E. Political Obligation (New York: Atheneum 1972)

Foot, Philippa. Moral Relativism, in Relativism: Cognitive and Moral (Michael Krausz & Jack W. Meiland eds.) (Notre Dame: Notre Dame Univ. Press 1982)

Fried, Charles. Contract as Promise (Cambridge: Harvard Univ. Press 1981)

Gale, George. Some Metaphysical Perplexities in Contemporary Physics, 26 Int. Phil. Q. 393 (1986)

Gandhi, Mohandas K. Non-Violent Resistance (Bharatan Kumarappa ed.) (New York: Schocken Books 1961)

Garner, Richard T. On the Genuine Queerness of Moral Properties and Facts, 68 Australasian J. Phil. 137 (1990)

Garofalo, Bruno. A Note on the 'Is/Ought' Problem in Hume's Ethical Writings, 19 J. Value Inquiry 311 (1985)

Garrett, Anthony J.M. and Peter Coles. Bayesian Inductive Inference and the Anthropic Cosmological Principle, 17 Comments on Astrophysics 23 (1993)

Gauthier, David. Morals By Agreement (Oxford: Clarendon Press 1986)

_____. Review Essay: The Roots and Roles of Normative Governance, 91 Synthese 219 (1992)

Gavison, Ruth. Natural Law, Positivism, and the Limits of Jurisprudence: A Modern Round, 91 Yale L.J. 1250 (1982)

Gellner, Ernest. Postmodernism, Reason and Religion (London: Routledge 1992)

George, Robert P. Recent Criticism of Natural Law Theory, 55 U. Chi. L. Rev. 1371 (1988)

Geroch, Robert. The Everett Interpretation, 18 Nous 617 (1984)

Gewirth, Alan. Reason and Morality (Chicago: Univ. of Chicago Press 1978)

_____. The Ontological Basis of Natural Law: A Critique and an Alternative, 29 Am. J. Juris. 95 (1984)

Gewirth's Ethical Rationalism (Edward Regis ed.) (Chicago: Univ. of Chicago Press 1984)

Gibbard, Allan. Wise Choices, Apt Feelings (Cambridge: Harvard Univ. Press 1990)

_____. Communities of Judgment, in Foundations of Moral and Political Philosophy (Ellen Frankel Paul, Fred D. Miller, Jr. & Jeffrey Paul eds.) (Oxford: Basil Blackwell 1990)

_____. Constructing Justice, 20 Phil. & Pub. Aff. 264 (1991)

_____. Normative Objectivity, 19 Nous 41 (1985)

Gibson, James L. The Political Consequences of Intolerance: Cultural Conformity and Political Freedom, 86 Am. Pol. Sci. Rev. 338 (1992)

Gilbert, Margaret. Agreements, Coercion, and Obligation, 103 Ethics 679 (1993)

Goldsworthy, Jeffrey. Externalism, Internalism and Moral Scepticism, 70 Australasian J. Phil. 40 (1992)

Goodin, Robert. Book Review of Morals By Agreement, 54 Economica 272 (1987)

Graham, Gordon. Religion, Secularization and Modernity, 67 Phil. 183 (1992)

Green, Leslie. The Authority of the State (Oxford: Clarendon Press 1990)

_____. Law, Co-Ordination and the Common Good, 3 Ox. J. Legal Stud. 299 (1983)

Greenawalt, Kent. Promise, Benefit, and Need: Ties That Bind Us to the Law, 18 Ga. L. Rev. 727 (1984)

Greenstein, George and Allen Kropf. Cognizable Worlds: The Anthropic Principle and the Fundamental Constants of Nature, 57 Am. J. Physics 746 (1989)

Gribbin, John and Martin Rees. Cosmic Coincidences (New York: Bantam 1989)

Grisez, Germain, Joseph Boyle and John Finnis. Practical Principles, Moral Truth, and Ultimate Ends, 32 Am. J. Juris. 99 (1987)

Grishchuk, L.P. and L.V. Rozhansky. Does the Hartle-Hawking Wavefunction Predict the Universe We Live In?, 234 Physics Letters B 9 (1990)

Grünbaum, Adolf. Creation as a Pseudo-Explanation in Current Physical Cosmology, 35 Erkenntnis 233 (1991)

_____. The Pseudo-Problem of Creation in Physical Cosmology, 56 Phil. Sci. 373 (1989)

Guth, Alan H. and Paul J. Steinhardt. The Inflationary Universe, 250 Sci. Am. 116 (1984)

Habermas, Jurgen. Discourse Ethics: Notes on a Program of Philosophical Justification, in The Communicative Ethics Controversy (Seyla Benhabib & Fred Dallmayr eds.) (Cambridge: MIT Press 1990)

Hacking, Ian. The Inverse Gambler's Fallacy: The Argument from Design. The Anthropic Principle Applied to Wheeler Universes, 96 Mind 33 (1987)

Hallberg, Fred W. Barrow and Tipler's Anthropic Cosmological Principle, 27 Zygon 139 (1987)

Halliwell, Jonathan J. Quantum Cosmology and the Creation of the Universe, 265 Sci. Am. 76 (1991)

Hampton, Jean. Should Political Philosophy Be Done Without Metaphysics?, 99 Ethics 791 (1989)

Harding, Sandra. After the Neutrality Ideal: Science, Politics, and "Strong Objectivity," 59 Social Res. 567 (1992)

Harman, Gilbert. Change in View (Cambridge: Bradford Press 1986)

_____. Moral Relativism Defended, in Relativism: Cognitive and Moral (Michael Krausz & Jack W. Meiland eds.) (Notre Dame: Notre Dame Univ. Press 1982)

Harris, Edward A. Fighting Philosophical Anarchism with Fairness: The Moral Claims of Law in the Liberal State, 91 Colum. L. Rev. 919 (1991)

_____. From Social Contract to Hypothetical Agreement: Consent and the Obligation to Obey the Law, 92 Colum. L. Rev. 651 (1992)

Harris, Errol E. Cosmos and Anthropos (Atlantic Highlands: Humanities Press 1991)

Hart, H.L.A. Are There Any Natural Rights?, 64 Phil. Rev. 175 (1955)

Hartle, James and Stephen Hawking. Wave Function of the Universe, 28 Physical Review D 2690 (3d series) (1983)

Hawking, Stephen W. A Brief History of Time (New York: Bantam 1988)

Healey, Richard. How Many Worlds?, 18 Nous 591 (1984)

Hebblethwaite, Brian. The Ocean of Truth (Cambridge: Cambridge Univ. Press 1988)

Henderson, Lynne. Authoritarianism and the Rule of Law, 66 Ind. L.J. 379 (1991)

_____. Whose Nature? Practical Reason and Patriarchy, 38 Clev. St. L. Rev. 169 (1990)

Herbert, Nick. Quantum Reality (New York: Anchor Books 1987)

Herzog, Don. Happy Slaves: A Critique of Consent Theory (Chicago: Univ. of Chicago Press 1989)

Hirschmann, Nancy. Rethinking Obligation: A Feminist Method for Political Theory (Ithaca: Cornell Univ. Press 1992)

Hittinger, Russell. A Critique of the New Natural Law Theory (Notre Dame: Univ. of Notre Dame Press 1987)

_____. Review of Jean Porter, The Recovery of Virtue, 8 Faith and Phil. 549 (1991)

Hobbes, Thomas. Leviathan (C.B. Macpherson ed.) (Harmondsworth: Penguin Books 1968)

Hocutt, Max. Must Relativists Tolerate Evil?, 17 Phil. Forum 188 (1986)

Hodgson, David. Mind Matters: Consciousness and Choice in a Quantum World (Oxford: Clarendon Press 1991)

Hokee, Minn. Creation From "Anything or Nothing," 105 Il Nuovo Cimento B 901 (1990)

Hudson, W.D. Hume on Is and Ought, 14 Phil. Q. 246 (1964)

Hume, David. A Treatise of Human Nature (L.A. Selby-Bigge ed.) (Oxford: Clarendon Press 1968)

Hume (Vera C. Chappel ed.) (Garden City: Doubleday & Co. 1966)

Hutcheson, Francis. An Inquiry Concerning the Original of Our Ideas of Virtue or Moral Good, in 1 British Moralists (L.A. Selby-Bigge ed.) (New York: Dover Publications 1965)

Isham, Chris J. Creation of the Universe as a Quantum Process, in Physics, Philosophy and Theology (Robert John Russell, William R. Stoeger & George V. Coyne eds.) (Vatican City: Vatican Observatory 1988)

The Is-Ought Question (W.D. Hudson ed.) (London: MacMillan 1969)

Jackson, Timothy P. The Theory and Practice of Discomfort: Richard Rorty and Pragmatism, 51 Thomist 270 (1987)

Jaki, Stanley L. God and the New Cosmologists (Washington, D.C.: Regnery Gateway 1989)

Jenkins, John J. Political Consent, 20 Phil. Q. 60 (1970)

Johnson, Jeffrey L. Inference to the Best Explanation and The New Teleological Argument, 31 S.J. Phil. 193 (1993)

Judgment Under Uncertainty: Heuristics and Biases (Daniel Kahneman, Amos Tversky & Paul Slovic eds.) (Cambridge: Cambridge Univ. Press 1982)

Kant, Immanuel. Lectures on Ethics (Louis Infield trans.) (Indianapolis: Hackett Publishing 1963)

Karmo, Toomas. Some Valid (but no Sound) Arguments Trivially Span the 'Is'-'Ought' Gap, 97 Mind 252 (1988)

Katz, Jonathan. Why There Is Something: The Anthropic Principle and Improbable Events, 27 Dialogue 111 (1988)

Kavka, Gregory S. Book Review of Morals By Agreement, 96 Mind 117 (1987)

Kenny, Anthony. What Is Faith? (Oxford: Oxford Univ. Press 1992)

Kent, Adrian. Against Many-Worlds Interpretations, 5 Int. J. Modern Physics 1745 (1990)

Kerruish, Valerie. Philosophical Retreat: A Criticism of John Finnis' Theory of Natural Law, 15 U. W. Aust. L. Rev. 224 (1983)

Klosko, George. The Principle of Fairness and Political Obligation (Lanham, Md.: Rowman & Littlefield 1992)

_____. Four Arguments Against Political Obligation From Gratitude, 5 Pub. Aff. Q. 33 (1991)

_____. Political Obligation and Gratitude, 18 Phil. & Pub. Aff. 352 (1989)

_____. Presumptive Benefit, Fairness, and Political Obligation, 16 Phil. & Pub. Aff. 241 (1987)

_____. Rawls's "Political" Philosophy and American Democracy, 87 Am. Pol. Sci. Rev. 348 (1993)

_____. Reformist Consent and Political Obligation, 39 Pol. Stud. 676 (1991)

_____. The Moral Force of Political Obligations, 84 Am. Pol. Sci. Rev. 1235 (1990)

_____. The Principle of Fairness and Political Obligation, 97 Ethics 353 (1987)

Kupperman, Joel J. Ethical Fallibility, 1 Ratio (n.s.) 33 (1988)

Kymlicka, Will. Contemporary Political Philosophy (Oxford: Clarendon Press 1990)

_____. Liberalism, Community, and Culture (Oxford: Clarendon Press 1989)

The Laws of Manu (Wendy Doniger & Brian K. Smith trans.) (New York: Penguin 1992)

Le Poidevin, Robin. Creation in a Closed Universe, Or, Have Physicists Disproved the Existence of God?, 27 Religious Stud. 39 (1991)

Leslie, John. Universes (London: Routledge 1989)

————. Value and Existence (Totowa: Rowman & Littlefield 1979)

————. No Inverse Gambler's Fallacy in Cosmology, 97 Mind 269 (1988)

————. Observership in Cosmology: The Anthropic Principle, 92 Mind 573 (1983)

Lessnoff, Michael. Social Contract (Atlantic Highlands: Humanities Press 1986)

Levinson, Sanford. Constitutional Faith (Princeton: Princeton Univ. Press 1988)

Lichtenberg, Judith. Subjectivism as Moral Weakness Projected, 33 Phil. Q. 378 (1983)

Linde, Andrei and Arthur Mezhlumian. Stationary Universe, 307 Physics Letters B 25 (1993)

————. Stochastic Approach to Tunneling and Baby Universe Formation, 372 Nuclear Physics B 421 (1992)

Lockwood, Michael. Mind, Brain and the Quantum (Oxford: Basil Blackwell 1989)

Lovell, Bernard. Emerging Cosmology (New York: Columbia Univ. Press 1981)

Lovibond, Sabina. Realism and Imagination in Ethics (Oxford: Basil Blackwell 1983)

Lyons, Daniel. The Odd Debt of Gratitude, 29 Analysis 92 (1969)

Lyons, David. Ethical Relativism and the Problem of Incoherence, 86 Ethics 107 (1976)

MacCannell, Dean. Empty Meeting Grounds: The Tourist Papers (London: Routledge 1992)

MacIntyre, Alasdair. After Virtue (Notre Dame: Univ. of Notre Dame Press 2d ed. 1984)

Mackie, John L. Ethics: Inventing Right and Wrong (New York: Penguin 1977)

_____. The Miracle of Theism (Oxford: Clarendon Press 1982)

Mannheim, P.D. Conformal Gravity and the Flatness Problem, 391 Astrophysical J. 429 (1992)

Mapel, David R. Democratic Voluntarism and the Problem of Justifying Political Bonds, 23 Polity 233 (1990)

Martin, Michael. Swinburne's Inductive Cosmological Argument, 27 Heythrop J. 151 (1987)

Martin, Rex. Rawls and Rights (Lawrence: Univ. Press of Kansas 1985)

Mauss, Marcel. The Gift (Ian Cunnison trans.) (New York: W.W. Norton 1967)

McConnell, Terrance C. Gratitude (Philadelphia: Temple Univ. Press 1993)

McGrath, P.J. The Inverse Gambler's Fallacy and Cosmology: A Reply to Hacking, 97 Mind 265 (1988)

McInerney, Ralph. Ethica Thomistica (Washington, D.C.: Catholic Univ. of America Press 1982)

McLean, Murdith. Residual Natural Evil and Anthropic Reasoning, 27 Religious Stud. 173 (1991)

McMullin, Ernan. Is Philosophy Relevant to Cosmology?, 18 Am. Phil. Q. 177 (1981)

McNaughton, David. Moral Vision (Oxford: Basil Blackwell 1988)

Medina, Vincente. Social Contract Theories: Political Obligation or Anarchy? (Savage, Md.: Rowman & Littlefield (1990)

Mercer, Mark Douglas. On a Pragmatic Argument Against Pragmatism in Ethics, 30 Am. Phil. Q. 163 (1993)

Meynell, Hugo. More Gaps for God?, in Origin and Evolution of the Universe: Evidence for Design (Alan Batten & John Robson eds.) (Kingston: McGill-Queens Univ. Press 1987)

Mill, John Stuart. On Liberty (Currin V. Shields ed.) (New York: Library of Liberal Arts 1956)

Misner, Charles W. Cosmology and Theology, in Cosmology, History and Theology (Wolfgang Yourgrau & Allen D. Breck eds.) (New York: Plenum Press 1977)

Moore, Michael S. Moral Reality, 1982 Wis. L. Rev. 1061

_____. Moral Reality Revisited, 90 Mich. L. Rev. 2424 (1992)

_____. The Interpretive Turn in Modern Theory: A Turn for the Worse?, 41 Stan. L. Rev. 871 (1989)

More, Thomas. Utopia (Mildred Campbell ed.) (Toronto: D. Van Nostrand Co. 1947)

Mortensen, Chris. Explaining Existence, 16 Can. J. Phil. 713 (1986)

Mulholland, Leslie A. Kant's System of Rights (New York: Columbia Univ. Press 1990)

Munitz, Milton K. Cosmic Understanding (Princeton: Princeton Univ. Press 1987)

Murphy, Jeffrie G. Consent, Coercion, and Hard Choices, 67 Va. L. Rev. 79 (1981)

Murphy, Nancey. Truth, Relativism, and Crossword Puzzles, 24 Zygon 299 (1989)

Nagel, Thomas. Equality and Partiality (New York: Oxford Univ. Press 1991)

Nakhnikian, George. The Principal of Reciprocal Obligations, 55 Phil. Stud. 195 (1989)

Neal, Patrick. Justice as Fairness: Political or Metaphysical?, 18 Pol. Theory 24 (1990)

The New Social Contract: Essays on Gauthier (Ellen Frankel Paul ed.) (Oxford: Basil Blackwell 1988)

Nielsen, Kai. John Rawls' New Methodology: An Interpretive Account, 35 McGill L.J. 572 (1990)

Nietzsche, Friedrich. On the Genealogy of Morals (Walter Kauffmann & R.J. Hollingdale trans.) (New York: Random House 1967)

Norman, Wayne J. Book Review of Moral Dealing, 101 Ethics 370 (1992)

Nozick, Robert. Anarchy, State and Utopia (New York: Basic Books 1974)

_____. Philosophical Explanations (Cambridge: Harvard Univ. Press 1981)

_____. The Examined Life: Philosophical Meditations (New York: Simon & Schuster 1989)

_____. Coercion, in Philosophy, Politics and Society (Peter Laslett, W.G. Runciman & Quentin Skinner eds. 4th series) (Oxford: Oxford Univ. Press 1972)

O'Neill, Onora. Between Consenting Adults, 14 Phil. & Pub. Aff. 252 (1985)

———. Ethical Reasoning and Ideological Pluralism, 98 Ethics 705 (1988)

Page, Don. An Enthusiasm in Cosmology: Review of S. Coleman, J.B. Hartle, T. Piran & S. Weinberg eds., Quantum Cosmology and Baby Universes, 256 Science 864 (1992)

———. Review of the Anthropic Cosmological Principle, 18 Foundations of Physics 479 (1988)

Pangle, Thomas L. The Ennobling of Democracy: The Challenge of the Postmodern Era (Baltimore: Johns Hopkins Univ. Press 1992)

Papineau, David. Reality and Representation (Oxford: Basil Blackwell 1987)

Parfit, Derek. Reasons and Persons (Oxford: Clarendon Press 1984)

Pateman, Carole. The Problem of Political Obligation (Berkeley: Univ. of Calif. Press 1985)

Penrose, Roger. The Emperor's New Mind (New York: Oxford Univ. Press 1989)

Perry, Michael J. Love and Power (New York: Oxford Univ. Press 1991)

Pico Della Mirandola, Giovanni. Oration on the Dignity of Man, in The Renaissance Philosophy of Man (Ernst Cassirer, Paul Oskar Kristeller & John Herman Randall, Jr. eds. and trans.) (Chicago: Univ. of Chicago Press 1948)

Pigden, Charles R. Logic and the Autonomy of Ethics, 67 Australasian J. Phil. 127 (1989)

Pitkin, Hanna. Obligation and Consent—I, 59 Am. Pol. Sci. Rev. 990 (1965)

Plamenàtz, John P. Consent, Freedom and Political Obligation (Oxford: Oxford Univ. Press 2d ed. 1968)

Plantinga, Alvin. Coherentism and the Evidentialist Objection to Belief in God, in Rationality, Religious Belief, and Moral Commitment (Robert Audi & William Wainwright eds.) (Ithaca: Cornell Univ. Press 1986)

Plato. Crito, in Euthyphro, Apology, Crito, and Phaedo (Benjamin Jowett trans.) (Buffalo: Prometheus Books 1988)

Platts, Mark de Bretton. Moral Realities (London: Routledge 1991)

Pogge, Thomas W. Realizing Rawls (Ithaca: Cornell Univ. Press 1989)

Polkinghorne, John. Reason and Reality (Philadelphia: Trinity International Press 1991)

_____. Science and Creation (Boston: New Science Library 1989)

Pollard, William G. Rumors of Transcendence in Physics, 52 Am. J. Physics 877 (1984)

Porter, Jean. The Recovery of Virtue (Louisville: Westminster/John Knox Press 1990)

_____. Basic Goods and the Human Good in Recent Catholic Moral Theology, 57 Thomist 27 (1993)

Prevost, Robert. Probability and Theistic Explanation (Oxford: Clarendon Press 1990)

Putnam, Hilary. The Many Faces of Realism (La Salle: Open Court 1987)

_____. A Reconsideration of Deweyan Democracy, 63 S. Cal. L. Rev. 1671 (1990)

Quantum Cosmology and the Laws of Nature (Robert John Russell, Nancey Murphy & Chris J. Isham eds.) (forthcoming)

Rae, Alastair. Quantum Physics: Illusion or Reality (Cambridge: Cambridge Univ. Press 1986)

Rawls, John. A Theory of Justice (Cambridge: Harvard Univ. Press 1971)

_____. Political Liberalism (New York: Columbia Univ. Press 1993)

_____. Justice as Fairness: Political not Metaphysical, 14 Phil. & Pub. Aff. 223 (1985)

_____. The Domain of the Political and Overlapping Consensus, 64 N.Y.U. L. Rev. 233 (1989)

_____. The Idea of an Overlapping Consensus, 7 Ox. J. Legal Stud. 1 (1987)

Raz, Joseph. The Morality of Freedom (Oxford: Clarendon Press 1986)

_____. Facing Diversity: The Case of Epistemic Abstinence, 19 Phil. & Pub. Aff. 3 (1990)

_____. Promises in Morality and Law, 95 Harv. L. Rev. 916 (1982)

_____. The Relevance of Coherence, 72 B.U. L. Rev. 273 (1992)

Redhead, Michael. Physics For Pedestrians: An Inaugural Lecture (Cambridge: Cambridge Univ. Press 1989)

Regan, Donald H. Law's Halo, 4 Social Phil. & Pol'y 15 (1986)

Renteln, Allison Dundes. Relativism and the Search for Human Rights, 90 Am. Anthropologist 56 (1988)

Rhodes, James M. Right by Nature, 53 J. Politics 318 (1991)

Richards, David A.J. Review of John Finnis' Natural Law and Natural Rights, 93 Ethics 169 (1982)

Rorty, Amelie Oksenberg. Varieties of Pluralism in a Polyphonic Society, 44 Rev. Metaphysics 3 (1990)

Rorty, Richard. Consequences of Pragmatism (Minneapolis: Univ. of Minn. Press 1982)

---------. Contingency, Irony, and Solidarity (Cambridge: Cambridge Univ. Press 1989)

---------. Philosophy and the Mirror of Nature (Princeton: Princeton Univ. Press 1979)

---------. Postmodernist Bourgeoise Liberalism, 80 J. Phil. 583 (1983)

---------. The Priority of Democracy to Philosophy, in The Virginia Statute for Religious Freedom (Merrill D. Peterson & Robert C. Vaughn eds.) (Cambridge: Cambridge Univ. Press 1988)

---------. Thugs and Theorists: A Reply to Bernstein, 15 Pol. Theory 546 (1987)

---------. What Can You Expect from Antifoundationalist Philosophers?: A Reply to Lynn Baker, 78 Va. L. Rev. 719 (1992)

Rolston, Holmes III. Review of John Leslie's Universes, 26 Zygon 317 (1991)

Rosen, Joe. The Capricious Universe (New York: MacMillan 1991)

---------. No Rumors of Transcendence in Physics, 54 Am. J. Physics 700 (1986)

---------. Self-Generating Universe and Many Worlds, 21 Foundations of Physics 977 (1991)

Rosenberg, Jay. Raiders of the Lost Distinction: Richard Rorty and the Search for the Last Dichotomy, 53 Phil. & Phenomenological Res. 195 (1993)

Ross, Steven L. A Real Defense of Tolerance, 22 J. Value Inquiry 127 (1988)

Roth, Robert J. Moral Obligation and God, 54 New Scholasticism 265 (1980)

_____. Moral Obligation—With or Without God?, 59 New Scholasticism 471 (1985)

Russell, Robert John. Theological Lessons from Cosmology: Two Case Studies, 41 Cross Currents 308 (1991)

Sapontzis, Steve F. Groundwork for a Subjective Theory of Ethics, 27 Am. Phil. Q. 27 (1990)

Sayre-McCord, Geoffrey. Being a Realist About Relativism (in Ethics), 61 Phil. Stud. 155 (1991)

_____. The Many Moral Realisms, 24 S.J. Phil. 1 (1986)

Scavone, Robert M. Natural Law, Obligation and the Common Good: What Finnis Can't Tell Us, 43 U. Toronto Faculty L.J. 90 (1985)

Scheppele, Kim Lane and Jeremy Waldron. Contractarian Methods in Political and Legal Evaluation, 3 Yale J.L. & Humanities 195 (1991)

Schlesinger, George N. New Perspectives on Old-Time Religion (Oxford: Clarendon Press 1988)

_____. The Anthropic Principle, 23 Tradition 1 (1988)

Schultz, Janice L. Is-Ought: Prescribing and a Present Controversy, 49 Thomist 1 (1985)

_____. 'Ought'-Judgments: A Descriptivist Analysis from a Thomistic Perspective, 61 New Scholasticism 400 (1987)

Seidler, Victor J. Kant, Respect and Justice (London: Routledge & Kegan Paul 1986)

Seneca, Lucius Annaeus. De Beneficiis, in 3 Moral Essays (John W. Basore trans.) (London: William Heinemann Ltd. reprint 1958)

Shearmur, Jeremy. Natural Law Without Metaphysics: The Case of John Finnis, 38 Clev. St. L. Rev. 123 (1990)

Siegler, Frederick. Plamenatz On Consent and Obligation, 18 Phil. Q. 256 (1968)

Simmons, A. John. Moral Principles and Political Obligations (Princeton: Princeton Univ. Press 1979)

──────. The Anarchist Position: A Reply to Klosko and Senor, 16 Phil. & Pub. Aff. 269 (1987)

──────. The Principle of Fair Play, 8 Phil. & Pub. Aff. 307 (1979)

Simpson, Peter. Practical Knowing: Finnis and Aquinas, 67 Modern Schoolman 111 (1990)

──────. St. Thomas on the Naturalistic Fallacy, 51 Thomist 51 (1987)

Singer, Peter. Democracy and Disobedience (New York: Oxford Univ. Press 1974)

Smart, J.J.C. Laws of Nature and Cosmic Coincidences, 35 Phil. Q. 272 (1985)

Smith, Quentin. A Natural Explanation of the Existence and Laws of Our Universe, 68 Australasian J. Phil. 22 (1990)

──────. Atheism, Theism, and Big Bang Cosmology, 69 Australasian J. Phil. 48 (1991)

──────. The Anthropic Principle and Many-Worlds Cosmologies, 63 Australasian J. Phil. 336 (1985)

──────. The Uncaused Beginning of the Universe, 55 Phil. Sci. 39 (1988)

Smith, Quentin and William Lane Craig. Atheism, Theism, and Big Bang Cosmology (Oxford: Oxford Univ. Press forthcoming)

Smith, Steven D. The Restoration of Tolerance, 78 Calif. L. Rev. 305 (1990)

Smolin, Lee. Did the Universe Evolve?, 9 Classical & Quantum Gravity 173 (1992)

Snare, Frank. The Nature of Moral Thinking (London: Routledge 1992)

_____. The Diversity of Morals, 89 Mind 353 (1980)

Soskice, Janet Martin. The Truth Looks Different From Here, 73 New Blackfriars 528 (1992)

Stannard, Russell. Grounds For Reasonable Belief (Edinburgh: Scottish Academic Press 1989)

Stein, Howard. The Everett Interpretation of Quantum Mechanics: Many Worlds or None?, 18 Nous 635 (1984)

Steinberg, Jules. Locke, Rousseau, and the Idea of Consent (Westport: Greenwood Press 1978)

Stenger, Victor J. The Universe: The Ultimate Free Lunch, 11 Eur. J. Physics 236 (1990)

Stevenson, Charles L. Ethics and Language (New Haven: Yale Univ. Press 1944)

Stewart, Robert M. and Lynn L. Thomas. Recent Work on Moral Relativism, 28 Am. Phil. Q. 85 (1991)

Stoeger, William. The Origin of the Universe in Science and Religion, in Cosmos, Bios, Theos (Henry Margenau & Roy Abraham Varghese eds.) (La Salle: Open Court 1992)

Stoljar, Daniel. Emotivism and Truth Conditions, 70 Phil. Rev. 157 (1990)

Stout, Jeffrey. Ethics After Babel (Boston: Beacon Press 1988)

_____. Truth, Natural Law, and Ethical Theory, in Natural Law Theory: Contemporary Essays (Robert P. George ed.) (Oxford: Clarendon Press 1992)

Sullivan, T.D. Coming To Be Without a Cause, 65 Phil. 261 (1990)

Swinburne, Richard. The Existence of God (Oxford: Oxford Univ. Press 1979)

_____. Argument from the Fine-Tuning of the Universe, in Physical Cosmology and Philosophy (John Leslie ed.) (New York: MacMillan 1990)

_____. Mackie, Induction, and God, 19 Religious Stud. 385 (1983)

_____. The Limits of Explanation, in Royal Institute of Philosophy Lecture Series no. 24: Key Themes in Philosophy 177 (A. Phillips Griffiths ed.) (Cambridge: Cambridge Univ. Press 1989)

_____. The Origin of Consciousness, in Origin and Evolution of the Universe: Evidence for Design (Kingston: McGill-Queen's Univ. Press 1987)

Symposium on David Gauthier's Morals By Agreement, 18 Can. J. Phil. 315 (1988)

Symposium on David Gauthier's Morals By Agreement, 97 Ethics 715 (1987)

Tannsjo, Torbjorn. Moral Realism (Savage, Md.: Rowman & Littlefield 1990)

Taylor, Charles. The Ethics of Authenticity (Cambridge: Harvard Univ. Press 1991)

Temple, Dennis. Hume's Logical Objection to the Argument From Design Based on the Uniqueness of the Universe, 28 Religious Stud. 19 (1992)

Tilley, John J. Moral Relativism and Hume, 69 Modern Schoolman 81 (1992)

Timmons, Mark. Putnam's Moral Objectivism, 34 Erkenntnis 371 (1991)

Tinder, Glenn. Tolerance: Toward a New Civility (Amherst: Univ. of Mass. Press 1976)

Tipler, Frank J. The Omega Point as Eschaton: Answers to Pannenberg's Questions for Scientists, 24 Zygon 217 (1989)

Titmuss, Richard. The Gift Relationship (New York: Vintage Books 1972)

Unger, Roberto M. Knowledge and Politics (New York: Free Press 1975)

Unruh, W.G. Is the Universe Natural?, in Origin and Evolution of the Universe: Evidence for Design (Allen Batten & John Robson eds.) (Kingston: McGill-Queen's Univ. Press 1987)

Unwin, Nicholas. Can Emotivism Sustain a Social Ethics?, 3 Ratio (n.s.) 64 (1990)

Veatch, Henry. Natural Law and the "Is"—"Ought" Question, 26 Catholic Lawyer 251 (1981)

Vilenkin, Alexander. Did the Universe Have a Beginning?, 46 Physical Review D 2355 (3d series) (1992)

Wald, George. Consciousness and Cosmology: Their Interrelations, in Bergson and Modern Thought (Andrew C. Papanicolaou & Peter A.Y. Gunter eds.) (London: Harwood Academic 1987)

Waldron, Jeremy. Locke: Toleration and the Rationality of Persecution, in John Locke, A Letter Concerning Toleration: In Focus (John Horton & Susan Mendus eds.) (London: Routledge 1991)

_____. Special Ties and Natural Duties, 22 Phil. & Pub. Aff. 3 (1993)

_____. The Irrelevance of Moral Objectivity, in Natural Law Theory: Contemporary Essays (Robert P. George ed.) (Oxford: Clarendon Press 1992)

Walker, A.D.M. Obligations of Gratitude and Political Obligation, 18 Phil. & Pub. Aff. 359 (1989)

———. Political Obligation and the Argument From Gratitude, 17 Phil. & Pub. Aff. 191 (1988)

Walker, Ralph. The Coherence Theory of Truth (London: Routledge 1989)

Weale, Albert. Consent, 26 Pol. Stud. 65 (1978)

Weinreb, Lloyd. Natural Law and Justice (Cambridge: Harvard Univ. Press 1987)

Weiskopf, Victor. The Origin of the Universe, 36 N.Y. Rev. Books 10 (1989)

Weiss, Roslyn. The Moral and Social Dimensions of Gratitude, 23 S.J. Phil. 491 (1985)

Wellman, Carl. Ethical Disagreement and Objective Truth, 12 Am. Phil. Q. 211 (1975)

Wertheimer, Alan. Coercion (Princeton: Princeton Univ. Press 1987)

Wheeler, John Archibald. Law Without Law, in Quantum Theory and Measurement (John Archibald Wheeler & Wojciech Hubert Zurek eds.) (Princeton: Princeton Univ. Press 1983)

Whitaker, M.A.B. On Hacking's Criticism of the Wheeler Anthropic Principle, 97 Mind 259 (1988)

White, Morton. Philosophy, The Federalist, and the Constitution (New York: Oxford Univ. Press 1987)

Wiggins, David. Moral Cognitivism, Moral Relativism and Motivating Moral Beliefs, 91 Proc. Aristotelian Society (n.s.) 61 (1991)

Wigner, Eugene P. The Unreasonable Effectiveness of Mathematics in the Natural Sciences, 13 Communications On Pure and Applied Mathematics 227 (1960)

Wiles, Anne M. Harman and Others on Moral Relativism, 42 Rev. Metaphysics 783 (1989)

Williams, Bernard. An Inconsistent Form of Relativism, in Relativism: Cognitive and Moral (Michael Krausz & Jack W. Meiland eds.) (Notre Dame: Notre Dame Univ. Press 1982)

_____. Subjectivism and Toleration, in Royal Institute of Philosophy Supplement no. 30: A.J. Ayer Memorial Essays 197 (A. Phillips Griffiths ed.) (Cambridge: Cambridge Univ. Press 1992)

_____. The Truth in Relativism, in Relativism: Cognitive and Moral (Michael Krausz & Jack W. Meiland eds.) (Notre Dame: Notre Dame Univ. Press 1982)

Wilson, Patrick A. What Is the Explanandum of the Anthropic Principle?, 28 Am. Phil. Q. 167 (1991)

Wolf, Susan. Two Levels of Pluralism, 102 Ethics 785 (1992)

Wolff, Jonathan. What Is the Problem of Political Obligation?, 91 Proc. Aristotelian Society 153 (1991)

Wong, David B. Moral Relativity (Berkeley: Univ. of California Press 1984)

_____. Commentary on Sayre-McCord's "Being a Realist About Relativism," 61 Phil. Stud. 177 (1991)

_____. On Moral Realism Without Foundations, 26 S.J. Phil. 95 (1986)

Wright, Crispin. Truth and Objectivity (Cambridge: Harvard Univ. Press 1992)

Wright, R. George. Should the Law Reflect the World?: Lessons For Legal Theory From Quantum Mechanics, 18 Fla. St. L. Rev. 855 (1991)

_____. The High Cost of Rawls' Inegalitarianism, 30 Western Pol. Q. 73 (1977)

Zimmerman, David. Coercive Wage Offers, 10 Phil. & Pub. Aff. 121 (1981)

Zycinski, Joseph M. The Anthropic Principle and Teleological Interpretations of Nature, 41 Rev. Metaphysics 317 (1987)

INDEX

A

Abbott, Philip 14, 18
Ackerman, Bruce 86
Adair, Robert K. 125, 126
Adams, Marilyn M. 129
Adams, Robert M. 14
Albert, David 128
Alexander, Larry xviii
Almond, Brenda 91
Aquinas, Thomas 14-18, 65-66, 93
Aquino, Corazon 81
Aristotle 57, 140
Arneson, Richard J. 47, 50, 51
Atiyah, Patrick S. 34
Atkins, Peter W. 94
Ayer, A.J 84, 90, 98

B

Baker, Lynn A. 96
Bakhtin, Michael M. 107
Balashov, Yuri 125
Ball, Steven W. xviii
Bambrough, Renford 107
Barnett, Randy 34
Barrow, John 116, 125, 132, 137
Beckstrom, John 94
Bell, Daniel 35
Ben-Dov, Yoav 128
Benhabib, Seyla 147
Bennett, Jonathan 94
Bentham, Jeremy 86
Beran, Harry 24-26, 32, 33
Berger, Fred R. 14-16

Berger, Peter 93
Bernstein, Richard J. 95
Betty, L. Stafford 123, 128, 132, 133, 135
Beyleveld, Deryck 147
Bix, Brian 90, 98
Black, Max xix
Blackburn, Simon 74-76, 84, 91-94
Boghossian, Paul 94
Bohm, David 137
Bond, E.J. 91, 110
Bourke, Vernon 66
Boyle, Joseph 13, 65, 90
Brandt, Richard B. 91
Breuer, Reinhard 125
Brilmayer, Lea 20, 27, 28, 30, 32, 33
Brink, David O. 90, 100, 101, 107
Brownsword, Roger 147

C

Camenisch, Paul F. 13, 16, 17
Card, Claudia 15, 16
Carloye, Jack C. 135
Carr, B.J. 127, 128, 131
Carson, Thomas L. 91
Chandrasekhar, Subrahmanyan 95, 123
Chappell, Vera C. xviii
Chavez, Cesar 82
Clark, Stephen R.L. 97
Clifton, Robert K. 127
Coles, Peter 133
Collins, P.D.B. 127
Cooke, Vincent M. 66
Copp, David 35, 90-92
Cordell, Bruce 123, 128, 132, 133, 135
Corey, M.A. 125
Craig, William Lane 131, 134, 135, 137
Cranston, Maurice 107

D

D'Agostino, Fred	96
D'Amato, Anthony	40, 49
Daniels, Norman	90
Dancy, Jonathan	89
Dante	140
Darwall, Stephen	69, 89, 92, 94
Davies, Paul	126, 129, 133, 136
Day, J.P.	30
del Campo, Sergio	127
Devine, Philip E.	98, 108, 133
Devitt, Michael	111
Derrida, Jacques	iii
Dieks, Dennis	129
Doppelt, Gerald	48
Dostoevsky, Fyodor	97
Double, Richard	xix
Drees, Willem B.	123, 124, 134, 135
Dummett, Michael	92-93
Dworkin, Ronald	45, 50

E

Earman, John	127, 130, 133
Eidelberg, Paul	95
Ellis, George F.R.	126
Epstein, David F.	109
Everett III, Hugh	128

F

Fallon, Richard H.	xviii
Fang Li Zhi	135
Finnis, John	xviii, 13, 53-67, 83, 92, 98, 110
Fish, Stanley	98
Fiss, Owen	110
Flathman, Richard	20, 30, 31, 33, 34

Foot, Philippa 91
Frankenstein, Dr. .... xii, xiii
Fried, Charles 32, 33

G

Gale, George 126
Gandhi, Mohandas .... xvi, 81, 98, 100,
.... 102, 105-09, 111
Garner, Richard T. 94
Garofalo, Bruno xviii
Garrett, Anthony J.M. 133
Gauthier, David 34, 35, 94
Gavison, Ruth 66
Gellner, Ernest 91
George, Robert P. 65
Geroch, Robert 129
Gewirth, Alan 86, 143-47
Gibbard, Allan 34, 69, 76, 77, 89,
.... 91, 92, 94, 95, 108
Gibson, James L. 109
Goldsworthy, Jeffrey 97
Goodin, Robert 34
Graham, Gordon 107
Green, Leslie 30, 31, 66
Greenawalt, Kent 42, 47, 49, 50
Greenstein, George 127
Gribbin, John 126, 136
Grisez, Germain 13, 65
Grishchuk, L.P. 135
Grünbaum, Adolf 136, 137
Guth, Alan H. 127

H

Habermas, Jurgen 147
Hacking, Ian 131
Hallberg, Fred W. 133
Halliwell, Jonathan J. 135, 136
Hampton, Jean 35, 39, 48, 49

INDEX

Harding, Sandra 143, 147
Harman, Gilbert 70, 91, 96
Harris, Edward A. 31, 33, 43, 47, 50
Harris, Errol E. 124, 126, 127, 129
Hart, H.L.A. .... ix, 47
Hartle, James 120, 121, 132, 134-37
Havel, Vaclav 81
Hawking, Stephen 120, 121, 126, 131,
 .... 132, 134-37
Healey, Richard 128, 129
Hebblethwaite, Brian 90, 129, 133
Heisenberg, Werner 121
Henderson, Lynne 110
Herbert, Nick 93
Herzog, Don 32, 34
Hirschmann, Nancy 47
Hitler, Adolf .... xvi, 86
Hittinger, Russell. 65-67, 92
Hobbes, Thomas 15, 58, 140
Hocutt, Max 108
Hodgson, David 128
Hudson, W.D. xviii
Hume, David .... x-xv, xviii, xix, 1, 11,
 .... 13, 17, 55, 110
Hutcheson, Francis 16

I

Isham, Chris J. 135

J

Jackson, Timothy P. 96, 97
Jaki, Stanley L. 131
Jenkins, John J. 30

K

Karamazov, Ivan. 80
Kant, Immanuel. 1, 11, 13-17, 28, 86, 140

Karmo, Toomas xviii
Katz, Jonathan 134
Kavka, Gregory S. 34
Kenny, Anthony 123
Kent, Adrian 130
Kerruish, Valerie 66
King, Jr., Martin Luther 81, 82, 98, 100, 102
Klosko, George 13, 16-17, 31, 32,
.... 41-45, 47, 49, 50
Kropf, Allen 127
Kupperman, Joel J. 98
Kymlicka, Will 39, 48, 102, 108

L

Langbein, R.F. 127
Le Poidevin, Robin 137
Leslie, John 114-17, 125, 126, 129-35
Lessnoff, Michael 32
Levinson, Sanford 96
Li Shu Xian 135
Lichtenberg, Judith 94
Locke, John 23, 100, 107, 108
Lockwood, David 128
Loewer, Barry 128
Lovell, Bernard 126
Lovibond, Sabina 91, 92
Lyons, Daniel 14
Lyons, David 92

M

MacIntyre, Alasdair 91, 123, 147
Mackie, J.L. .... xviii, 89, 97, 125
Madison, James 102
Malcolm X 81
Mannheim, P.D. 134
Mapel, David R. xix
Martin, Michael 123

INDEX

Martin, Rex	49
Mauss, Marcel	13
McConnell, Terrance	13-15, 18
McGrath, P.J.	131
McInerney, Ralph	65
McLean, Murdith	132
McMullin, Ernan	124, 126
McNaughton, David	xviii, 93, 107, 108
Medina, Vicente	33
Mercer, Mark Douglas	96
Meynell, Hugo	125, 133
Mill, John Stuart	42, 49, 100, 102, 108
Milton, John	100
Minn, Hokee	135
Misner, Charles W.	135
Moore, Michael S.	89, 90, 92, 96, 109, 110
More, Thomas	111
Mortensen, Chris	131
Mulholland, Leslie A.	16
Munitz, Milton K.	135
Murphy, Jeffrie G.	30
Murphy, Nancey	92

N

Nagel, Thomas	49, 110
Nakhnikian, George	47
Neal, Patrick	49
Nielsen, Kai	47-49
Nietzsche, Friedrich	xv, 27, 33
Nightingale, Florence	81
Norman, Wayne J.	35
Nozick, Robert	xviii, 30, 34, 40, 48, 49, 80, 97

O

Ockham, William	117
O'Neill, Onora	33, 147

P

Page, Don	124, 132
Pangle, Thomas L.	96
Papineau, David	89, 90
Parfit, Derek	89
Pateman, Carole	31
Penrose, Roger	126
Perry, Michael	90, 103, 107-10
Phillips, D.Z.	xix
Pico della Mirandola, Giovanni	97-98, 147
Pigden, Charles R.	xviii
Pitkin, Hanna	32
Plamenatz, John P.	30
Planck, Max	89, 90, 126
Plantinga, Alvin	90
Plato	13, 57, 79
Platts, Mark de Bretton	91, 109
Pogge, Thomas W.	49
Polkinghorne, John	123, 126, 127, 129, 130, 132, 133, 135
Pollard, William G.	133
Porter, Jean	66, 92
Prevost, Robert	123
Prometheus	xv
Putnam, Hilary	81, 95, 97, 107

R

Rae, Alastair	130
Railton, Peter	69, 89, 92-94
Rawls, John	ix, xviii, 33, 37-42, 47-49, 86
Raz, Joseph	30, 34, 48, 49, 90
Redhead, Michael	135
Rees, Martin	126, 127, 131
Regan, Donald H.	xviii
Renteln, Allison Dundes	108
Rhodes, James M.	67
Richards, David A.J.	65

INDEX

Rolston III, Holmes 129
Rorty, Amelie Oksenberg 107-09
Rorty, Richard 78-81, 95-97
Rosen, Joe 114, 124, 125, 134
Rosenberg, Jay 96
Ross, Steven L. 109
Roth, Robert J. 67
Rousseau, Jean-Jacques 57
Rozhansky, L.V. 135
Russell, Robert John 126

S

Sapontzis, Steve F. 90, 97
Sayre-McCord, Geoffrey 90, 92, 93
Scavone, Robert M. 65, 66
Scheppele, Kim Lane 31, 33, 34
Schlesinger, George N. 124, 134
Schultze, Janice L. .... xviii, 66
Schumpeter, Joseph 35
Seidler, Victor J. 14, 15
Seneca 1, 13-16
Shearmur, Jeremy 66
Siegler, Frederick 30
Simmons, A. John .... xviii, 3, 14-18, 23,
.... 30-33, 50
Simpson, Peter .... xviii, 66
Singer, Peter 21, 22, 31
Smart, J.J.C. 51
Smith, Quentin 124, 127, 129, 130,
.... 131, 133, 136
Smith, Steven D. 109
Snare, Frank .... xviii, 92
Socrates 1, 7-9
Soskice, Janet Martin 142, 147
Stalin, Joseph .... xvi, xvii, 100
Stannard, Russell 123, 128, 129
Stein, Howard 128
Steinberg, Jules 30, 31
Steinhardt, Paul J. 127

Stevenson, C.L. 84, 90
Stewart, Robert M. 90
Stoeger, William 129
Stoljar, Daniel 94
Stout, Jeffrey 82, 97, 123
Sullivan, T.D. 124, 137
Swinburne, Richard 92, 123, 127, 133, 134

T

Tannsjo, Torbjorn 94
Taylor, Charles 97, 98
Temple, Dennis 126, 129, 131
Thomas, Lynn L. 90
Tilley, John J. 110
Timmons, Mark 89, 97, 108
Tinder, Glenn 110
Tipler, Frank 116, 125, 128, 132
Titmuss, Richard M. 13
Torquemada . . . . xvi, xvii, 100
Tutu, Desmond 81

U

Ulysses 145
Unger, Roberto 82, 83, 97
Unruh, W.G. 132
Unwin, Nicholas 94, 95
Utilitarianism 7, 25-28, 32-34, 55, 56, 58,
. . . . 59, 62, 72, 80, 139, 142

V

Veatch, Henry. . . . . xviii, 66
Vilenkin, Alexander 137

W

Wald, George 126, 133, 134
Waldron, Jeremy 31, 33, 34, 65, 75, 84,
. . . . 98, 107, 109

INDEX

Walker, A.D.M. 1, 13, 15-17
Walker, Ralph 90
Weale, Albert 30
Weinreb, Lloyd 66
Weiskopf, Victor 135
Weiss, Roslyn 15, 16
Wellman, Carl 93
Wertheimer, Alan 30
Wheeler, John Archibald 89, 130-32
Whitaker, M.A.B. 131
White, Morton 109
Wiggins, David 92, 110
Wigner, Eugene P. 134
Wiles, Anne M. 91
Williams, Bernard 91, 98, 99, 107, 108
Wilson, Patrick A. 133
Wolf, Susan 108
Wolff, Jonathan 48
Wong, David B. 90-93
Wright, Crispin 95
Wright, R. George 48, 110, 130

Z

Zimmerman, David 30
Zycinski, Joseph M. 126, 127, 129, 130